The Origin
of
Economies

Christopher
Meakin

THE GOODCHILD PRESS

LONDON • OSLO • WASHINGTON D.C.

August 2017

First published 2017 by
THE GOODCHILD PRESS
London, United Kingdom
www.Goodchildpress.co.uk
Reg. Off: Redwoods, 2 Clystworks, Clyst Road, Topsham, Exeter EX3 0DB

A catalogue record of this book
is available from the British Library
ISBN : 978-1-897657-03-4

Set in Garamond 12.5 on 14.6 pt and designed by the author
Printed and bound in Great Britain by
Short Run Press Limited, Exeter
www.shortrunpress.co.uk

The Origin of Economies

CONTENTS

Acknowledgements

With unending gratitude to my family for putting up with it while the book was thought about and written. To Christopher Walker, of the British Museum, for his broad outlook, great insight and massive encouragement. To Geoffrey Gardiner, my close collaborator in economics, and beyond, for thirty years. A nod of gratitude to fellow editors of Wikipedia. Respectful thanks to members of the 'Gang Of Eight' transatlantic group of iconoclastic economists, of whom nine more are included below. To all of the following (at least thirty of whom have since died) for their panoramic knowledge, deep wisdom, writing inspiration and sublime encouragement (frequently unknowing) before and during the distraction-prone years in which this complex and challenging book was unsystematically assembled.

Tariq Ali	Walter Eltis
Rupert Allason	Mark Firth
Bernard Argent	Mike Freeman
Norman Ashton-Hill	Norman Fowler
Anne Atkins	Beryl Gardiner
Tony Baron	Richard Geldart
Michael Beloff	Michael and Monica Gilbert
James Bourlet	Jonathan Gili
Gyles Brandreth	Peter Gillman
Leon Brittan	Mary Goldring
Sam Brittan	Peter and Alison Gould
Frances Cairncross	Stephen Green
Prof Averil Cameron	Peter Gummer
Hugh Chapman	Miranda Hardie
Nathaniel Clapton	Prof Mike Harloe
Fiennes Cornwallis	Len Harris
Mark Couch	Ralph Harris
James Cumes	William B Harrison III
Arno Mong Daastøl	Peter Hawksley
Prof Peter Davison	Tim Heald
Georgia Derrico	Bill Hefferle
Paul Dimond	Prof Mike Hill
Alan Duncan	Patricia Hodgson
'Billy' Effron	John Horam
Joe Egerton	David Howell

Acknowledgements

Bernard Hunn
John Hyde
Joseph Hyde
Wendy Hyde
John im Thurn
Peter Jay
Prof Tim Jenkinson
Keith Joseph
Stephen Kahn
Dave King
Uwe Kitzinger
Conrad Kozak
Geoffrey and Susan Lace
Damon de Laszlo
Roger Laughton
Michael Lewis
Henry C. Liu
Pat Limerick
Dmitri Lvov
John Maples
Colin Matten
Christopher Meyer
John Mills
Prof Patrick Minford
Prof Basil Mitchell
Edward Mortimer
Marianne Neville-Rolfe
Gordon Newton
Steven Norris
Christopher Ogg
Greg Opie
Noel Picarda
David Pinder
Rod Porter
Tim Potter

Letty Payod
David Quarmby
Michael Preston
William Purves
Bob Rangecroft
Philip Ransley
John Raven
Clem Redesdale
William Rees-Mogg
Robyn Robertson
Keith 'Tick' Robinson
Rony Robinson
Peter Rodgers
Richard Ryder
David Sainsbury
John Scarlett
Prof Tony Seaton
Arthur Seldon
David Senior
Alfred Sherman
Ian Spence
Chloë Stallibrass
Diana Stein
Stewart Steven
Ned Swan
Rachel Tingle
Gunnar Tomasson
Nigel 'Bert' Towers
Philip van der Elst
Nigel Vinson
Jack Waterhouse
Prof Richard Werner
Evelyn Westwood/Cox
Hugh Whinfrey
Prof Randall Wray

Dominus Illuminatio Mea

Chapter One

A Science That Never Was

The experience of being disastrously wrong is salutary;
no economist should be denied it, and not many are.
JOHN KENNETH GALBRAITH in *A Life in Our Times*

WRITING THIS BOOK HAS taken a long time, for while it was still in hand, the world of economics and finance was turned upside down. There was nigh on a worldwide collapse in banking in 2007-2008. The worst such calamity for eighty years, the phenomenon was mainly financial, but in part it was also intellectual. Almost overnight, economic wisdom which until then had been widely accepted as infallible suffered a mortal blow. Ordinary people in their millions came to the conclusion that the self-acclaimed 'science' of economics was little more than a pantomime.

Yet there is a morsel of good in almost everything : the financial calamity helped remove a major impediment to completing the book. If it ain't broke, don't fix it. What would be the point of arguing that economic teaching is deeply flawed when everything seemed to be working so smoothly?

Until the financial fiasco in the summer of 2007, it had been broadly agreed among economists in both commerce and academe, among politicians of all parties and media commentators, among trendy authors of fashionable books about economics, that the civilised world had put any such economic incompetence firmly in its past.

According to these experts, the machinery for everlasting economic progress was now all firmly in place. The financieri were now totally and wisely in charge, no longer governed by serendipity nor by circumstances beyond the leader's control. According to the nabobs and pundits, economic anxiety, the former nightmares of boom and bust, even the trauma of inflation had at last been consigned to the dustbins of history.

It was an extensive mutual admiration society reaching both sides of the Atlantic. There was broad agreement - especially among themselves - that people now running central banks, national treasuries and finance ministries, the directors of retail and investment banks, of stock markets, hedge funds and mortgage companies were all masters of their craft.

The roaring success of London and New York as global financial centres was apparently proof of that. Along the way it meant that the purpose of bank lending was distorted, and the individual annual bonuses of some bankers grew almost obscenely large. This self-inflicted largesse did not trouble finance ministers one iota. Their coffers were being filled with more and more high-rate income tax.

Since the early 1990s it had all become a sophisticated, proven, highly profitable routine. In Great Britain a triumphant Chancellor of the Exchequer was hailed by his colleagues as one of the greatest ever. He was regarded, and probably saw himself, as unprecedented. Yet all this acclaimed omnipotence disappeared like mist in the dawn when suddenly, disastrously it all went wrong. Now, apparently, it was everyone else's fault but their own. They had never been in charge in the first place.

With the economic calamity of Summer 2007, ordinary people in their hundreds of millions saw for themselves how that cosy consensus of financieri and their political friends had really been a high road to disaster. The devastating bank liquidity collapses, credit starvation and wrecked public finances of 2007-2008 were not the first economic disaster to hit the developed world by any means, and sadly the odds are they will not be the last either. Cynics could fairly argue that another calamity is imminent as soon as the last person to have experienced the previous calamity at first hand finally retires from active service.

NOR WAS IT JUST the cynics. As the Queen was moved to ask when she visited the London School of Economics in Spring 2009, *Why did no-one see it coming?* The man she was addressing, the director of the LSE had by then been head of the Financial Services Authority, head of the Audit Commission, director-general of the CBI and a deputy governor of the Bank of England. Surely if anyone had an ideal vantage point to see it coming it would have been he. Sadly not, it seems.

Amid all that financial merry-making one wonders whether anyone had the authority to persuade the party-goers of the errors of their ways. Even so, not everyone had agreed with the cosy consensus of the financieri. A few egregious economists, including academics, had voiced doubts for years. Unfortunately there are few folk less beguiling than those who say 'I told you so' but this book must wave a respectful flag on their behalf.

The opening salvos of the book that follows were fired in a lengthy lecture[1] in late 1998, almost ten years before the cataclysm. It was anchored in what was then a wholly unfashionable belief that not all was well in the ministries, seminars, board rooms and think tanks of economic power.

In part this book is anchored also in a belief, shared with John Maynard Keynes, that too many of those in charge of economies prefer to look backwards when devising their strategies: *'practical men, who believe themselves to be quite exempt from any intellectual influences, are usually the slaves of some defunct economist.'* This book does not agree with Keynes on everything by any means, but in that famous observation he was absolutely spot on.

Economics has to be anchored in something. Adam Smith sought to anchor it in wealth and land, and to a lesser extent in the workings of the market, his 'unseen hand'. The *Wealth of Nations* has been described by some as a publicity tract for Scottish landowners. His successors embellished Smith's foundations until Karl Marx turned them upside down.

Instead Marx sought to anchor economics in the contribution of labour, but like Smith he still saw the subject as an outpost of politics, his revolutionary Communist Manifesto an exceptional form of political economy. By the end of the 19th century, Alfred Marshall and others were trying to move away

1. *Given at the School of Economic Science in November that year, following a shorter version given at the British Museum to a seminar on Mesopotamian Finance in 1996. Variants on the theme were given to the Economic Research Council in 1999 and at Birkbeck College, London in 2009. That somewhat iconoclastic account of the origins of economies became the basis of this book.*

from such politicisation. Instead they attempted to anchor economics in 'supply and demand'.

The contribution of Keynes in the 1930s was to bring political economy back to centre stage, with his practical advocacy of deficit financing by government, in effect inflation, to cure the then dominant problem of economic depression. The monetarists of the 1970s then rejected Keynes by anchoring their thinking in some older theories about inflation and in the beneficial mechanisms of unfettered markets. In the subsequent misuse of the latter doctrine can be seen the seeds of the economic catastrophe which struck in 2007.

The book which now follows seeks to move on once more, a change which after eighty years is perhaps overdue. Its preference is to anchor economics in the evolution of methods for understanding and recording credit, and in the remarkable influence they have exerted over the shape of human society.

THE GENERAL STUDY of economics must ultimately serve a practical purpose, otherwise it is merely a glass bead game. People may of course come up with any purpose they wish but so far as this book is concerned, economics should first show politicians how they may attain two strategic aims: to increase the sum of material prosperity, and how to balance its distribution fairly between rich and poor. Economists then need to show how the second should be prevented from confounding the first. You cannot make the poor rich by making the rich poor.

Finally they must show how the mechanisms of economics may be protected from bringing the whole edifice crashing down. The subject was originally called Political

Economy with such purposes firmly in mind. Compared with those of medicine, or of chemistry, or of physics, the sciences rewarded with Nobel prizes, even the basic principles of economics are still far from conclusive. As a specific field of enquiry, there is little evidence the subject existed at all before Adam Smith (1723-1790) and the eighteenth century French physiocrats who had influenced him.

Although it was never called economics, the work of The School of Salamanca[2] in the sixteenth century is now seen by some to have paved the way, a link back to the earlier 'economic' thoughts of classical writers such as Aristotle. However the entire 'science of economics' as a recognise field of enquiry is still only 250 years old. It continues to blunder around looking for magic formulae, broadly at the same stage of development that chemistry had reached with its medieval alchemists.

In a mature intellectual discipline, the golden rule is to change the theories to fit fresh evidence as it emerges, no matter how disruptive that new evidence may be. Too much of economics, that teenager among academic pursuits, that adventure playground for would-be philanthropists, still seeks to do the reverse: to reshape the evidence so that some moribund theory they admire may be kept alive.

It is a pervasive habit. Nowhere has it been more apparent than in the metaphysical calculus of supply and demand, in the quasi-religious belief that a free market is the solution to almost anything or in the hocus-pocus of seeking to measure 'money' supply. Worst of all is an imperishable conceit that when the chips are down, the wise nannies of Whitehall and Westminster -

2. (See Bibliography)

or Washington - will always know best. That peculiar notion has held sway since the Second World War, the offspring of powerful influences brought to bear by John Maynard Keynes on his many admirers in central government.

'Scientific' economists are confronted by a further problem. The essence of any genuinely scientific procedure, in marked contrast to a magic trick, is that it can be repeated and verified. That has been the unswerving requirement since the days of Pythagoras, the founding father of our western intellectual tradition, and probably the first man to distinguish between science and magic.

FROM HIS DAY ONWARD, magicians have been people whose professionalism demands they never repeat their tricks. In complete contrast, scientists are those whose professionalism demands that they must always do so. Amid such demands the 'science' of economics finds itself caught in the crossfire

On which test bench, or laboratory mouse, or guinea pig, can anyone conduct a scientific test for some artifice of economic management? Meanwhile where is the exactly identical bench, mouse or guinea pig kept untouched as the 'control' for scientific comparison? In the real world there can be none, and the Law of Unintended Consequences rules supreme.

Again, can any economist ever be certain that his favourite device, used a first time to modify an economy, will have just the same effect when applied a second time? In a genuine science, such repeatability is fundamental. It simply cannot be done in economics, ever, because all the people out there in the economy now know what the manoeuvre is going to involve and take due precautions. They are now knowingly prepared for what will come next. It is the same old problem facing all magicians and the underlying reason they never repeat a trick.

There are yet more difficulties to consider. Economic devices to implement public policy are put into effect amid powerful and constantly changing economic interruption. The environment is the diametric opposite of 'laboratory conditions' required for a legitimate scientific experiment, where unwanted contamination is avoided at all costs. The prospect of ever conducting a live economic 'experiment' under sterile conditions is hopelessly unrealistic.

THE PRECEDING FIVE PARAGRAPHS set out the principal theme of this chapter. Measured by the wise rules for legitimate scientific method, the pursuit of economics fails on all counts. It is a science that never was. Unable to test scientifically whether some economic trick really works as intended, too many conventional economists down the years have been left clinging to their defunct hypotheses, while the real world of industry, commerce and government moves on.

Rather than cherishing their time-worn axioms, obsolete rubrics and questionable assumptions, it would be wiser for economists simply to accept that human ideas and behaviour will change continuously. As recently as the 1960s, for example, the idea promoted by Alfred Wegener that entire continents might be gradually sliding around the globe was still being laughed out of court by most serious geographers.

Yet in the following decade his notion of continental drift was transformed from ludicrous speculation into canon principle, and the transformation was done by geographers and geomorphologists themselves. If geographers can change the basis of their understanding so radically, why cannot economists as easily do the same?

Biologists were speedy enough to concede that their subject had been turned upside down by publication of Charles Darwin's *Origin of Species* in 1859. Physicists willingly accepted Sir Isaac Newton's re-writing of the fundamental laws of their discipline. Economists, despite the youth of their subject, have been far more resistant to change. Too many still seek to turn it into a sub-school of mathematics, when all the evidence shows it is one of the humanities, like history or philology.

Yet worn-out ideas about economics still litter the corridors and smoke filled rooms of political economy. Keynes referred to their proponents as defunct economists. Or as Keynes's biographer Sir Roy Harrod once succinctly put it: *"statesmen have a hard task these days. If we are to have a sound economic policy, certain new aptitudes are called for. The small group of ministers concerned with economic decisions need to have some understanding of economics. This is indeed a formidable requirement."*

It could have been written last week, but in fact it was originally written to describe the immediate postwar government in Great Britain. It has been equally applicable on numerous occasions before and since. As Harold Macmillan once commented as Chancellor of the Exchequer, his task was like trying to run the economy using last year's Bradshaw - his Victorian term for a railway timetable. Had professional and academic economists over those first 250 years got it right, or anywhere near right, then catastrophic credit crashes would no longer happen. Unemployment would be voluntary, the trade cycle would be ancient history while the mechanisms of public finance would lubricate rather than debilitate the rest of the economy. Mr and Mrs Joe Public's savings nest egg would be as safe as houses. At least.

The public services such as education, transport, health and welfare would no longer languish as the impoverished recipients of spasmodic political largesse. The Third World would by now be just as prosperous as the First.

At all times economic wisdom deserves to be judged, not by its philanthropic aspirations, but by its discernable effects. Future historians could easily conclude that the 20th century was a prolonged disaster for economic theorising - nowhere more so than in centrally-governed Great Britain.

FOR NO REASON OTHER than artless economic management the UK spent at least half that century sinking lower in the league table of economically successful nations. Like first world war generals noting casualty figures from the Western Front, Britain's dignitaries gazed on in impotent serenity while some inflexible economic dogma wiped out whole industries, or small businesses, or farms, or jobs or family firms in their tens of thousands.

The mass extermination was grandly proclaimed to be 'clearing out the dead wood' or 'modernisation' or 'the post industrial era'. Exuberant catch-phrases such as 'the freedom of the market' or 'economic planning' or 'the third way' or 'nationalising the commanding heights of the economy' or 'controlling the money supply' were wheeled out as the latest miracle cure amid reverent applause, only to fizzle out in the years that followed.

Such misplaced confidence extended well beyond the shores of the United Kingdom. Governments in many countries looked around for a coherent wisdom to drive their economic policies. The economists who were heeded most were those with the catchiest slogans. It was not so far removed from magic after all, as the snake oil salesmen of economics charmed gullible customers around the world's treasuries and finance ministries.

Governmental enthusiasm for their nostrums was never dampened by the salutary lessons of reality. As Eddie George, Governor of the Bank of England once helpfully explained "There are three kinds of economists: those who can count, and those who can't." John Kenneth Galbraith coined another pithy epithet in 1958 in his book 'The Affluent Society'. He observed a slide toward 'private affluence and public squalor'. His memorable criticism failed to reverse the slide, which by the end of the twentieth century was gaining fresh momentum.

Such criticisms have been rehearsed many times, and paint a stark backdrop to this book. It seeks neither to rehearse them any further, nor to propose yet another of those miracle cures which have peppered economic discussion for more than 150 years. For those who still need them, there is already an ample supply of economic witch doctors.

Rather than join the conventional debates of economics with yet another set of only superficially distinct arguments, this book has a contrasting aim: to urge the teachers and theorisers of economics onto a different tack. The architecture of economics surely needs to change. No author can claim to be immune from lifetime influences which have shaped their thinking. This book is the outcome of a career studying economics at school and university, then through serious business journalism, qualifying in the City as a trader in commodity derivatives, then policy formation for Chambers of Commerce and the Confederation of British Industry to working in the tough worlds of international banking, finance and commerce. It has been anything but a safari through the whispering cloisters of academe.

Nor is there any covert career agenda in what follows. Only books which escape that lethal cockpit of academic backbiting may pursue originality unsupervised. Since 1998 the influences upon this book have included a global network of economists, one which only became feasible with the emergence of the internet.[3] The network has included inquisitive businessmen and financiers, enquiring academics, unorthodox bankers and a former Australian ambassador, all of them sharing scepticism about the wisdom of modern economics.

Any encouragement needed by the author to question conventional wisdom was bolstered immeasurably as a young feature writer for the *Financial Times*. The educative surprise revolved round an emergency economic package introduced by Prime Minister Harold Wilson on Wednesday 20 July 1966.

In those days, such budgets and quasi-budgets created a peculiar problem for the FT, one of only three Fleet Street papers printed solely in London. To inform their readership in Scotland or in the far west of England and Wales, such

3. *Known as the 'Gang of Eight' - although its members were numerous than that - it was founded by the author in September 1998. The members included at least one economist considered close to Nobel Prize standard, and the internet discussions flourished until about 2015.*

newspapers had to deliver their first edition to overnight newspaper trains from Paddington, Euston and Kings Cross by 9.30pm. Using old-fashioned hot metal technology, virtually all copy had to be in the hands of the typesetters by around 6.30pm. Only a couple of hours after the final edition of London's *Evening Standard*, it was an exceptionally early hour for a newspaper ostensibly datelined the following morning.

Unfortunately it was the habit of Chancellors and other parliamentary performers to withhold announcement of all the juiciest bits of their budgets and economic packages until the last possible moment, usually around 4pm. Perhaps they hoped to retain the interest, and so attendance, of as many members of parliament as possible. This did however put a critical squeeze on the *Financial Times, The Times* and maybe on the *Sun*.

THE ONLY WAY ROUND THIS famine of time, at the FT anyway, was for its senior editors to hazard a guess what might be in the government's economic package then parcel out those topics to members of the staff who could write feature articles quickly. Their task was then to do all their research beforehand, and ideally hit the ground running when the crucial moment came.

The present writer, being the most junior of that July 1966 writing team, was allocated travel allowances as the least likely prospect. Late in the afternoon the meat of what the Prime Minister had to say began spewing from the tape machines, and in a trice the ground shook. *"Has anyone researched travel allowances?"* exclaimed the paper's deputy news editor John Hay as he stooped over the Press Association tape machine.

His surprise was audible. *'Wilson's only gone and slapped an annual £50 limit on them.'* The deadline clock began its remorseless ticking. So it was now time for a slice of journalistic ingenuity. Just three weeks previously there had been a news story about the launch in Britain of Barclaycard. It was the nation's first-ever credit card, in effect a rebranded version of the BankAmericard. The launch had been accompanied by a substantial public relations fanfare on 29 June. I had helped cover the story.

Any Bank of England expert, Treasury official or leading politician could have read the news with equal ease, a textbook example of the blindingly obvious. Yet as I ploughed through all the PA tape, UNS tape, Reuters tape, and press releases from sealed packages sent by the Treasury and plonked on my desk, there was not a mention of credit cards in any of them.

ON THE FACE OF IT any resourceful traveller could drive a coach and horses through Mr Wilson's £50 allowance. I rang the number at the Treasury given for further enquiries, and drew to their attention the remarkable absence of credit cards in the reams of material. *"Aha, Mr Meakin, that one's just a bit too technical for us."* said quite the smoothest press spokesman Whitehall ever recruited. *"I will however give you the direct number at the Bank of England of the man who actually drafted this part of the new regulations."* The unmistakable clatter of a passing buck echoed down the line.

Next I rang the direct number at the Bank and asked the nameless man who answered it if he was the one who drafted the Prime Minister's statement on the £50 travel limit. *"I am indeed. And how can I help you?"* I was in a hurry, deadlines loomed. *"Well*

I've read through all the material and can see no mention anywhere of credit cards". There followed a very long silence, as the man at the Bank of England pondered this obvious omission. It had a crippling impact on the legislation set before Parliament about fifteen minutes earlier, and maybe on his own career at the Bank of England. The egg on his face was almost audible.

At length he said *'Christ'* extremely loudly. His un-Bank expletive was followed by a gabbled explanation, something about a Source File dating back to 1948. *"Let me help you."* I volunteered. *"Way back in 1948, of course, there were no such things as credit cards in this country."*

He agreed with me, meekly. Worse by far, his proposals for the £50 limit must have been examined by his superiors at the Bank, passed through various levels of scrutiny at the Treasury, processed by policy apparatchiks at Number 10 and ultimately reviewed by the Prime Minister himself.

No-one, not one of them, had spotted the blindingly obvious. As it stood, the newly-announced £50 travel limit was next to useless, all thanks to a credit card launched only three weeks previously. That same Harold Wilson once said a week is a long time in politics. Quite clearly three whole weeks in politics were a mind-numbing eternity, in which the faintest recollection of former events was long ago consigned to oblivion.

At the time I was ten weeks short of my 23rd birthday. The travel allowance fiasco could not have been better timed. It explains why the book which follows frequently makes a beeline for the most obvious places. Too often such places prove to be the least visited. After all, if they cannot see it coming, it is even less likely they can see it when it is standing still.

It surely falls within the frontiers of legitimate enquiry, even in economics, to ask what actually happened. How did today's commercial structures originally come about? Amid all the machinery of familiar economic activity, which component came first? How soon did money first make its appearance? Upon what earlier foundations, for example, was banking later constructed? In the best traditions of the Oxford English Dictionary, the version of economics which follows is built on historical principles. Anyone looking for mathematical equations as the basis of the subject will find it all a huge disappointment.

THE HISTORICAL UNDERSTANDING of economies proves to be full of intriguing and educative surprises, yet it is hardly ever explored. Unknowingly, mankind was laying the foundations of modern structures for a good ten or twenty millennia before Adam Smith wrote *An Inquiry into the Nature and Causes of the Wealth of Nations*. The subject of 'economics' clearly does not start in 1776, as Smith himself freely acknowledged. Sadly many of his intellectual successors have been far too willing to overlook that reality.

Nor does economic activity commence, as many respected economists would still have people believe, at some fanciful moment in prehistory when primitive man grew bored with barter and suddenly decided to invent money instead. It was not that simple, not even by many thousand years.

The true origin of economies is far more convoluted than that. This book departs from a long-established habit of conventional economists. Its principal sources are not to be found in that ponderous body of literature, the history of economic thought. Those intellectual traditions of economics are not rejected outright, and some of their myriad notions find a comfortable niche in the saga which follows. Here the aim is to build a fresh framework, or architecture. Others may embellish it with patent economic nostrums should they so wish.

Few economists can have written their books while surrounded by all the research advantages of the internet. Many real-world observations vital to their endeavours have not been available to economists for very long. This book could not have been written without them. Remarkably one of the most telling is derived from the discoveries of scuba divers, an exclusively modern pursuit. Readers must wait until the end of Chapter Three to learn the significance of that.

So this book's principal sources are to be found partly in empirical observation, but also in modern advances of archaeology, in ancient and modern history, in the annals of banking, sometimes in geology, in the widely differing realms of anthropology and accountancy and in the diligent research of numismatists. As an alternative to a history of pioneering economic thoughts, what follows is a history of pioneering economic deeds. Our quest for the origin of economies therefore begins, not in some simple eighteenth century pin factory at the dawn of the Industrial Revolution, but long before that in the tribal world of hunter-gatherer man.

Chapter Two

Before 1500 BC

There are more things in Heaven and Earth, Horatio,
Than are dreamt of in our Philosophy.
WILLIAM SHAKESPEARE, HAMLET

T
O GRASP THE BASICS of economics properly it is wisest to trace right back to the beginning of humanity's time, back to times when there was no such thing as an economy. Only in that way can one start from scratch and see how things subsequently began and, most importantly, in what order. This quest is to find the origin of economies. Jumping in half-way through the narrative means overlooking fundamentals which have come, and gone, and long since been forgotten.

More than that. The time spent in each major stage of mankind's early development proves of great significance to an effective understanding of economies.   Humanity's evolutionary story is long and anything but simple, with very different time-scales in different parts of the world. It is also very sketchy; its unfolding archaeological record is based on roughly a bus-load of fossilised skeletons spanning perhaps two million years.

Mankind's ancestors began to emerge when a higher ape *australopithicus* evolved into the earliest hominin, pioneering handy man *homo habilis*. That advance is now thought to have been driven mainly by diet. Archaeological traces reveal that, from roughly two million years ago, these advanced apes began making and using tools.

The skeletal remains at Olduvai Gorge in northern Tanzania have been dated back as far as 1.9 million years ago. Unsurprisingly mankind's first deliberate stone tools were weapons for killing other animals, and blades for cutting meat. The previous pre-humans had been restricted to a largely fruit and vegetable diet, just as the higher apes are still vegetarians today.

Such a strictly vegetarian diet would have been monotonous and time-consuming for the preceding *australopithicus*. Its low nutritional value, by contrast with protein, meant they needed to spend most of their time feeding, and most of the energy so obtained was promptly expended on digestion. They would probably eat grubs and small creatures as well - a more efficient source of protein, and something which was easy to catch. Their digestive system easily evolved to handle that.

Possibly the first meat from a large animal eaten by those proto-humans had been scavenged from the kill of a big cat. That could have happened many times. Then at some point one of them worked out how to kill fresh game for himself, or lead a family group to do so collectively. That pioneering meat-eating *australopithecus* was clearly very clever, because it killed by guile rather than by superior physique, as of course do big cats. Some archaeologists nowadays consider they were still more ape than human and prefer *australopithicus habilis.* It is perhaps semantic exactly when, but at some point they became human beings. Perhaps we might reasonably call their leader Adam, even though his brain was still no larger than that of a modern chimpanzee.

THE BIRTH OF MANKIND wasn't an apple offered to Adam by Eve. It is far more likely to have been a fresh liver. There must have been some first such occasion when killing and eating big meat was done with premeditation by a team, and that underpins the transition from higher ape to pioneer human. We may reasonably guess that one tasty dead animal led to another. If there was a handy cliff, animals could be herded over it to kill them and just possibly that might have become a practised routine.   Living in proximity to gorges and ravines, perhaps?

Suitable cliffs with big game atop them are, however, few and far between. Sooner or later Adam or his offspring must have used a big stick as a club. Then specialised stone tools such as spears were manufactured and thereby the first uniquely human, non-animal like traits began to emerge.

It is now reckoned that the earliest humans evolved from an exceptionally clever meat-eating ape. Steadily *homo habilis* evolved into *homo erectus* and it has been thought that species migrated out of Africa to inhabit coastal areas of much of the old world; the 'Out of Africa' thesis.   They were probably forced to move when hunting savannas of the Sahara were reduced to inhospitable desert by climate change.   Some consider this 'Sahara pump' to have caused emigration from northern Africa in four separate phases over a very long period, most recently to distribute our own species of *homo sapiens*. Why was this large region a probable nursery for the origins of a cleverer mankind? Adverse changes in climate can demand greater ingenuity for survival. Necessity, not ability, is the mother of invention. The hunter-gatherers emerging from the capricious Sahara would have been ingenious people.

To begin with the process of human evolution was almost imperceptibly slow. It still requires a lot of energy to digest raw meat, as anyone who likes their steaks bleu, or who eats steak tartare, will readily confirm.   Meat which has first been cooked is much easier to digest, leaving a greater surplus of nutritional energy for higher activities other than simple digestion.

WITH THAT GREAT advance human evolution could, and did, accelerate. The archaeological record is not surprisingly, rather diffuse. There are some hints of using fire much earlier, but much available evidence currently points to around 450,000 years ago. Given future archaeological discoveries that time-scale could of course change.

By that date there are clear signs of humans using fire as far afield as China, modern Israel, Spain and Suffolk in England. It seems meat-eating humans had taken at least a million years before they learnt how to cook. How quickly that happened once they had learnt to control fire to keep warm we cannot tell; it was not intuitively obvious to burn meat before eating it. We may speculate that one day someone inadvertently dropped a chunk of meat into a fire, or found an animal that had been killed, and cooked by a fire caused by lightning or a volcano. Such flukes do happen. Norway's traditional Christmas dish of lutefisk is dried cod which is then soaked in water dosed with lye, or potash, the chemical obtained from fire. It probably started when a wooden fish-drying shed burnt down, and there was nothing else available.[1] As it unfolds, the story of economic advance is full of helpful happenstance like that.

With the passing of time, cooking meat became a widespread and regular human practice. We may guess that it passed from tribe to tribe by word of mouth, or perhaps through an instructive marriage. By that advance, however, the human race distanced itself from the rest of the animal world. Many animals hunt for food, a few even devise crude tools, but none of them can make or control fire. All animals other than human beings merely fear it.

Requiring less energy for digestion, cooked food left more nutrition available for other uses. The organ greediest for this extra nutrition is the brain, with a specific need of its essential fuel, glucose. The human brain had been growing since handy man and now it could grow much more quickly. Skull analysts have clearly demonstrated that it did.

The first evidence of Neanderthals emerges in Europe more than 350,000 years ago. They had larger brains and various other distinct and beneficial characteristics, compared with other strains of humanity. Originally they were considered a separate sub-species. No longer. It is now considered the early Neanderthal humans

1. *My thanks to Arno Daastøl, the international moderator of Gang Eight, for pointing out this splendid example of culinary serendipity.*

carried the genes which cause lighter-coloured skin, essential to absorb sufficient vitamin D and thrive in cloudy, higher latitudes.[2] Neanderthal genes have been found in *homo sapiens* races of Eurasia, but in none in the races of sub-Saharan Africa. Emigrating from the "Sahara pump" had clearly meant travelling north or east. Going southwards across the Equator was probably too hot for them, while to the west lay the Atlantic Ocean. It seems the white skin gene itself was not so geographically confined. The Bushmen, aboriginal peoples of southern Africa, are also a white-skinned people.

WE NOW ENTER a fascinating field of study which anthropologists fairly regard as a golden era for their subject. Ability to interpret the human genome expands every year and the investigation still has far to go. Where it meshes with conventional archaeology, the results are profound. One consequence is that ideas about the relationship between *homo sapiens* and Neanderthals are being reconstructed.

The old notion the latter were not as bright as 'pure' humans is being progressively abandoned. This is proving to be yet another of those academic shifts, not unlike the geographers' sudden switch to Continental Drift outlined in the previous chapter. By their collective flexibility of mind, today's anthropologists show today's economists an effective way forward.

It has been worth devoting several paragraphs to the changes in the fundamentals of their thinking. Anthropologists have

2. The genomic landscape of Neanderthal ancestry in present-day humans. *Sankararaman, Mallick, Dannemann et al.* Nature, *29 January 2014*

progressed their discipline because of research tools which were not previously available. Yet faced with such radicalism in their own discipline many professional economists would simply back away. They consider it, not so much a golden era, rather an unwelcome intrusion on their own established academic position and a threat to their earlier publications. Worst of all, they might even be forced to start teaching their subject differently.

Confident professional disciplines readily embrace change. Others, lacking the necessary intellectual maturity, will instead fear change and seek to deflect it. As noted in the first chapter, Keynes declared that *'practical men, who believe themselves to be quite exempt from any intellectual influences, are usually the slaves of some defunct economist.'* Perhaps out of politeness to his colleagues, he did not spell out its logical corollary, namely that too many professional economists are themselves slaves of defunct ideas.

Not so anthropologists. They have now shown that by 130,000 years ago, completely Neanderthal characteristics had developed. In some places a strain of unmixed *homo sapiens* continued to evolve, but at a different rate. At two sites in South Africa, the Klasies river mouth and border cave, such *homo sapiens* fossils have been dated to around 60,000 to 80,000 years ago.

Until recently those relics were assumed to be the earliest known example of modern human beings, and from that emerged an oft-cited notion that we all trace back to Africa. However in the light of subsequent evidence, thinking is changing on that as well. Such sub-Saharan African races, lacking any Neanderthal admixture, may not be everyone's ancestors after all. Either way the result was that people emerged who were much like modern human beings. Brains had evolved to present-day proportions. Brain size is easy to measure from fossil skulls and can be dated; carbon-dating helps. Working out how those human brains functioned intellectually is, however, a different matter.

No amount of skull measurement can ever explain that. In pursuing the origin of economies, we need to know how profoundly those ancient humans could think. One of the key requirements for fathoming their ability to undertake economic activity is knowing how far they could think in the abstract, and therefore communicate abstract ideas among themselves. Fortunately there is at least one archaeological test for that.

D ELIBERATE, CEREMONIAL BURIAL of the dead is a sure sign of essentially human, in contrast to animal, awareness and intelligence. As is frequently observed, elephants may have 'graveyards' but they do not erect memorial stones nor employ tools to excavate family graves.

Unlike most of his other activities, early man's burials, his marked graves and subsequently tombs can and have survived down the millennia. Those ancient human graveyards have bequeathed evidence of unequalled value to today's archaeologists. Their significance has grown through the millennia : when they were dug, death and burial rituals probably accounted for just a small fraction of the hunter-gatherer routine. They are much more important now, in the absence of other durable remains or artefacts.

People who deliberately dug memorial graves must have understood death in the abstract; such activity embodies a clear sense of reverence for the dead. So those early humans would in all probability have the capacity to discuss the afterlife. It follows they thought and communicated understanding of abstract ideas - rather than just grunt at one another about the weather or where the next meal was coming from. Even one field of abstract thought is enough to demonstrate that others were feasible as well. If they couldn't do any of that, human beings would have expired where they sat, unremarked and unrecorded, as most animals just expire.

A deliberate burial site in Sierra de Atapuerca, Spain, known as Sima de los Huesos has so far yielded around 1600 bones from 50-60 different bodies, just a small fraction of the likely total. The observed skull capacity, and therefore brain size, is not greatly different from that of modern man.[3] Yet the site is Pleistocene and dates back more than 300,000 years, in other words way back into Neanderthal times, and much earlier than the *homo sapiens* relics from the coast of South Africa.

Future such discoveries may push the key thresholds of human evolution even further back in time; they cannot bring them forward. As archaeology makes progress, time's arrow always flies in a reverse direction. With that proviso about future discoveries, it is now possible to sketch a coherent account of mankind's developing physique and his innate intellectual capabilities; it is a long one. In seeking to explain the origins of economies, however, we do need to identify that further and exclusive achievement of true human beings,

3. *Nature, 8 April 1993, p534.*

the capacity for communicating abstract ideas. In sum : people with at least our dexterity, most probably our level of intelligence, most probably our sense of purpose have been living on this planet for a very long time. In marked contrast, human activity meriting the term 'an economy' is far more recent than that. Why? A purpose of this chapter is to examine that time discrepancy. Doing so begins to exposes a crucial shortcoming in the basic architecture of current economics.

BEFORE EVEN THE SIMPLEST economy could start to emerge, an advanced language using abstract concepts was needed throughout an entire community; the rationale for that is explored later. It was a language far beyond the dancing of bees, the whistling of dolphins, the chattering of apes or the groaning of whales.

The original structure and vocabulary of that first human language are long gone, yet philologists may just detect some of its lingering traces in languages we still use today. It is probably significant the word "Papa" is shared by about seven hundred of a thousand different languages examined by French academics; it is one of the earliest natural sounds a baby makes.

Traces of prehistoric human language could stretch back to the earliest days of *homo sapiens* and even earlier. Recent research has focussed on the hyoid bone, essential for speaking as it supports the root of the tongue. Lacking that feature, other species of animals cannot speak. Some Neanderthals have hyoid features similar to modern humans which could well be evidence of early language.

Nor was the hunter-gathering of *homo sapiens* just some arbitrary animal-like wanderlust. To succeed in their quest for food, men who hunted had to search many miles over increasingly unfamiliar territory and, most importantly, find the way back home to their families with their kill afterwards. Theirs was a task which demanded tenacious single-mindedness. The families of those men who failed to find their way home again would have starved. Memory is important; apparently squirrels forget where they have hidden 80% of their nuts. To survive ancient man had to do better than that.

Only the children of the most capable men survived, Darwinian selection at its most striking.   And so of necessity navigating ability became a highly-developed male instinct. As such it is not exclusively human; it is also found in many animals, impressively so in homing pigeons, many other migrating bird species and most remarkably in salmon. Or in the gigantic migrating herds of the open savanna.

Mankind's navigating expertise was probably conscious and verbal; in it we may once again identify the early emergence of complex language; probably only humans can explain the difference between left and right. As those hunters amassed their knowledge of animal tracks and migration patterns, it was handed down verbally from father to son. There were no maps. Through the millennia men evolved with an instinctive and powerful sense of direction; one might add it seems to have embodied a deeply-ingrained enthusiasm for spotting interesting things. Bruce Chatwin's book *'Songlines'* paints a vivid picture of the purely verbal techniques which Australian aborigines in our own times have developed to memorise, communicate and navigate long journeys across open terrain, and do so without maps or writing.   Instead they sing their maps.

Such melodic wisdom has been handed down from father to son, the accumulated learning of many generations. It is a boy thing; daughters learn other important skills. Evolution had now taken humans beyond the stage at which all members of a community, males and females alike, had to forage side-by-side for most of their waking day. Species which only eat plants cannot afford the luxury of permitting the males to do one thing and the females another.

WITH MEAT-EATING HUMANS the male hunters if successful would bring home sufficient food for all. The men hunted while the women gathered, though there would have been scope for individual exceptions to that. Notably athletic women would join in the hunt, while older or physically infirm men would stay behind gathering. For all that, hunter-gatherer men and women steadily developed different aptitudes. They remain with us today. Sadly they have become embroiled in a silly obsession with 'political correctness.'

Early traces of a fundamental element of economies, a division of labour, began to manifest themselves even as mankind diverged from the *australopithecus* apes. Human evolution after that separation steadily developed instinctive differences between the sexes. If we observe, we can clearly see those difference among ourselves and not just in that hackneyed comparison between single-minded men and multi-tasking women.

Hunting and fishing, pursued nowadays primarily for sport, are still predominantly male pursuits. Modern men are living out a deep-rooted survival instinct to search for food dating from two million years ago. Gardening, by contrast, particularly attracts women, living out a quite different set of instincts. Like their hunter husbands they too are pursuing their own means of survival. Many of our deepest human instincts are still those of hunter-gatherers.

Men's ancient abilities for direction-finding and navigation are revealed most clearly in the modern culture of the motor car. A twenty-first century male *homo sapiens* driver will valiantly seek to identify main points of the compass, noting the changing position of the sun and the hour of the day, or observe the natural downhill paths of rivers and the shape of nearby hills.

It is instinctive. Sitting at the driving wheel of his Ford Mondeo he is still seeking to reach his destination using the skills of a practised hunter-gatherer. At heart he is still merrily on the open range, using ancient faculties to build a mental map which he can naturally read from any direction.

Hunter-gatherer women were not generally expected to lead hunting packs across unmapped countryside. So they developed no equivalent map-generating or map-reading instincts. That probably explains why so many of their distant 21st century map-reading daughters are still obliged - often with evident desperation - to turn a map upside-down when the car is heading south. That was never their job. Instead hunter-gatherer women became naturally skilled at remembering the local landmarks. Women still are: try finding your way unerringly round IKEA without one.

Men find it easier in today's corporate world to understand and cope with hierarchies because that is how it always worked in the hunting pack. Today's women, in contrast, will often find male hierarchies inimical. Their equivalent instinct is much more strongly territorial: it is almost always women who complain 'get out of my space.' The vital task of hunter-gatherer women was not to hunt collectively with the pack but to maintain an individual clean household, especially for the health and survival of their children.

To this day, women are much more adept at observing dust and disorder around the home than men will ever be. The domestic complaints are interminable. Once again, that has been their distinctive talent, and essential task for the past two million years. Maybe the male equivalent is a fascination with finding out how things work, dismantling and repairing them. It was an instinct which developed the genius of both George Stephenson and Henry Ford; detail on that must wait until a later chapter.

There are many other ancient gender distinctions but the salient point in the origin of economies is surely made. The earliest notion of a "division of labour" really is as old as that. None of it should surprise or upset anyone; as the French say most appropriately, 'vive la différence.' Meat-eating humans were to spend two million years, perhaps 100,000 generations, selectively honing their instincts and genes and adopting the best ones for ensuring survival. As is shown later almost all our ancestors were hunter-gathers and that is where our present-day instincts evolved.

The two genders developed different priorities because they had different tasks to perform. Quite separately they had become either hunters or home-making gatherers - no longer just all-purpose foragers. In short, they developed a distinctive two-fold division of labour. Amid all this, and in much more besides, we can observe Darwinian natural selection of not just the fittest, but of the cleverest, the most appropriately talented, the most ingenious.

At the most, our agricultural ancestry stretches back five hundred generations, just a tiny fraction of mankind's total. So most of our basic human instincts, for all our supposed sophistication, still remain those of a meat-eating hunter-gatherer.

THOSE EARLY HUMANS lived in small communities of people who knew one another well, and latterly at a subsistence level sufficiently 'affluent' to allow recreational pursuits. Although they had no activity we might call an economy in any modern sense, they would have made transfers of rudimentary property. Anthropologists, inferring from primitive tribes in our own times, speak of them as the 'bride-price' and 'fines'.[4] There would have been disputes about hunting grounds when different tribes came into contact with one another.

Their patch of open range was their livelihood. Hunter-gatherers would have been every bit as jealous of their territory as any grouse moor-owning Scottish laird in our own era, indeed like all kinds of landowners down the ages. Probably there were tribal fights to begin with, but sooner or later such disputes must have evolved into a basis of mutual respect.

4. *My thanks for this insight to Randall Wray, then professor of economics at Missouri University, Kansas City, and a fellow founding member of Gang of Eight.*

WITH THAT ANOTHER essential component, recognising property rights, was welded into place in the origin of economies. More ominously, leaders of one tribe would be obliged to make conciliatory payments to a tribe next door. It probably had more in common with a protection racket than with free trade, but an early semblance of commodity exchange was slowly emerging.

There was no money, nor yet anything even remotely like money, to make such payments. Fines were likely to be honoured with slaves, attractive women, choice food or treasured possessions. Words for concepts such as 'payment' which were later woven into economics gradually came into being. The process was a little different from barter; it also carried a moral imperative.

There can be no doubt that prehistoric cultures developed many skills. Archaeology can only reveal a few artefacts, the most durable ones which have survived the millennia since. They are a tiny fraction of what prehistoric man made or used; almost all of it decayed to nothing. That said a renowned archeological site in the central Russian province of Voronezh is situated in a steep ravine at Kostenky.

Among other artefacts it has yielded a carved bone female figure, the '*Venus of Kostenky*' of the Aurignacian culture of the Upper Palaeolithic, dating back to 30,000BC. So we know hunter-gatherers did intricate carvings; such dexterity provided the same physical skills and mental aptitude later needed for writing. Yet surprisingly, for some, that does not emerge for another 25,000 years or more.[5] From the early Stone Age, man learnt how to knap flints to manufacture fine spear heads, axes and other cutting tools. In Britain alone they date back almost a million years. Stone Age expertise and dexterity were well-developed. Such deliberately-shaped flints and other treasured stones of their time have been unearthed far from their geological source. That probably involved trade rather than expropriation; or an early kind of trade by treaty, exchanging what today are called 'diplomatic gifts'.

Such 'trade' could equally have been achieved by a simple kind of barter, but money was still many millennia away and many more economic concepts and mechanisms were necessarily to emerge before that stage could be reached. Pre-occupation with barter has been an abiding and misleading characteristic of primitive economists and of many other people since.

It has been too readily assumed that one day prehistoric man grew bored with barter - and so invented money instead; even more implausibly that one led straight into the other. Reality was rather more complicated than that. A historically sensible version of what actually happened, one difficult step at a time, is the focus of the following Chapter. Proper understanding of economies depends on understanding their origins. A full awareness of the complexities of money and how it gradually came into being is fundamental to

---

5. *Dr Diana Stein, an archaeologist at Birkbeck College, London University, points out that even earlier examples are now known. The author is grateful for her voluntary diligence in attempting to cleanse this chapter of anachronisms. More may have crept in subsequently.*

grasping all that followed.   There is no short cut. The grossly simplistic link to barter is no more than that.

Among the many Stone Age tools found by archaeologists, some were of greatest use to carpenters, and therefore to boatbuilders. The rafts or boats they built would primarily have been used for fishing, yet it was not just their brave fishermen who put to sea. Stone Age women and children crossed the ocean too.

T HE MIGRATION OF EARLY PEOPLES shows those early boats were sufficiently reliable to colonise islands, even the water-locked continent of Australia by, at its most recent, 60,000 BC.   Maybe one could relate that in time to the near-contemporary 'Klasies river mouth' *homo sapiens* in Africa (see p.25) although the difference in technological ability appears to have been substantial.   Nor was colonising Australia some isolated instance; there is much work to be done.

Anthropology, augmented by blood-group and DNA analysis,   shows there was much overseas human migration in hunter-gatherer times. Seaworthy passenger vessels able to transport whole tribes[6] could not have been knocked together by some slapdash do-it-yourself enthusiast. Given the restricted workshop of Stone Age hand tools available, boat-building must have been a well-respected, specialist trade. Hunter-gatherer achievements were

6. *By folk tradition, the Welsh consider they originally arrived in Wales in thirty large boats from the land which is modern Spain. Increasingly there is linguistic and genetic evidence to indicate the tradition could well be right.*

reaching well beyond the staple needs of food and warmth. Their society had skilled artists too. In surviving cave paintings we can witness powers of observation exercised by practised draughtsmen.

They were working in difficult conditions just by dim candlelight - another innovation. Their choice of animal subjects reveals what was on their minds. They were probably painting what they hoped they would catch. The paintings even show animals which are now extinct; they provide an intriguing snapshot of fauna in prehistoric times.

Archaeologists now consider some of the painting was achieved by spitting a frothy coloured mixture onto cave walls. Whatever painting technique was used, given the limited range of natural pigments available it involved considerable skill, while hand prints indicate that many cave artists were women. One might surmise it was simply a social pastime, collective morale-lifting while their menfolk were away hunting. Rather than deeply-profound religious symbolism, or a place of reverence, it was quite possibly a far from primitive precursor of today's recreational painting classes enjoyed by the over-fifties.

Cave paintings have been shown to have remarkably early dates. Those at Lascaux in France go back over 17,000 years. Paintings at El Castillo in Spain are older still, dating to 40,000 BC. Such an aesthetic culture would have bards and minstrels as well. It is plausible that, by trial and error, hunter-gatherer peoples understood medicinal herbs and rudimentary healthcare. So it is a fair guess that a wide range of specialist skills had developed, yet their economic application was still far into the future. It all fell far short of any kind of fully-fledged economy we would acknowledge as such. Within a small hunter-gatherer community, fair distribution of whatever was produced, if ever a bone of contention, could be decreed by tribal elders.

Any 'financial' structure was unnecessary. Disputes about 'work' or 'pay' could be settled by collective arbitration. Fairness and justice were more or less instantaneous. There was no requirement to carry over precise records for many years or even months. There was, in truth, little or no necessity to look at any activity in the longer term. Passage of time was unimportant.

The archaeological record already sketches a culture embracing many different skills, from artists to flintsmiths to boatbuilders. By the intellectual calculus of Adam Smith, primitive man had a well-developed division of labour. Yet the step from that Stone Age culture to the earliest economy had to wait many thousands of years. That said, our quest for origins is at least on its way. Given all his physical, and social skills, hunter-gatherer man was roughly halfway towards an economy. Crucially he was no further advanced than that. Something was still missing.

So at that point we start to look beyond the early insights of Adam Smith. His explanation set out in *Wealth of Nations* was not wrong, simply insufficient. A division of labour is not a full explanation of economic activity. As indicated at the outset of this chapter, to build a complete picture one needs to go back to the beginnings of humanity and then proceed a step at a time. Only in that way can we comprehend how things started, and in what order they did so, so to grasp the real origin of economies. Further, it is significant that hunter-gatherer society as explained so far had a conspicuously timeless quality about it. There was no hurry, there were no deadlines to meet. There was neither need nor financial means to catch meat to take to market, nor to build boats for onward sale. Any such economic sophistication was still far into the unknowable future. Boats were ready when they were ready; ambitious cave paintings took their time. A tribe of hunter-gatherer man was dependent on no-one else and least of all on a timetable; such a notion would have been meaningless.

A FTER SOME TWO MILLION years living in his primeval Garden of Eden, mankind now began to move out of it and into a village. He was about to become a farmer instead. The next few pages of this chapter examine that fundamental change, and in particular the attendant and lasting delay before it took place.

Tribal hunter-gatherers would have passed through several stages of progressive development, each probably lasting many thousands of years, before settled agriculture became the norm. The change itself had to be rapid. The fascinating transition from highly accomplished, socially cultured hunter-gatherer to effective farmer has been fairly designated the 'Neolithic Revolution'.

In terms of daily lifestyle the change was dramatic, demanding huge shifts in cultural attitudes. Seeking to unearth a precise sequence of events in that mysterious period, archaeologists must contend with many unknowns. Different archaeologists have their own ideas about what happened when, where first and so in what precise order. The picture is blurred, but the rapid emergence of agricultural society is the greatest single economic advance mankind has ever achieved. It was marked by a switch to living in permanent settlements, a giant step forward from semi-nomadic groups camping in caves or perhaps tents. There had to be some practical stepping-stones on the path to full-time agricultural man.

WHAT SOME NOW CALL 'village sedentism' could not become a regular way of life until organised agriculture was properly established. Only then could enough food be grown and supplied in confidence to a fixed location for successive generations. By a wide margin and for all its strengths, the previous hunter-gatherer society had fallen well short of any such 'civilisation' - a word whose root indicates a city-dweller. Hunter-gatherers, no matter how cultured, were never that.

Although it was to be a further six thousand years before early peoples devised their first true towns, with the Neolithic Revolution mankind had at least embarked on his journey. In the millennium after 10,000BC, the most advanced societies consigned simple hunter-gathering activity to their cultural past. We may guess there were numerous failed experiments along the way.

One practical lifestyle, however, would have been transhumance, an annual routine of following a repeated migration route in canny anticipation of weather patterns, or of closely-related movements of wild herds. Alongside that repeating lifestyle, hunter-gatherers could well have moved beyond simply gathering and start transplanting fruit bushes along their established annual trail.

As centuries advanced, such peoples would learn how to control herds and become pastoralists. Once that happened it cannot have been long before primitive man realised that managed, domesticated animals benefit from winter fodder, so it had to be grown and stored for the cold season.

So some fundamentals of agriculture were already on the horizon. However organised farming came into being at widely differing times in history in different regions. Unhelpfully the physical record of those earliest farms has generally been obliterated by more recent agriculture; a good place to farm then is still a good place to farm now. Archaeological research to solve the conundrum necessarily relies on finding seeds of domesticated plants in ancient settlements. That is not an easy task, demanding scrupulous care.

T he earliest signs of permanent agriculture found so far are in the foothills of the Taurus and Zagros mountains of Turkey, Syria, Iran and Iraq. The region thus broadly equates to the territory of the modern Kurdish peoples. The climate of the region was no doubt supportive as was the gradual retreat of the Ice Age but, most important of all, it was one corner of the ancient world where emmer-wheat, einkorn-wheat and barley all grew wild.

An intriguing debate continues among painstaking archaeologists about which grain seeds they discover are wild and which were domesticated varieties, and how far that is evidence of organised as opposed to 'chance' agriculture. The point at which wild varieties of edible grain become domesticated varieties is perhaps semantic, but historically important nonetheless. However domestication of wheat eventually went much deeper than that. Normally hybrids are F1 hybrids which are infertile. Yet at some point along the way, early agricultural man achieved a remarkable breakthrough. Probably more by happenstance than by design he had stumbled upon a fertile hybrid. Many modern plant breeders would like to know how to do that.

THE OLDEST KNOWN HUMAN settlement showing clear evidence of organised farming is at Zawi Chemi Shanidar, near the upper Zab river in northern Iraq. Among huge deposits of bones and discarded stones there are querns, mortars and sickle-shafts, as well as engraved bone tools, beads of limestone, green stone and pretty native copper.

　　Those earliest farmers were still living in New Stone Age. The subsequent Bronze Age, considered later in this Chapter, was still totally unknown, in the far distant future. The shift to bronze was another great cultural achievement. Moreover manufacturing vital implements for farming was not some hunter-gatherer pastime like cave-painting.

　　It was a tough and slow necessity for the new agricultural man. Although there are no signs of cultivated seeds - as distinct from chance wild seed varieties - it is unlikely inhabitants of that settlement by the River Zab would bother to make reaping and milling equipment unless a supply of grain was dependable.

Comparative time-line to the emergence of farming

event	years ago	generations before us
First meat-eating toolmaker	two million	100,000
First tool-maker in Britain	900,000	45,000
First use of fire for cooking	450,000	22,500
First large-brain Neanderthal	350,000	17,500
First organised farming anywhere	11,000	550
First known farming in Britain	5,000	250

Human generations have been calculated on simple formula of one generation every twenty years, or fifty in a millennium. A more precise estimate would be hard to justify; and for this comparative exercise, not essential anyway.

That earliest farming settlement has been dated to 8900BC, give or take. So adding some preceding generations in which farming tools were conceived and devised, that takes us to roughly 9000BC for the earliest identifiable evidence of properly-developed agriculture. As such it becomes the first specific date in the origin of economies, for the time being anyway. Future discoveries could push the date back further in time; there could in principle have been farming before that of which all traces have totally disappeared.

The comparative time-line helps summarise the explanation so far. It also leads to some noteworthy, surprising conclusions. In fairness the chronological evidence is still somewhat awry: archaeologists have also found charred remains of wild wheat and barley at sites by the Sea of Galilee which have been dated to much earlier times than the first identified farms of northern Iraq. However and as noted, agriculture must have started where the different nutritious grasses grew wild; only later with much greater understanding would seeds be transported elsewhere.

O NCE FARMERS KNEW HOW TO gather seed and sow, and knew what kinds of land was easy to till and produced good crops, they would look for pastures new. The date for the first farmers is not cast in stone : further archaeological discoveries if there are any, could only push the critical dates further back in time. They cannot bring them forward: as noted earlier, time's arrow in advancing archaeology always flies in the reverse direction.

Searching for the origins of economies, the most striking thing about the time-line is the eternal delay before agriculture emerged.   As noted above on page 28, *"people with at least our dexterity, most probably our level of intelligence, most probably our sense of purpose have been living on this planet for a very long time"*. Such people had the mental capacity and physical ability needed to devise farming way back in Neanderthal times. Yet they did not. Why?

As the time-line shows, there have been around 17,000 generations of such capable people living on this planet.   Their cultural achievements were substantial, from flint-knapping to sculpture and latterly to boat-building. The early human colonisation of Australia, alone, indicates there have been well over 3,000 generations of skilled boatbuilders. Meanwhile organised farming still eluded humanity, anywhere on the planet. Even in the earliest iteration there have been no more than 550 generations of farmers. Is boat-building really so much easier than farming? Hardly. Here in Britain a modest 250 generations of people have been farmers.

The huge difference in duration between the epochs is striking, and is the subject of much of what follows in this chapter. Understanding and explaining the contrasting time-scales is a key to a better understanding of economies.

By way of further comparison, it is worth noting how today's United States of America has been built in just twenty-five generations since its Pilgrim Fathers arrived on the Mayflower. In the wider picture that is just a single tick on the historic clock of humanity. As an economic yardstick, the building of the American economy, creating a new kind of material civilisation, provides a telling example of what can be achieved by ordinary people in just a few hundred years, let alone tens of millennia.

Those responsible for building America were not MBAs nor did they have university degrees in economics. Far from it. As Emma Lazarus declared in her sonnet inscribed at the foot of the Statue of Liberty, they were '*the tired, the poor, the huddled masses, the wretched refuse of your teeming shore*'. Such people would not necessarily be anyone's first choice to build the world's greatest economy.

In terms of dexterity, level of intelligence or sense of purpose (see p.28) America's pioneers were little different from capable people who have been living on our planet for a very long time. Yet the speed with which America's ordinary folk, many of them little-educated immigrants from traditionally poor countries, built their nation into what we see today speaks volumes. Just twenty-five generations of people collectively devised a revolutionary kind of civilisation with unprecedented wealth for almost all. Prosperity was no longer an exclusive perquisite of the few. On the contrary, they devised the mass-consumer society, a change for all time. In so doing they have shown the rest of humanity what can be achieved in material terms given the vision, and given the necessary aptitudes.

No economist, no philosopher nor single visionary told the peoples of America how to build a nation, how to devise the American civilisation. There was never an instruction manual. Indeed as is shown in a later chapter, Adam Smith probably went out of his way to inhibit the process. Poignantly his celebrated, ground-breaking book *The Wealth of Nations* was published in 1776, the same year as the American Declaration of Independence.

Taking a pragmatic yet ambitious step at a time, the new peoples of America just made it up as they went along. Given its sheer speed it has surely been the world's greatest-ever triumph in do-it-yourself economic progress. American never received any foreign aid. Certainly there were individuals of great talent and vision who led the way in 'opening up' the West, primarily by building its railroads and establishing its banks.

That is significant too. Without finance or effective transport not much could happen. Hard on the heels of the railway barons and the banking magnates came the specialist businessmen, men of commerce and industry who devised everything needed to build an economy. They were anything but practising economists, nor was America's expansion pre-planned by professionals in the art of political economy. They were nowhere to be seen. So is economics even a learned profession in which, like doctors or lawyers or architects or engineers, its exponents get their hands dirty? Given the practicalities of those professions, it is a question worth asking.

The broad comparison with America prompts another : why did the Neolithic Revolution, the emergence of agriculture, takes quite so long? The difference in speed between America's self-made economic revolution, and the slowness with which people much like us painstakingly brought about the Neolithic Revolution, needs to be explained.

It is a paradox of economics which should not be ignored. In terms of Adam Smith's requirement that he could devise a division of labour, hunter-gatherer man had arrived at the take-off point for agriculture long ago. So what exactly was he waiting for? The time-line above is eloquent. *Homo sapiens* possessed all the necessary aptitudes for many millennia before he made his advance into farming. That momentous step was almost implausibly recent.

O R PERHAPS NOT. Much depends on what one regards as the 'necessary aptitudes'. If it had been a simple matter of his physical strength and dexterity, his reasoning ability or technical skills, then mankind's eternally long delay before his Neolithic Revolution, moving from accomplished hunter-gatherer to full-time farmer, would be difficult to explain convincingly. It is an economic question and a fundamental one. It was not a question of superior physique or sudden change in reasoning capacity. In our quest for the origin of economies, answering that central question provides a vital key. In fathoming that delay we begin to close a yawning gap in the conventional architecture of economics.

Doing so changes the structure of the subject quite markedly, and arguably for the better. For that insight, however, we must now move beyond Adam Smith's observed principle of the Division of Labour and look for something more. Fortunately there is another way to approach the issue, one which is far removed from pin factories or the jealous entitlements of Scottish lairds, a preoccupation of *Wealth of Nations*.

As is shown above that pioneering division of labour insight of Adam Smith - let's now call it the 'Specialist Principle' - is only a part of answering one of the unanswered questions of economics. It is a necessary, but not of itself sufficient, structural component to construct a durable architecture for the discipline.

The 'necessary aptitudes' were not just an ability to scratch seeds into the earth, or work out which plants were fit to eat, or comprehend how tiny seeds may be coaxed into large and fruitful plants. The range of necessary aptitudes was at least as much cultural as such intelligent observation and practical skills.

One further step was the willingness to accept a debt in confidence, thereby providing credit. The crux of the matter was explained over twenty years ago: *"the earliest specialist farmer found himself with a problem: many of the things he needed from other members of the community were needed day by day, but his harvest came in just a few days each year. The solution was obvious: he was given goods in return for a promise to supply food at harvest time. Credit had been invented."* [7] That fundamental economic mechanism is still evident in every bank account or credit card and can be traced all the way back to the birth of the Neolithic Revolution. The mechanism was one necessity; another is closely related, the systematic measurement of time. There is more to be said of that much-overlooked human accomplishment shortly. Neither achievement was anything like so obvious at the outset as they might seem today.

W HEN THEY WERE MASTERED for the first time, as twin components of the origin of economies, they were both massive steps forward. Yet today both have all but disappeared into the intellectual undergrowth, and most people have lost sight of their economic significance. Rather they are just taken for granted.

As was pointed out at the start of this chapter: "jumping in half-way through the narrative means overlooking fundamentals which have long since become obscured." No matter how serious the intellectual oversight, they remain two of mankind's most profound, yet least acknowledged cultural achievements.

The first real farmer was, by definition, a specialist. He was more than just a hunter-gatherer with a part-time smallholding - if indeed that was ever feasible given that true hunter-gatherers must keep moving on. True farmers, in marked contrast, must stay put; if for no other reason that to defend their fields.

---

7. *Geoffrey Gardiner in 'Towards True Monetarism' published by the Dulwich Press in 1993. He is a founding member of Gang of Eight.*

Quite apart from their technical agrarian skills, farmers also needed a social structure enabling them to strike trustworthy bargains with their neighbours in confidence. They all had to uphold deals that would stay in place for months at a stretch, well beyond the fallible memory span of a typical human being.

FARMING BROUGHT WITH IT not only a greater degree of mutual dependence. A widely-accepted and upheld system for debt and credit was vital as well. As the following pages seek to show, it was a cultural achievement with several tricky components. Instead of living hand-to-mouth and day-by-day as their hunter-gatherer forefathers did, the Neolithic revolutionaries now thought in terms of an entire year.

They were operating on a much longer time-scale than any hunter-gatherer ever needed to contemplate. During the many months when their crop grew from bare fields to harvest-time, farmers still needed day-to-day supplies to support themselves and their families. In anticipation of their harvest they also needed technical equipment of all kinds such as stone scythes, or reed baskets in which to gather their crop.

The Stone Age expert flint-smith or basket-maker perforce awaited their eventual payment in food. There was no money, nor any other physical means to store credit. It was all entirely a matter of trust. Such pioneer entrepreneurs would need to establish credit agreements among themselves by other means - in practical terms using a prehistoric version of the system we nowadays categorise as 'trade credit'.

Governed by the annual harvest cycle, the peoples of even the earliest agrarian community had nothing, apart from their own good intentions, to offer one other. It is simply not feasible to 'barter' good intentions without some form of credit. Farming (as distinct from gardening) invariably involves producing greater quantities than the farmer needs for himself. Willingness to plan and produce a deliberate surplus depends on a high level of confidence that the eventual customers, the creditors, will deal fairly.

So the revolutionary transition from hunter-gathering to farming was not only technological or a matter of intelligence. It called for some basic changes in outlook and culture. That had other components too. Previous hunter-gatherers could not plan their food supply very far ahead, nor did they ever need to do so. In such a precarious existence, primitive peoples take what comes.

A Stone Age farmer, by contrast, had to plan his seasonal activities for many months ahead. An ability to understand and measure the changing seasons now became an essential part of the farmer's craft. All of that, rather than his reasoning power, dexterity, determination or physical strength distinguished him from his hunter-gatherer ancestors.

By their mastery of the annual harvest calendar, and with an effective grasp of debt and credit, farming peoples gained far more control over where they lived and, much more than previous cultures, how they lived. There was a price to be paid. Farming brought men face to face with the familiar disciplines of the harvest. Effort throughout many days of each year would bring useful reward on just a few.

Worse still, some untimely storm, or flood, or drought, could destroy an entire year's effort. Hunter-gatherers had never experienced such a prolonged calamity; they simply moved on. For farmers facing the risk of a poor or failed harvest, it has always been essential they build a surplus into their calculations. In years when, happily, there are no catastrophes, such surpluses come to fruition - and then they risk another set of problems with a glut. Surpluses bequeathed by and famines imposed by nature were an intrinsic feature of farming, in 9000BC and have been ever since.

In that one respect agriculture is wholly unlike any other process of premeditated production. The necessity for, and safeguarding of, farm surpluses led to the construction of granaries, now to be seen as some of mankind's earliest stone buildings. Using stone for construction was a sure way to keep marauding bears and other large animals away from vital stores of food.

Beyond that, different crops being harvested at different times of the year generated another new problem. Farming folk had to rely on one other's benevolence, not for just for the odd day or two, but for months at a stretch. So human frailty now came into the reckoning. Over prolonged periods of weeks or months, people can all too conveniently forget what they owe to whom.

Forgetful debtors have been among us as long as debt itself. Resulting disputes cannot be resolved by brute force, with aggrieved creditors giving those forgetful debtors a good thrashing. If that were norm, then who would supply anything on credit, or lend anything, to a strong man? Some more cordial arrangement in the earliest agricultural community was a prerequisite.

Around this point some readers will be tempted to devise ingenious models of early agriculture which avoid any need for debt, and therefore for credit. It is a lovely idea based on a touching belief that everyone would be benign. There is little point in so doing for when, many thousand years later, organised agriculture does emerge into the light of recorded history, among its most conspicuous features is now a meticulous management of debt and credit. Both concept and practice reached a high degree of sophistication during the dark ages following the Neolithic Revolution.

W HEN DEBT AND CREDIT do eventually show up in written records, they are intimately associated not only with commerce but with the religious lore dictating its ethics. A lot of hard-won experience must have marked the intervening six thousand years.

Some social historians are wont to assume that the first agricultural communities were benevolent co-operatives - everyone shared in making baskets in the winter, then mucked in for the big heave at harvest time. They believe instead that such prehistoric co-operatives, collective farms - or kibbutz or soviet or any number of utopian experiments - would generate surpluses which could be bartered, seemingly with itinerant merchants in spot transactions. One might perhaps ask who financed the merchants.

Such idealists then argue that credit was unnecessary. Their speculation barely conceals a doctrinal urge to demonstrate how philanthropic communism, which so conspicuously collapsed in the twentieth century, might have somehow flourished 10,000 years previously. The notion of from each according to his ability, to each according to his needs is an irresistible dream for celestial minds.

If Communism could not be made to succeed in recent historical times, then maybe there had to be some Golden Age in prehistory when it could. Or so the utopian mindset imagines. It is not, however, immediately apparent why mankind's benevolence should have so diminished with the passage of time. And if, as some historians are inclined to suggest, it began with trade representatives from one clan 'bartering' their community surplus with trade representatives from another in some credit-free transaction, that in turn introduces another logical difficulty. Two communities would need to offer one other something different. There was little to be gained by offering to barter simultaneous surpluses of barley.

In seeking the origin of economies, it is much more illuminating to consider the various talents, disciplines and accomplishments which were necessary to make possible first-ever credit agreements even possible.   Those high ethical requirements live on; their absence has dire economic consequences. Almost all poor countries in our twenty-first century need to eliminate the gross corruption which destroys their economic prospects. Without an ethically watertight system for credit, and trading generally, the cancer of corruption is the bane of the Third World.

Until they can escape from the insidious corruption trap, they will remain impoverished countries no matter how much 'foreign aid' is poured into their ever-open coffers. In a real sense too much of today's third world is still trapped in the self-centered subsistence of early hunter-gatherers forty thousand years ago.

Y et somehow, eleven thousand years ago, those pioneering humans had developed the sophisticated ethical structure which enabled them to take up farming. As Geoffrey Gardiner remarks in the passage quoted above "credit had been invented". It was not just an airy-fairy concept. Of necessity it was a living system which the Neolithic revolutionaries used every day of their lives. To enable that to happen, debtors had to be trustworthy. Ethically that earliest of mankind's revolutions was already some way ahead of today's self-pitying Third World countries. One hopes they will take note.

ANYONE IS WILLING TO become a debtor, it is the easiest skill in the world. The test comes when it is time to cough up, as the debt falls due. Without some watertight reassurance of repayment, there would never be any creditors in the first place. The mechanisms which make credit and debt possible and sustainable are not self-starting. Just because they so are familiar today, we should perhaps remind ourselves that they were once just unattainable fantasies.

The first prerequisite, which took millennia to achieve, was evolving a suitable language. It was not just a primitive patois about fire, rivers or berries. That language held an entire dictionary, embracing a wealth of difficult abstract concepts such as trustworthiness, fair play, indebtedness and future time. From what we have since learnt about the slow evolution of languages - especially their lexicon of basic abstract concepts - it is fair surmise that generally agreeing a language sufficiently advanced to sustain a credit system took aeons.

In such respects, a modern language like English shows little advance on Sanskrit. By the fourth century BC that Indo-European root tongue had advanced to the point at which its illustrious philologist Panini could codify the entire language, its grammar and its morphology, into just 4,000 mantras. Not even the Oxford English Dictionary would be able to do that today. Even the passing of the last couple of thousand years has added little to the basic structure of human language. For some concepts old Sanskrit is still more effective than modern English, as indeed is classical Greek.

At such a gentle rate of progress, *homo sapiens* would have needed much of the previous five hundred millennia for his languages to have developed from an assortment of amiable grunts to the level at which 'to respect' and 'to obey' may be universally understood and differentiated.

For those earliest credit agreements to survive, people needed unquestioning consensus on the exact meaning of those subtle abstract words. When credit was still new, everything would be questioned. Not only was an advanced language with those concepts essential, but its usage could not be confined (as was Sanskrit) to an exclusive caste of educated priests.

FARMERS SPOKE IT TOO. Of necessity, advanced words such as honesty, fairness, debt, or obligation were accepted beyond dispute throughout the community. If someone tried to gain unfair advantage by questioning *'Ho-nes-ty? Why, does that funny noise mean something?'* any attempts to establish credit agreements would have collapsed instantly.

Widespread agricultural activity had to respect, and if necessary impose, exacting ethical standards. Defaulting on a debt became a wickedness which everyone condemned. Farmers and traders alike needed some mechanism, which everyone supported, for recording, remembering and settling those earliest trade debts. A legal concept of rightful ownership was equally vital. If society deemed it acceptable to let some hapless optimist grow his crop, then condoned the neighbours moving in to expropriate the lot according to crude principles of hunter-gathering, organised farming was pointless and would never have come about.

The Neolithic Revolution was not a sudden transition from uncouth savagery to civilised harmony. Hunter-gatherers must have been assembling the necessary linguistic and ethical foundations for millennia before it could even begin; they were all equally necessary from Day One. Seen in that light, it is no longer quite so surprising that agriculture emerged so late in humanity's day.

Nor does that revolutionary change make much sense as some kind of military confrontation. The process looks less like warring tribes driven into bloodthirsty conflict by their conflicting needs, more one of chilled-out hunter-gatherer hippies at repose in their congenial lifestyle, observing with benign amusement the dogged persistence of yuppy farmers in fertile clearings down the valley. Neither hippies nor yuppies could have possibly known, at the time, they were taking part in mankind's greatest-ever revolution.

Quite apart from the cultural requirements to make credit possible, the farmers of the Neolithic Revolution were totally dependent on something else. If longer-term credit involved a thorough appreciation of elapsed time, planning the harvest depended not only on knowing what happened each season, but knowing in advance when they were about to happen.

Yet there was no organised system of reliably counting the days. A prehistoric farmer could hardly check his diary or look at a newspaper. Reading and writing were unknown for another six thousand years. Few if any men would have the practical means to count to 365, understand why they needed to do exactly that, and then start all over again at square one.

The earliest farmers did not inherit a named calendar from their hunter-gatherer forefathers. For those remote happy-go-lucky ancestors, life had been just an unnumbered, undifferentiated succession of days and nights. For hunter-gatherers, giving names to individual days, then grouping them into counted weeks and named months, as we do automatically nowadays, would have been almost absurd. It would have been an unthinkable comprehension about an unknown future.

W E REPEATEDLY ASK "what date is it today?" and "what time is it?" in our daily lives. To the pioneer farmers of the Neolithic Revolution, those esoteric questions would still have been meaningless. Hunter-gatherer man bequeathed no dates, nor clocks, to farming man.

It is unlikely he even knew how to count. Primitive societies, even in our present world, can still find counting an unattainable mystery. Some languages only go so as far as "one, two, many". They then leave it at that.

Andamanese have only two words for numbers, meaning "one" and "more than one".   In their practical experience nothing more advanced is necessary and, as noted before it is necessity, not ability, which is the mother of invention.   The concept of large numbers with names is beyond their comprehension.

Such attenuated grasp of number is still part of our own twenty-first century. Turn the clock back 11,000 years and counting accurately to as large a number as three hundred and sixty five - without dissent - would have been an expertise mastered by very few.   Working Neolithic farmers relied on a body of experts to do it for them, in much the same way that we rely on a body of experts to understand and anticipate the weather.

Specialists who could be trusted to measure a whole annual calendar accurately became the sages and mystics of a farming community.   Their time wisdom was a prominent and much-admired mystery. Without knowing accurately when to sow and when to reap, while ignoring what day-by-day weather might unhelpfully suggest, an entire community could be putting its well-being at risk. So prehistoric farmers turned to their time lords.

Such mystics almost invariably seek to render their mysticism impressive; knowledge is power and they typically seek to hold ordinary people in their spell. We can but guess the preceding sequence of events. Some if not most would-be farmers experienced harvest catastrophes because their annual timing was wrong. Without a diary to rely on, looking only at clouds, they probably got it wrong many times. They had no counting ability. Why should they? Rather like today's Andamanese, they might well have simply counted 'one' and 'more than one.' We have no reason or evidence to suggest farmers of the early Neolithic Revolution were any more numerate than that.

From their accumulation of hunting expertise gained on the open range, however, people would come to realise that the alignment of the sun determined the varying length of days, while sunrise and sunset gradually moved around the horizon. The further from the equator the more obvious the effect would be.

With sticks in the ground they would observe how their shadows varied in length as days went by, and that hotter days had shorter shadows. Whoever it was first worked out that the solar year had around 360 days, and was able to number them accurately, was extremely clever. It was a huge advance on counting 'one, two, many'. No-one had done anything like it before.

However working in base three hundred-plus-plus arithmetic would be a considerable challenge even to anyone today. So their next achievement was to keep a record of six times sixty instead. They used base-60 arithmetic. In view of what was to happen later, they could once again have been keeping their daily count using sticks in the ground - or whatever came to hand.

Unlike any previous simple observation of shadows, it had now become an exercise in fairly complicated arithmetic. The wise men needed to know how many days would elapse before the longer and shorter shadow pattern began to repeat itself. Those early mystics were devising an arithmetical sophistication well beyond any more obvious decimal system based on the number of fingers or number of toes, or even on the two added together. Unfortunately nature had not decreed any convenient numerical correlation between the number of days in a solar year and the number of our digits. Detailing the annual pattern and length of seasons involved a far more demanding arithmetical system. We may conclude that complex method of calculation to be as old as agriculture itself, in other words about 11,000 years.

Perhaps the first ancient man who could work it all out precisely on his solar calendar was admired in awe as the pioneering Ancient of Days. Base-60 almost solves the problem, but not quite. It can only get as close as 360. The awkward gap between that versatile number and the unhelpful number 365 (divisible only by two prime numbers, 5 and 73) has perplexed arithmetical-minded astronomers for many hundreds and probably thousands of years. The calendar of the Mayan civilisation offers one way round it: the Mayans had five days in the year known as 'days without name'.

WE STILL USE base-60 arithmetic in our own era, for the specific purposes of dividing days into smaller units and measuring the parts of a circle. Maybe it is a little surprising we don't also have sixty shorter hours in the day, and then again sixtieths of that. Each day would then have 3600 shorter units of time instead of the present somewhat arbitrary 1440 minutes. It would be logical but that did not happen.

However time measurement did, of necessity. Without it the exact annual routine of the harvest would have been too fraught. Seeking the origin of economies, our interest deserves to focus on what happened, its history and geography, to achieve agreement on measuring the otherwise arbitrary passing of time, and giving its units names. Much flows from that.

Where did it all originate? The answer is not hard to find. Pioneering time measurers emerge in the Near East, the same territory which first devised farming. It is surely no coincidence. Around nine thousand years later it was still 'Wise Men from the East' who were following a 'yonder star'. They would have been Babylonian astronomers, adepts of what had become an ancient lore.

Consistently successful farmers needed a reliable calendar; without it they would not have a clue when to sow and when to reap. Building on that we can guess there was much folklore, and not a little personal rivalry and superstition, about the best possible moment for those key farming decisions. It would be quite like today; a modern rule of thumb says that frost can occur in Britain on any day up to 24 May. That is all very well if you now what May means, why it is different from June and you happen to have a diary.

The annual calendar was not just an entertainment; it was a prerequisite to any kind of premeditated, seasonally-adjusted agriculture. The typical weather of Atlantic maritime England was almost certainly as unpredictable then as it is now. One could discern little of significance by staring at a perpetual succession of clouds.

Britain's earliest farmers undoubtedly experienced much the same frustration as Britons of our own time, switched-on people who watch the news, then valiantly stay up half the night to witness a widely-acclaimed comet, an unusual stellar conjunction or the remarkable showers of Perseid shooting stars in mid-August. *"It was too cloudy. We missed it."* is the normal comment in the following days.

Harvest calendars not dependent on daily weather would have been a central feature of every farming community. Many dating from the earliest days of agriculture in Britain are to be seen still, although their workaday function appears to have been long forgotten. The language spoken by the people who built them is long gone as well, so we do not know what they were called at the time. So we call those farmer's calendars "wooden henges".

They were the definitive version of sticks casting shadows on the ground, seemingly aligned with the rising and setting sun. The name itself is a modern concoction, simply a back-formation from "Stonehenge" - all the things quite like it but not made of stone. As is often the case with mystery edifices, they have been hastily labelled 'religious cult' and it is left at that. More of Stonehenge shortly, it is probably the most remarkable ancient stone monument north of the Alps. The first task, however, is to delve into farmers' calendars.

WOODEN HENGES MAY still be identified in numerous places in southern England, where subsequent agriculture has left them relatively undisturbed. There should be no mystery about their true purpose. They were an essential calendar for successful Stone Age farming, and it is a fair guess they became the village centrepiece in the millennia following the Neolithic Revolution. The notion that a communal calendar, and a device to record it, stands at the heart of a community has been around for a long time. Note the following which describes the function of the Temple in Jerusalem, written about events in 56 AD: *"The rôle of the Temple in*

Jewish life cannot be understated. The Temple serves as calendar and clock for the Jews; its rituals mark the cycle of the year, and shape the day-to-day activities of every inhabitant of Jerusalem. It is the centre of commerce for all Judea, its chief financial institution and largest bank" [8]. Although it cannot have been a true bank, its commercial rôle is distinctive and may be traced right back to the 'temples' of Sumer, themselves a crucial first step in economic activity explained later in this chapter.

As Reza Aslan's description makes abundantly clear, the revered temple and its timekeeping were the focus of Jewish religious and commercial life. There is nothing unusual about that; in Britain we are all familiar with same principle. Well into the twentieth century and even since, the parish church with its prominent clock has been the baton which orchestrates British rural life.

In each village the time of day was measured locally, much as it had been since the start of the Neolithic Revolution. Until the nineteenth century church clocks were tuned to the visible behaviour of the sun in the neighbourhood. Their 'noon' was determined by the zenith of the sun locally. As a result, 'noon' in one town never quite coincided with 'noon' in the next.

For thousands of years that did not really matter. Only with the advent of the east-west running Great Western Railway in the nineteenth century did that localised time discrepancy first become a nuisance. Because of it, trains running westwards from London to Plymouth appeared to be forty minutes faster than those running

8. *Recorded by the American scholar of religions Reza Aslan, writing in his* "Zealot : the Life and Times of Jesus of Nazareth" *and published by the Westbourne Press in 2013.*

eastwards from Plymouth to London. That awkwardness rendered the Great Western railway timetable, enshrined in Bradshaw, something of a nonsense. So the GWR organised a conference to resolve the problem. That was the forum which devised a standardised system of clocks for railway timetables. Church clocks and others soon complied, a huge change: noon no longer meant where the sun could be seen locally at its zenith.[9]

THE LANDMARK AGREEMENT of Britain's railways in turn inspired a historic conference in Greenwich which determined the system of Time Zones now used throughout the world. Britain's unique tradition of measuring time had been led by John Harrison's solving the Longitude problem with great precision, essential to determining exactly where ships were when far out to sea. There had been too many catastrophic wrecks in the Royal Navy because captains were unsure of their exact location.

Harrison's highly accurate chronometers took their place in Britain's history of time measurement. It goes back to the henges of the Neolithic Revolution, and it is a tradition which was still being

9. *In the twentieth century the London North Western Railway, and later the LMS, played a vital rôle. Each day a highly accurate chronometer was set precisely at the Greenwich Observatory, and taken to Euston Station. There it was handed to the safe keeping of the guard of the prestige 'Irish Mail'. At Holyhead he handed it similarly to the purser on the Irish Sea ferry, and so it reached the main Post Office clock in Dublin. " Taking the Time to Ireland " was a daily railway ritual which continued - despite Irish independence - until 1939.*

upgraded five millennia later by the Great Western Railway - whose main line to Plymouth runs just twelve miles north of Stonehenge.

Our measurement of time is still being refined today. We may recall how the information technology industry almost drove themselves and their customers into a frenzy by the change to a different millennial date on 1 January 2000, a problem they cryptically labelled 'Y2K'.

In terms of its disruption potential, it was reminiscent of the problems of the Great Western Railway over a century previously. In terms of contrived collective neurosis it stood fair comparison with the neurosis of people who claimed they had been cheated out of eleven days of their lives by the decision to shift from the Julian to the Gregorian calendar.

Economists may care to note how those three apparently simple steps in measuring time accurately were to have a profound effect on sea transport in the 17th century, on rail transport in the 19th century and on information technology in the 21st. As the saying goes, from small acorns great oak trees grow.

THE MEASUREMENT OF TIME is something of a paradox, a characteristic it shares with many other major advances. To begin with almost everyone is troubled by the prospect of change and most hope it won't happen. Then they get used to the idea and it becomes the norm.

Finally people grow so accustomed to the new arrangement they take it for granted, and then forget the change was ever necessary or even controversial. [10] As this book is being finally put together, Britain is experiencing that controversial sequence with Brexit. Turn back the clock 5,000 years, and gradual acceptability is surely what happened as Britain entered its agricultural age. Novelties became the norm, including the wooden astronomical calendar on which farmers depended. Much like the Temple in Jerusalem 3000 years later, or the English village church 4,500 years after that,, each of them has been the baton which orchestrates a farming community's annual harvest cycle.

A helpful clue to the original purpose of the henges is generously provided by the archaeological timescale. As noted the first systematic farming in Britain dates from approximately 3000BC. So after 17,000 generations of intelligent hunter-gatherer humans had lived in these islands, they eventually became full-time farmers.

Such intelligent humans would have been at least as curious as we are about the sun and the night sky. Then after around 17,000 generations of looking at the stars with passive fascination, in approximately 3,000BC they suddenly took an active interest and started building their astronomical henges. That remarkable cultural coincidence should provide diligent archaeologists, as they wield their trowels, with some nourishing food for thought.

Inevitably any archaeological trace of the vast majority of farmers' henges long since disappeared beneath ploughed fields, as is the case with so much other valuable evidence. It is the bane of archaeologists that they are granted only a tiny keyhole through

10. *"All truth passes through three stages : First, it is ridiculed. Second, it is violently opposed. Third, it is accepted as being self-evident." (Schopenhauer)*

which to observe the almost boundless activities of the past The above farming explanation of henges should put one seeming archaeological mystery to rest.

Unfortunately such a down-to-earth rationale has been deflected by the awesome World Heritage structure of Stonehenge. In recent decades it has become a tourist attraction of major importance, before which is was just the boring old 'stones' but that has not added much to comprehension. With very little to go on other than knee-jerk reactions inferred from the religious lore of the Old Testament - entirely unfamiliar to ancient Britons, and not written down for another two thousand years - Stonehenge has also been endowed with some mystical, sacrificial, religious purpose.

STONEHENGE CELEBRATES something quite different, namely grand and ostentatious wealth. It was most likely one of the earliest examples of conspicuous expenditure, quite the precursor in our own time of the film star mansions to be seen in the Hollywood hills, or the assortment of Premier Division footballer mansions to be viewed south of Manchester.

Five thousand years ago the extravagance of building Stonehenge would have been well beyond the wealth accumulation of any workaday Stone Age farmer, or even that of a feudal lord taking a rake-off, and that was probably the chief intention. It was a typical example of the "I can afford it and you can't" rich man's mentality which explains most of the super yachts normally moored and going nowhere, just to be admired, in Monte Carlo harbour. Egypt's pyramids, contemporary with Stonehenge in its most splendid phases, provide another enduring example of conspicuous expenditure, and on a colossal scale; the only surviving Wonder of the ancient world. They had little practical use : their purpose was political, to inspire the people's awe at the might of the pharaoh, and to show that the latest pharaoh had been even more divine than his predecessor. There is really nothing new under the sun.

Similarly, in building Stonehenge there was no practical necessity to import massive stones all the way from Mynydd Preseli in the far south west of Wales, other than to demonstrate that the builder, or owner, was simply rich enough to do so. And also that he had worked out how to do it. Even today, systematic attempts to imitate that ancient achievement have met with rather more headaches than convincing answers.

It is a distance of 140 miles as the crow flies. The stones from Preseli had to be taken by sea the length of the Bristol Channel or, an even longer way round when every yard was a test of transport ingenuity, brought to Stonehenge by crossing the River Severn further upstream. Working out exactly how Preseli's stones were moved over such a great distances remains a celebrated mystery. While civil engineers ponder that, economists could well ponder the source of the wealth which paid for it all. An explanation of that leads to some more economic basics.

The financial jigsaw puzzle of Stonehenge starts with emergence of the Bronze Age, also dated to around 2500-2300 BC. Once again a remarkable historical coincidence should provide some food for thought. Bronze was also a remarkable achievement. Adding tin to soft copper it was now possible to produce a hard alloy of huge military advantage, or even for the manufacture of much tougher ploughshares as the Stone Age gradually petered out.

There was a problem, however, which was why the preceding Copper Age was prolonged. The problem was the scarcity of tin. In the ancient world, workable deposits of copper were relatively commonplace. The island of Cyprus, at the very heart of the ancient world, has ample deposits; the words 'Cyprus' and 'copper' even derive, originally, from the same verbal root.

OBTAINING COPPER WAS relatively easy, with tin was anything but. In our own era it has been obtained from as far afield as Malaysia and Chile, territories far beyond the horizons of prehistoric man. So the perplexing question is where did the ancient world obtain its tin to make bronze? There have been suggestions there were deposits in today's Germany and in Afghanistan, but the best-attested ancient sources were those of England, a source known to the later Phoenicians as "The Tin Islands".

Tin may have been found in the Mendip Hills, but the most likely source and the one best-known today is Cornwall. From ancient times and into the twenty-first century tin has been mined there, and even now Cornish tin production comes and goes as the shifting world price for the metal means the mines hover tantalisingly on the brink of economic viability.

Evidence of an early 'international' tin trade further afield is also readily available. Around 2000BC if not earlier, the advanced civilisation of ancient Sumer established a trading community at

Kanesh on its western outposts, importing tin from the West. The archaeological traces of Kanesh in Anatolia are not far from Kayseri, about 150 miles south-east of Ankara.

The nearby River Kizilirmak quite probably marked the boundary of the Sumerian empire; the headwaters of the River Tigris are only about seventy miles to the east of Kayseri. Between them is the watershed; the Kizilirmak flows westwards through Ankara and down to the southern coast of the Black Sea. The Tigris, and the nearby Euphrates flow in the opposite direction. They have been the principal thoroughfares linking the successive civilisations of Mesopotamia with the Persian (nowadays the Arabian) Gulf for at least ten thousand years.

Recorded history shows that Kanesh was importing tin from the West, but if it originated in ancient Britain how did it get as far as that? Seeking an answer to that opens up some key questions about the way economies had to evolve. The interesting questions are how such expensive Cornish tin could be transported over such a distance and how it was paid for. Money as we know it nowadays was still well over a thousand years away in the unknowable future.

First, what was the most likely trade route for a journey of about 4,000 miles as the crow flies? In the third millennium BC the necessary transport method would have been primarily overland, or navigating rivers, and thus passing through many different, maybe antagonistic, tribal territories. Looking at a map the likeliest tin route would have crossed southern England heading for the Thames estuary, along the route of today's A303 trunk road. Is it significant that route goes straight past Stonehenge? Historically the River

Thames could be forded in the vicinity of Westminster. Just downstream from there the Romans chose the first point travelling upstream which had firm land on both opposite banks.

Their original London Bridge blockaded the river and so became the upper limit of navigation. That became a simple port, and Roman London was born. A basic rule of economic geography is that upper limits of navigation and crossing points have been the site of major conurbations for millennia. The ancient site of Paris traces to the same principles of transport and navigation. New York, San Francisco and Sydney, among other key cities, all share the advantage of a magnificent natural harbour instead.

Taking the practical termini of England's tin trade as Exeter and central London, then Stonehenge is just about half-way between the two. In passing we might note that such ancient trading activity provides a helpful clue to the functional origins of London itself. Was it originally a wealthy Neolithic sea terminal ideally placed for the short sea crossing to continental Europe? In turn that might explain its mysterious name : the originally form 'Lundun' is ancient, derived from a forgotten language. When they arrived the Romans adopted it, giving it the Latinised form 'Londinium'.

Beyond the easy crossing of the North Sea towards the Rhine estuary the tin route is fairly clear. It would have headed east across modern Belgium, then up Rhine as far as today's Mainz. From there the River Main opens up an easy route near Nuremburg linking with the Danube. Today it is marked by a large canal only forty miles long. The Danube then provides a route all the way to the Black Sea. South along its coast leads to modern Istanbul. Could that ancient trading city, once Byzantium, have been involved in the tin trade at the beginning of the Bronze Age? The metal working skills of the region figure in the next great leap in mankind's economic progress.

To the east of Istanbul on the Black Sea coast is the estuary of the River Kizilirmak, the natural route inland to the frontier of the Sumerian empire, and so to its ancient tin trading centre at Kanesh. From cuneiform records we know that is where tin was traded into what was then the most sophisticated civilisation in the known world. It was a strategic metal, quite the uranium of its day.

S UMER WAS THE BIRTHPLACE of the Bronze Age, or so it appears. That begs the question of where bronze was originally invented. It had to be somewhere that natural copper and natural tin were found in close proximity. In those conditions sooner or later an alloy of the two would be discovered, probably by accident, to create bronze. In much the same way, agriculture appears have started where emmer wheat, einkorn wheat and barley were also all found in close proximity.

At South Crofty tin mine in modern Cornwall, deposits of the two metals can be seen within a hundred or so metres of one another. Geologists might care to look for other places in the ancient world where the two key ingredients of bronze occurred so close together. If Cornish tin did find its way right across Europe to Sumer, the local geographical knowledge required was immense.

There were no maps nor any road signs, nor any decent roads for another two thousand years. Transport except on rivers would have been by mule or donkey. The entrepreneurial effort and diplomatic skills needed to undertake trade in tin trade all the way from England to Anatolia, through tribal territory after tribal territory, would have been immense and are examined later in this chapter. The wealth generated by that tin trade would also have been immense, quite probably sufficient to finance Stonehenge.

For the time being, the overland tin route proposed above is merely surmise, knowing only its geographical starting and finishing points.   It would be intriguing to know whether there are any archaeological traces, or surviving place or river names, along the way providing some clue to that ancient trade.

Whatever route it followed, that ancient tin trade would have created a cultural link between Britain and the Fertile Crescent. That could answer another question : the transfer of base-60 arithmetic. We know it originated in ancient Mesopotamia, where farming also originated. It then reappears at Stonehenge and even more in nearby Woodhenge, about two miles to the east. With the conspicuous numbers 15, 30 and 60 in its three concentric circles, Woodhenge clearly adopts the same, originally Mesopotamian, distinctive base-60 arithmetic.

Britain's everyday wooden henges only incorporated basic astronomy of the kind needed by farmers. Stonehenge goes several steps beyond that; it is a highly sophisticated astronomical calculating machine.   Had the man who caused it to be built become familiar with the superior astronomical wisdom at the distant end of the tin route? If so he may well have invited those exotic astronomers to come to Britain and show his fellow countrymen how it should be done, a good prehistoric example of knowledge transfer.

Eventually the overland tin route was replaced. Improved navigational skills, the prowess of a people familiar with the treacherous Bay of Biscay, meant the trade could now go much more economically by sea instead. The new maritime traders were the somewhat mysterious Phoenicians, and they referred to Britain as the "Tin Islands". Had such skilled navigation been technically feasible in 2000BC, the frontier trading centre of ancient Sumer would not have been built in central Asia Minor, but more sensibly on the coast of the Levant.

THE PHOENICIANS AND THE Biblical Canaanites were the same people. They called themselves the Kena'ani; in Hebrew the word has the secondary meaning of 'merchant'. Seeking Tyrian purple, it was the ancient trading Greeks who labelled them the Phoenicians.

That name is derived from the Greek word *phoinix* or *phoinios*, meaning purple or crimson, as they sought the much-prized Tyrian purple dye for their aristocratic garb. So the Levantine traders became the pioneering Purple People. The Phoenicians then handed on the compliment by labelling Britain the Tin Islands, following much the same logic of commodity nomenclature.

Among Phoenician metal traders, St Michael's Mount in Cornwall became the recognised trading landmark. Evidently they knew it well. Somewhat beyond the mainstream pursuit of this book, there is now interesting speculation that the upstart Phoenicians themselves had originated from the Atlantic littoral. Herodotus explained they originated on the shores of the 'Erythraean' sea, which has generally been taken to mean the Indian Ocean. A wrong assumption may well have been made about his word 'Erythraean'. It can equally mean the Western Sea.

The notion that the Phoenician 'Pilgrim Fathers' heading for the Levant dragged their ships over 100 miles of desert across the Suez Isthmus is less plausible than the idea they originally sailed in easily from the Atlantic through the Pillars of Hercules, as the Straits of Gibraltar later became known.

Their superior seamanship now in warmer, less turbulent seas would have quickly outstripped the locals in the benign, almost tide-free Mediterranean. The Phoenicians founded a trading centre and city of their own in north Africa, namely Carthage, which became the sworn enemy of Rome. Their society and culture was re-labelled 'Punic' by the Romans; and that was the usual name of their own and interesting language.

Although basically a Semitic tongue Punic makes use of lenition, a peculiarly distinctive mutative treatment of consonants in forming adjectives which is also found in Irish and Welsh.[11] Academically it all adds up to watch this space. The various connections would however explain why the seafaring Phoenicians - unlike the landlubber Sumerians - knew exactly where to go to find plentiful supplies of scarce tin from beyond the Mediterranean, once they discovered they had a rich market for it in the Near East.

The tin story, the base line of the Bronze Age, has many ramifications, too many of them still unexplored. Temptingly so. It

11. *The author is grateful to classicist Geoffrey Gardiner (q.v.) for his intriguing insight into the likely origins of the seafaring Phoenicians.*

is at least as interesting, and economically more important, as investigating the Silk Road. Stonehenge could well be part of the Tin Story : the geology, the geography, the astronomy, the arithmetic and the economics all fit the picture. The indications are that Stonehenge had little to do with the agricultural lore of henges, and as such has been a powerful archaeological distraction. Workaday wooden henges were more important, even if they hold far less fascination for the tourists of the twenty-first century.

ONE MAJOR CONSEQUENCE of the change from hunter-gathering to agriculture was population levels. Hunter-gatherer tribes had required a large swathe of territory to themselves, if their food supply was not to become too scarce. Farmers, by contrast, produce surpluses of necessity and benefit from concentrations of people. Once agriculture took hold, its traces indicate farming spread into fresh territory quite rapidly. Sons and daughters probably set up new farms next door to their parents.

The new breed of farmers needed help and co-operation on a significant scale. Along the Tigris two brothers working alone could spend years fruitlessly trying to dig a ditch, perhaps thwarted by shifting river channels or seasonal floods. Twenty men working as a team could dig it in a single season. Even if each family lived somewhat in isolation, they needed an accessible centre to trade their produce and obtain their supplies, and within reasonable walking distance. Again, farming communities co-operated to protect their fields, and their crops, from unwelcome intruders.

In the fullness of time, the numerical supremacy of farmers, and their more advanced social and economic structure, enabled them to supplant hunter-gathering as a way of life. All that and more came together because those early farmers trusted one another and worked together - in both senses they gave one another credit.

When we seek to reconstruct the economy of that first agricultural society, some simple form of trade credit is essential from the outset. Credit serves two essential functions.

First, it is the basic device necessary for balancing different product timetables, something direct barter can never do. The barley crop would come at a different time from other crops. Someone had to wait; someone had to give credit.

Second, credit is the only way to organise activities requiring a chain of producers. No-one can consume osiers directly, they would only be useful for making harvest baskets. The woodsman who cut them must perforce wait until they have been put to good use in harvesting something he wanted. In the meantime he had to give the farmer credit.

His commitment was an embryo form of business risk. He could not be sure the debt would be honoured. There had to be ethical control in some form. Even a simple Neolithic farming village depended on a spider's web of such credit agreements among its varied suppliers and customers. The more credit agreements their system could manage honestly, then the greater extent of specialisation their society could support.

C REDIT IS A BASIC building-block of all economic activity, and the pattern described so far gives rise to what is now labelled the *Creditary Principle*, a new concept to be adopted for the remainder of this book. Many earlier economists have looked at credit but not seen it in that light. Above all, it is the economic mechanism which enables the division of labour to flower into full-grown economic activity. In effect, the Creditary Principle gives life to Adam Smith's Specialist Principle.

Logically, the more credit agreements an economy can sustain, then the greater the division of labour it may attain. That is a timeless relationship and, as this book seeks to demonstrate, deserves to become a cardinal principle of economics. It has been hitherto overlooked.

Adam Smith was a philosopher with exceptional insight and in *Wealth of Nations* he unveiled a first component of the origin of economies - as well as showing there was a whole academic discipline to be unveiled, a more durable achievement. However surrounding, relevant knowledge from many other disciplines has moved on a long way since the mid-eighteenth century.

Since Smith wrote his early economics, archaeology in particular has revealed the wealth of mankind's achievements during many millennia before his Industrial Revolution. The division of labour made its appearance far, far earlier than man's first attempts to trade with strangers. People had a multitude of specialist skills long before the Neolithic Revolution. Adam Smith can have known little or nothing of that. He might have guessed, but he didn't.

Simply joining the saga at the Industrial Revolution, in Britain from around 1750 onwards, is much too late, a fundamental point made at the start of this chapter.

This book requires a further two chapters explaining economic, and specifically creditary, achievements before it can sensibly reach that point. By exploring modern knowledge, the basic architecture of economics can at last be brought up to date.

In the process a spurious mythology about the invention of money can be laid to rest at last, and with it a widespread misunderstanding of what money is and how it functions. The easiest way to fathom all that is to look at its origins, a step at a time, the principal concern of the following chapter. The development of money, the coinage or currency, took many centuries. Beyond that looms the complicated invention of banking; that too took many centuries. Some classical Greek philosophers could envisage the prospect but it then required the best part of two thousand years to bring their ideas to fruition. Banking is not easy to understand or explain and much of it is counter-intuitive [12].

This book devotes Chapter Four to the invention and development of banking. By starting from its origins, all the subsequent layers of sophistication, especially central banking, become easier to comprehend. Too many modern economists, and even some bankers, fail to understand some or even all of it correctly. Keynes, even, got lost in the intellectual maze.

---

12. *The present writer learnt as much the hard way as principal spokesman, in succession, for what are now the two largest banking groups in the western world.*

THE SPECIALIST PRINCIPLE made its appearance long before civilisation came into being. As noted the mechanical division of labour, the basic building block of economics according to Adam Smith, precedes urban civilisation by millennia. It was one necessary component to trigger economic activity, but far from being the whole story.

The other essential component was - and still is - cultural and ethical, not just mechanical. It is the Creditary Principle. The principle embodies the level of trust and confidence among people needed to reach their lending and borrowing agreements, and therefore everything else which such agreements alone will facilitate.

For a society to develop to the point at which is which can generate a flourishing economy, the essential creditary principle requires the full development of abstract language, of universal consensus on meanings such as 'honesty', of respect for property rights and of some process of fair legal enforcement.

Without any of these, permanent agricultural society would have been impossible. Every bit as much as Adam Smith's division of labour, they too are the architecture, the basic tools, to make sense of economies. An economy which could assemble a division of labour was not just a consequence of self-interest, technical ingenuity or manual dexterity. There is rather more to it than the non-benevolent, much-vaunted 'hidden hand'.

Once one grasps the fundamental creditary principle, it becomes apparent that major cultural and ethical components are every bit as indispensable. So the essence of economic activity is not merely the pleasure of rude mechanicals.   It is not, nor should ever be, imprisoned in a box simply labelled 'sub-school of mathematics', despite today's phalanxes of business economists, consultant prognosticators and handsomely-remunerated City soothsayers determined to convince people otherwise.

With its fundamental ethical, moral, human components in their proper place economics is no longer the dismal science. It is not merely an arid calculus with no place for morality or benevolence. Nor can its fundamental mechanisms and principles be extrapolated from tables of statistics. That is no more feasible than fathoming how a steam locomotive works from railway timetables.

So long as one looks no further than Adam Smith's specialisation principle, or his easy observations on buying and selling, it seems possible to explain how all economic activity is constructed on the market alone.   It so becomes an amoral calculus, and economics is then derided as that dismal science. The urge to identify such a simplified economic mechanism was particularly prevalent in the 1970s and 1980s. The mechanically-efficient market had become the be-all and end-all.

Yet understanding the market alone was not sufficient - anything but. When coining his endlessly-quoted rubric about 'Not From Benevolence' to explain how butchers, brewers and bakers come together to make an economy work, Adam Smith was missing the point. The equally essential creditary, ethical keystone of all economic activity quite escaped his attention. At most he only had half the answer.

THE CREDITARY PRINCIPLE now introduces a quite different, moral component. Doing so exposes a fundamental flaw in any blueprint of economics which finds no place for some collective sense of high morality and fair play. The economic system may not rely directly on philanthropic benevolence among Adam Smith's self-seeking butchers, brewers or bakers; however they all rely absolutely on the constant benevolence of authority to ensure their spider's web of debts is recognised, recorded and honoured.

A man may twist and turn to hypothecate ways to contrive a division of labour as many ways as he likes, but somewhere along the line the creditary principle is an essential part of the picture. That is the only means to transform those good intentions of risk-bearing businessmen into the reality of production.

Nor is there any reason to confine this fundamental economic synergy to the primitive societies of the Neolithic Revolution. The creditary principle has supported all economic activity for eleven thousand years since, from those first-ever farmers through the Industrial Revolution and into the financial complexities of our own times. As much as any advance in technology, some advance in creditary technique is a pre-requisite for any further step down the long road to economic prosperity.

The unassertive, yet fundamental creditary principle is the necessary twin to Adam Smith's much-remarked specialist principle. The two serve side by side, welded into the driving force of all economic activity. They are of exact equal importance with one another, spiraling through time, bound together in one of those double helixes. Specialisation creates risk. Credit absorbs risk. The two must always be in balance.

Although they are the inseparable forces of economic activity, a yin and yang, the creditary principle is easily the more fragile of the two. Where creditary willingness breaks down, then people will no longer risk a commercial division of labour. That must collapse too.

It is destruction of an effective creditary system, rather than sudden forgetfulness about the workings of factories or farms, which drives once thriving economies into decay and decline. Creditary failure is the normal cause of economic collapse. It lies at the heart of every bank failure.

As already noted above, the absence of an effective creditary system is the certain hallmark of any poverty-ridden society. A so-called 'developing' country lacking access to a trustworthy creditary system will inevitably remain an impoverished country. No matter what euphemisms are coined to ease its politicians' sensitivities, it can never 'develop'. Lack of creditary effectiveness is the surest evidence of a country condemned to poverty. Given the shibboleths of political correctness the creditary logic, though inevitable and readily apparent, is too rarely admitted.

Wealthy citizens from such countries shy away from their basic responsibility to drive its economy forward; they shun any such entrepreneurial opportunity. They prefer to squirrel their often illegitimate wealth away in the reliable banks of countries - typically Switzerland - whose creditary system is quintessentially trustworthy, so making that country the world's most prosperous instead. There is no more telling sign of a failing nation than one whose government, legal system and economic potential are rejected by its own wealthy citizens. Instead they prefer to live in a developed country abroad, enjoying a sumptuous idle lifestyle at the cost of their fellow citizens back home living in poverty and squalor.

Economically their countries are languishing where 'the West' was several millennia ago. If they wished the Third World's absentee plutocrats could easily follow the American example and lift their own countries out of their dire predicament. Far too many of them duck that desirable rôle. A continuous round of cocktail parties in Mayfair or Monte Carlo, or in expensive villas around the Swiss lakes, is a far more tempting way of life, for those who can afford it. The pleasures of the First World do seem to be diverting the attention of those who, alone, could transform the Third.

DEVELOPING COUNTRIES NEED their own home-grown Turnip Townsends, their George Stephensons, their Henry Fords, their Rockefellers. Instead they import foreign entrepreneurial skill by selling franchises to international oil companies and mining corporations. Their politicians then have the gall to make speeches at the United Nations blaming everyone but themselves. Behind the scenes their habitual, incessant corruption knows few bounds.

It is no coincidence that the America was developed by its private enterprise banks and railroads. They drove their new country almost two thousand miles into untapped territories beyond the Mississippi. Although the fuller economic significance of transport must wait until later, it is worth noting now. It has been plausibly argued that 100,000 kilometres of new, reliable roads built throughout the continent of Africa would transform its economy, enabling it to become more than self-sufficient in such staples as food. It is not the complete solution but it is an essential prerequisite.

Provided it also had a reliable creditary system that would bring to an end Africa's appalling cycle of famine and starvation. There is no other way. Once country-dwelling people can transport their produce to market, and return home within the day, only then will they have the self-interest to become commercial farmers. Transport is also part of Smith's 'unseen hand'. Until that is available, there is no point in anything above mere local subsistence.

One man who recognised that simple truth was a founding father of today's USA, Henry Ford. He regarded his Model T car, and its truck version, as tools for America's country-dwellers to become commercial farmers. A century later, the ubiquitous pick-up truck is still the basic tool of farming the world over.

The full measure of Ford's vision and achievement is explored in the final chapter. Meanwhile it is pathetic that his simple transport and commercial logic has yet to be grasped by the world's political know-alls of economic development. Grand conferences are staged, splendid banquets are enjoyed, globe-trotting politicians spout platitudes - but little actually happens.

A society with no creditary basis cannot have an effective economy. It is a 'nation' which is little more than a primitive dispersal of more or less capable Robinson Crusoes. Lacking the building blocks of economies, any notion of 'nation' as in Smith's

'*Wealth of Nations*' is rendered meaningless. They find it hard to progress beyond tribalism. It is almost inevitable such tragic people will remain trapped in Thomas Hobbes' state of nature where life is nasty, brutish and short.

Even more, the density of population in our times has grown hugely because of the Neolithic Revolution and its aftermath. There can be no going back to some idealistic world of amiable hunter-gathering. No matter how many hippies dream of reverting to a world of self-sufficient Robinson Crusoes, their dream is hopelessly unrealistic. With seven billion people now inhabiting his planet, mankind's sparse-populated Garden of Eden is gone forever.

ATTENTIVE READERS will have noted, in passing, a deliberate loose end in the logic so far. Back on p. 57 it was observed that *"farmers and traders alike needed some mechanism, which everyone supported, for recording, remembering and settling those earliest trade debts."*

So exactly how was that prerequisite achieved eleven thousand years ago? Of necessity the mechanism was something rather more effective than the eternal stalemate of 'one man's word against another'. The inviolable ethic of credit and trust had to be championed by the village community at large. It also needed a figurehead to shape and uphold that collective morality.

Perhaps in the preceding hunter-gatherer era, the most important figure in the tribe had been its swiftest runner or strongest spear-thrower, or maybe the man with the clearest sense of direction or best understanding of wild animal behaviour. In an agricultural community, by contrast, the most important figure would have been the person with the most respected memory and best sense of fair play, the fatherly chieftain. Here was another great sociological step forward. Upholding a steadfast ethic of credit and trust ultimately hinged on the one individual in the community who had most to gain by violating it.

It was a chieftain's own commitment to truth and justice, far more than that of any other individual, on which advance towards a durable debt-credit system depended.   How long, one may wonder, did prehistoric men need to wait until several neighbouring tribes simultaneously provided themselves with such chieftains, each one of whom set the greater good of the broader community above and against their own personal gain?

As one observes the medieval financial antics of post-colonial potentates in Africa, or indeed the expenses-claiming antics of British members of parliament or House of Lords in our own time, such leaders are still hard to find. For the Neolithic Revolution ever to unfold, in his later incarnation hunter-gatherer man must have been a profoundly principled soul.

As already noted, anyone is prepared to become a debtor. It is the easiest thing in the world. The tricky part is to find someone willing to become a creditor. In the extended family unit of a single tribe, an acknowledged father figure can impose simple justice on everyone, a degree of authority more than adequate to supervise any rudimentary short-term debts. As soon as the interwoven community extends to a number of different families, each with their own father figure, then the matter becomes more complicated.   Discipline

CHAPTER TWO : BEFORE 1500 BC 89

within a single family group on its own is good, but no longer quite good enough. To make their creditary system function, people now require a *modus vivendi* with the neighbours as well. At the heart of that interdependent community must have been some respected debt-rememberer.

B ACK IN PREHISTORY, the rôle of debt-rememberer may have been discharged by the chieftain directly, or more likely by a respected gathering of tribal elders. Or by another specialist - the function which several thousand years later evolved into that focus of collective morality, the priest.

As the quotation from Reza Aslan on p.64 points out, the Jewish temple was the centre of both morality and religion, but also its centre of commerce, the chief financial institution of Jerusalem. Both debt-rememberer and priest alike had to be at the fulcrum of morality and fair dealing.

Yet whichever of these various figures was respected as the debt-rememberer, the task depended on the unaided human memory alone. Safely recording a cat's cradle of agricultural debts would have required great memory capacity, a known feature of pre-literate societies in our own time.[13] A creditary system relying on human memory alone to record who owed what to whom would suffer from obvious limitations. Murder the debt-rememberers, and it would be quite the equivalent of wiping everyone's overdrafts from the computer at HSBC. They had to be protected by their community.

~~~~~~~~~~~~~~~~~~~~~~~~~~~~~~~~~~~

13. Nissen, Damerow and Englund (see bibliography)

THE RECORDING CAPACITY of such a technique was not great, probably sufficient to retain the creditary network of a large village and not much more. Archaeological evidence suggests the earliest levels of Jericho supported a population of around 2,000. We can only marvel at the human ingenuity, using memory techniques alone, underpinning its creditary system. Back in 7000-8000BC nothing else was yet available. All the debt recording systems which today we take for granted were, at the time, still 4,000 years and more into the future.

For all that, creditary ability based on memory techniques alone lasted longer than any of its successors has since - so far anyway. It is the surmise of this book that such a creditary system, relying on human memory to record its debts, dependent on uniformly-respected abstract words, incorporating sound legal principles with property rights, protecting its creditary network presided over by respected debt-remembers, steadily emerged to establish Neolithic farming communities by around 9,000 BC. Reliance on the human memory then survived without fundamental change for some 6,000 years, in some places until much later still, even into our present era.

Archaeologists are already stretched to reconstruct a comprehensive picture of the material lifestyle of prehistoric man, so scant is the surviving evidence. Creditary economists would now pose an even tougher challenge. They would wish to know, not so much what prehistoric peoples possessed or were able to manufacture, but rather how they treated one another. How did the earliest farmers manage credit agreements with their suppliers? Throughout history and right into our own era the constant indebtedness of the farmer, or rather the fragile resilience of his creditors, has been an unremitting challenge. Why should things have been any different back in 9000 BC?

Constructing a viable creditary system was a far greater achievement at the time than it might appear after it has been taken granted for so long. Mankind's pioneering commercial creditors were taking a courageous, as well as an historic, step. Early credit deals could have been no more than simple one-to-one agreements. They agreed to provide something now, in exchange for a dependable promise of something in return later. Such deals, once recorded with authority offered little scope for further reshaping.

It was all very straightforward. Debtor and creditor remained the same people from the moment the deal was first struck, until it was finally honoured. There was still no money for such transactions: they can only have been agreed in commodities, and that was to remain the case for the next 5,000 years.

The earliest credit arrangements long predate the invention of anything even approximating to a coinage, which was not to appear until long after physically-recorded, as distinct from memorised, debt had become the norm. As noted, above suggestion that 'primitive' man nonchalantly decided to invent money one day as a superior system to 'barter' have been a pervasive myth among economists for the best part of two centuries.

People who simply barter on the spot do not have debts; they deal and say farewell. Primitive farmers must have had debts, even though they lacked any form of, or even concept of, money to enumerate them.   With just one improvement, that ancestral creditary method is still widely used in our own era. Perhaps 11,000 years after it was first devised, we know it today as trade credit. Modern economic analysts and especially statisticians too easily ignore the huge volumes of trade credit when constructing their monetary models in an attempt to tweak an economy. Just because it is difficult to measure is no reason to exclude it from the analysis.

In our own times, trade credit still provides a mainstay to much economic activity. It functions unobtrusively. Although it is now denominated in money, today's trade credit retains a central characteristic of those earliest-ever farming debts : debtor and creditor are the same people throughout the life of their one-to-one agreement.   Once the creditary system began to evolve that restricting characteristic would be the first to go.

That prehistoric creditary system was still resilient enough to sustain farmers through harvest failures or attempts by dishonest people to disavow their debts.   Where disputes arose, creditors would turn to the community's debt-rememberer, who would have become the focus of its honesty and justice.   His, or her, or probably their, ruling was of necessity reinforced whenever needed by the chieftain's authority and ultimately backed by some kind of public assembly.

Without that recognition and support, any creditary system would soon have collapsed and taken its embryo agricultural economy down with it. Even today credit still works that way in parts of the world, as the following anecdote well illustrates. The village elders of a community in the former Rhodesia - some time after the Second World War - approached a respected figure of their local community and asked him to buy a bicycle for one man, and meanwhile to accept three weeks' free gardening from another.[14]

These small but important business transactions were the two loose ends of debts and credits extending throughout the community. Village debt-rememberers had already netted most of them off, while a bicycle was reckoned to be near enough of equal value to three weeks' labour. The relief within the community, once their chosen debt-settler agreed the deal, was palpable. Clearing the cat's cradle of inter-woven debts and credits had taken weeks.

ANOTHER SUCH ANECDOTE relates to land-owning records in rural Ghana. To negotiate a purchase of land, a European was directed to the group of tribal elders whose task it was to remember who owned which fields. Once they were satisfied due payment had been made, they adjusted their collective memory to embrace the new landowner.

Modern anthropologists still have a depth of this oral record-keeping to explore, and in so doing teach us much about the creditary capacity and thus economic prospects of prehistoric communities. However it meant that in one respect those clever prehistoric farmers were unable to make much significant progress.

---

14. *As related by the former Greater London Council member for Putney, Len Harris, whose father was the respected neighbourhood figure at the centre of events. When discussing early ideas for this book, he told the author this illuminating story directly.*

That was the maximum size of their settlements. So long as their creditary structure was dictated by the capacity of human memory alone, people would be unable to co-operate reliably in anything larger than a substantial village or, as seen in prehistoric Jericho, at most a fairly small town.

Much the same goes for the size of settlements using oral records in our own time. With such a basic creditary structure, cities would be unthinkable. The current enthusiasm for discovering even more ancient cities of India - which it has said have long since disappeared beneath the sea - faces the same problem. What written creditary system did they use?

The notion that large communities need a substantial creditary system has yet to be factored into archaeology and now provides an intriguing challenge. Without written debt and credit, such ambitious projects as Egypt's pyramids would have been impossible. They could never have been managed by debt-rememberers. Is it a coincidence the earliest pyramids date from the same era as origins of Egyptian writing?

As already shown in the case of the Hebrew temple in Jerusalem, there are some clear similarities between the powerful morality of debt and the tenets of religion. In the ethics of recording, remembering and enforcing debts may be seen roots both of religious concepts and of legal codes.

One such linkage between them is now familiar: the original meaning of a 'jubilee' was both a religious festival and a philanthropic cancellation of debts. In recent years it became a *cause celebre* among activists campaigning to reduce the indebtedness of poorer nations.

Far older than such predicaments among third world countries, the
Legal Code of Hammurabi, king of ancient Babylon, displays a
remarkable fixation with debt. Uniquely it still exists as a carving
and has been dated to about 1750BC. In the surviving stele there is
a gap in its 280-odd series of legal illustrations (between numbers 65
and 100) and that gap significantly falls between two cases both
setting out illustrations of routine commercial ethics.[15]

So if we assume the Code followed some ordered sequence
then the missing illustrations 66-99 arguably involved commerce too.
Its section dealing with creditary ethics must have been thorough,
well reflecting the preoccupations of Babylonian society. Armed
with the creditary principle, maybe some Babylonian scholars will
now be tempted to take another look.

BY THE TIME OF BABYLON'S Hammurabi, writing
was being used for political and legal purposes but that is
not how it started. The earliest use of writing was to record
debt and credit. That breakthrough to written debt
recording techniques, bringing a much higher capacity than the limits
imposed by human memory, took ages.

It was the achievement of the earliest accurately identified
people of Mesopotamia, the Sumerians. They lived to the east of
mankind's pioneer farmers of several millennia previously, further
along the Fertile Crescent. Their way forward was to create physical,
instead of human memory, debt records. This great move forward

15. *The original stele of the Code of Hammurabi is the Louvre, with a full-size copy
in the British Museum.*

took a long time to incubate. Sumer's inventiveness led first to the invention of written number, and then to writing itself. We all now acknowledge the fundamental importance of writing to mankind, but Sumer's inspired inventors would have had no inkling of that.

Unlike every society since, there was no ready-prepared creditary path for them to adopt as they invented first the rudiments then the sophistication of writing. They were making it up as they went along, following their noses, and their principal concern was commerce. There was no instruction manual for them to follow. Long before the appearance of fully-fledged writing, the earliest hints of physical counting and even accounting in Mesopotamia are to be found in simple stone and clay tokens which have survived more than 8,000 years. That places them far back into the prehistory of agricultural man. To being with, inevitably, progress was slow.

From around 6000 BC onwards, those made of baked clay were deliberately formed into an assortment of deliberate and systematic shapes. Archaeologists have concluded such tokens represented either a sheep, or perhaps a measure of grain or some other unit of useful produce. There is precious little to go on.

Nor is it immediately apparent exactly how such tokens worked. However the evidence of other civilisations, much later but no more advanced, rather suggests they may have been some kind of primitive unit of account for valuing other commodities. Such tokens would begin to make some sense if they were used to represent transferable ownership in some way - a form of debt and credit. How that was achieved without forgery remains a mystery. Clay tokens are a distinct feature of the archaeological record in

Mesopotamia.   Much effort, and not a little puzzlement, has been spent on their interpretation.   If there was ever any doubt that their true function was commercial, it is however dispelled by what happened next.

Sealed ball-shaped clay envelopes are then found, nowadays called bullae, containing whole sets of such tokens.   Bullae were clearly designed as tamper-proof records, but of what and between whom is not immediately apparent. In the absence of other and more obvious needs, the recording and management of debts seems an attractive and likely explanation.[16]

THE NEXT INNOVATION was to improve on such bundles of tokens by denoting number with simple markings directly onto a single clay token. This practical method of economising on clay had a further and historic side-effect. It also represents mankind's earliest-known achievement of written number.

In the late Uruk period (about 3200 BC) another sign of growing sophistication appears, the individualised cylinder seal. Around three to four centimetres long and perhaps a centimetre or so in diameter, they were intricately carved in stone with recognisable figures and objects. Each pattern was almost certainly unique to one identifiable owner.   Rolled across moist clay, the cylinders left an impression which secured the integrity of a clay

16. *Again, excellent examples of all these are to be seen on display in the British Museum, among other places. A bulla is a seal, and that usage of the word survives in 'Papal Bull'.*

document, and simultaneously identified one party to a deal - logically the debtor.

They might be considered the earliest ancestor of the signet ring, or for that matter the embossed company seal still applied to business and legal documents. Many man-years of work still remain to be done on these early Sumerian artefacts. They pose several important questions. Are they the remnants of mankind's first ever physical creditary system? Or are they simply one, from among other such systems, which just happens to have survived?

Yet the artefacts also answer some important questions. They begin to reveal features in the Sumerian economy which all seem quite familiar to us. Those emerging structures and patterns confirm one thing more. Whatever else had been going on in the preceding dark age of several millennia during which Neolithic agriculture evolved, it is evident that concepts of debt and credit, and the means to affirm them, had been developing apace.

ON THE BEST EVIDENCE available, the Sumerians of Mesopotamia were the world's pioneers of written debt records. The climate and soils of Mesopotamia are well-suited to preserve ancient artefacts over many millennia. The evidence is not only empirical but circumstantial too. As soon as the creditary breakthrough to written records was achieved, the direction and pace of economic advance were greatly accelerated The expanding economy of Sumer was driven by human innovation of a very high order. Its expansion had much to do with the next and greatest achievement - the development of writing. Well over two thousand years before any sign of civilisation in Greece, writing first appears in Sumer with proto-Cuneiform, around 3200 BC.

Then over the next few centuries proto-Elamite, and the earliest versions of hieroglyphic in ancient Egypt, also begin to emerge. It should be seen as no coincidence to any creditary economist that around the same time, Sumer began to develop large-scale settlement and thus its first urban centres. They were the first-ever cities, and archaeologists now regard that as the origin of true civilisation anywhere in the world.

Its pace of development from the pioneering urban centres, to the later construction of large irrigation earthworks in the Tigris-Euphrates system was remarkably rapid, just a few centuries. So the much later high-speed development of the United States of America does have a fair historical precedent after all.

Once clay tokens begin to include cuneiform writing, archaeologists switch to the word 'tablet' to describe them. Over a short historical period, tablets crop up as a commonplace feature of the archaeological record.[17] They were clearly a great success. Sumer's tablets list many different commodities, although linking

---

17. *In 1994 the author was introduced to Christopher Walker of the British Museum, its acknowledged expert on cuneiform tablets, and the man who has been so helpful in inspiring this part of the book. "Sometimes I used to take a few Sumerian clay tablets home to Ealing and read them to our dinner guests as entertainment. On one occasion one of them, a banker, said 'Chris, you have just read out a list of banker's acceptances.' I did not include it in my paper because, as an archaeologist, I was not entirely clear what a banker's acceptance did."*

individual cuneiform characters to specific commodities as we would know them is not easy. It is far from simple, for example, to decide whether a particular character denoted 'tin' or 'lead'.

Sumer's creditary records are so accessible today largely because they used such a durable material. Cuneiform inscriptions, made on clay with a reed cut to an oblique point, may be seen in many museums. They well demonstrate the intricacy and diligent workmanship of this, the earliest known writing. It was precise clerical work. The translations however reveal that the pioneers of Sumer did not invent writing to proclaim some grand religious or philosophical principle, nor to flatter a king, but to meet the decidedly prosaic needs of their everyday commerce.

This mundane reality has in the past been a disappointment to archaeologists and sent them searching elsewhere for better sport. For years the exact function of cuneiform tablets in the Sumerian civilisation was just a mystery. Creditary insight can now provide them with a down-to-earth answer.

It does not assist creditary interpretation that so many early clay tablets were thrown aside by earlier archaeologists as debris, so destroying whatever chronological or commercial sequence they may once have had. That said, the clay tablets so found may never have been stored in a methodical manner in the first place.

Once the debt they originally recorded had been discharged, they were of no further obvious use anyway and discarded. Sumerian clay tablets have probably languished on some rubbish heap or other, be it ancient or modern, for much of their long existence. Given the cuneiform evidence so far, the earliest known writing is about five thousand years old. Given the longevity of *homo sapiens*, that date is remarkably recent. Why did mankind not invent writing much earlier? Few people seem to bother asking that question. Discoveries of carefully notched bones have been dated to 28,000 BC, almost as far back as the Venus of Kostenky (page 34). Analysis has suggested that their notation is a sequence rather than a number; as already noted above, who needed to count?

Such carvings show people already had more than sufficient insight and dexterity to make precise records, doing so right back in hunter-gatherer days. They even devised a suitable technology. So why did mankind then wait a further 25,000 years before applying such intelligence and dexterity to inventing writing and number?

CREDITARY ECONOMICS CAN now supply an explanation for that as well. Not until hunter-gatherer man's agricultural descendants had evolved a system of credits and debts based on memory; then exploited that rudimentary memory system to its limit, did writing and counting become worth pursuing. As noted earlier in this chapter on several occasions necessity not ability is the mother of invention.

The earliest-known writing emerged in Sumer from around 3200BC onwards. Within a couple of centuries, city-states large enough to be worthy of that name had developed, in what archaeologists label the Early Dynastic period, approximately 2900-2400BC. During this time, *'specialisation increased, with many categories of craftsmen - potters, metalworkers, jewellers, makers of cylinder seals, leather workers, masons, manufacturers of textiles'* [18]. One might reasonably add to that list numerous other skills and trades concerned with building, supplying foodstuffs and what today we would classify as 'services' of which few if any artefacts can have survived.

The division of labour, the specialisation principle, was burgeoning as never before. Archaeologists have yet to propose a direct cause-and-effect link between the invention of writing, originally for commerce, and the phenomenal economic expansion which followed shortly afterwards. The principles of creditary economics, by contrast, provide a precise and inseparable link between the two.

A city with many thousand inhabitants, or any populous settlement, could flourish only when it could cope with an extensive and intricate web of debts and credits. The more credit agreements an economy can sustain, the greater the degree of division of labour it may attain - the basic creditary rule. Once any debt-recording mechanism reached its maximum capacity and then began to disintegrate, creditors would naturally refuse to agree further debts.

So the size of human settlements made only limited progress from the first agricultural society in around 9000BC, to the first urban civilisation in about 3000BC. It rather suggests that the creditary breaking-point may have been reached on numerous occasions in that dark epoch.

Even a Stone Age village's debt-rememberer must, like Homer, have nodded from time to time. The concept of written debt records may seem simple and obvious enough to us, but at the

18. *Prof H W F Saggs in* Civilisation before Greece and Rome, *p.38*

time in would have been both courageous and challenging. To be willing to accept an inanimate chunk of clay as dependable evidence that someone will pay you back one day was no mean achievement.

The implied trust and confidence becomes more impressive once debt tablets began to circulate. How, then, did you go about enforcing a debt now owed to you by someone else rather than by the original debtor? Sumer's clay tablets, no matter how unexciting they may have once appeared even to early twentieth century archaeologists, were the very breakthrough which man's economic advance had been awaiting for perhaps five thousand years.

H OWEVER IF MODERN ARCHAEOLOGISTS perhaps overlooked that aspect, modern economists have overlooked another. Since the 1970s it has been fashionable to champion 'the market' as the origin of all economic activity. On that basis one might presume that Sumer started with a free market system and only later moved toward some form of centralised., directed economy.

The surviving archaeological evidence, however, indicates the opposite. The heart of Sumer's early economy was an institution which has come to be called the 'temple', or in literal translation the 'big house' or the 'estate'.

Both in name and function, it was the direct ancestor of the Jewish temple in Jerusalem of three thousand years later (see p.64). Far from being some embryonic free market, the pioneering Sumerian economy was a cumbersome bureaucracy. The temple owned anything up to a quarter of agricultural land. It was endowed with livestock and issued labouring contracts. It found employment for war widows and orphans, and for the sick and infirm. Rent was received in the form of sharecropping agreements..

So the Sumerian temple was the first ever absentee landlord. It was also the focus of Sumer's most intricate economic activities. It ran the first-ever craft factories, to begin with owning them directly. Later on, production was sub-contracted to suppliers controlled with a bureaucratic exactitude which would gladden the heart of any modern supermarket chain.

Some miserly suppliers must have been trying to fiddle the system with gusto. The ingredients of such staples as textiles and beer were stipulated to a high degree of precision, spelled out with fastidious accuracy on surviving clay contracts. The pettifogging regulatory officials of our twentieth century and since ply their doleful trade in the spiritual afterglow of Sumerian bureaucrats who beat them to it by about 4,800 years.

Labour employed by the temple in its factories was nourished on temple produce and was later hired out to entrepreneurs. The Sumerian temple was the world's first bed and breakfast employment agency. From its factories, the temple supplied stocks of products to licensed merchants; in some ways it was tantamount to franchising.

Temple records also show how these pioneers of commerce were also helped to pursue international trade. Merchants belonged to temple guilds which equipped them and supplied stock on credit, in due course receiving payment at a mark-up. It is the earliest known example of making a commercial loan and then charging a rate of interest for the facility. Some kind of export trade with distant societies was essential. First Sumer, then Assyria, needed a range of raw materials not available on its alluvial plains, especially once the Bronze Age began to unfold from the mid-third millennium onwards. Tin, mentioned earlier, was obviously one such necessity.

Although archaeologists use the word 'temple' to describe a Sumerian institution which sounds rather more like a chamber of commerce, its connection with the basics of religion was still quite marked. One of the numerous titles of Sumer's principal god was 'The Great Trader'. The rôles of priest and commercial scribe were closely comparable and overlapped, both involving rigorous training.

Among the many clay records which have survived are the classroom exercises of trainee cuneiform scribes. Even if recording commercial debts and contracts was their eventual objective, all the disciplines of a religious seminary were necessary to ensure everything was learnt and done correctly. Sumer's creditary architecture wholly depended on precision and honesty.

F OR ALL ITS ECONOMIC innovation, Mesopotamia gave rise to city states, nothing larger, each with their own self-contained economy. Although kings claimed the allegiance of several such cities into what are today labelled 'empires', the nation state as we would understand it did not yet exist. Nor could it. Under various rulers Mesopotamian dynasties waxed and waned and their succession of different societies has been given a variety of names. A Semitic tribe, the Amorites, succeeded the Sumerians and their rivals the Akkadians, and gradually emerged as the Babylonian 'empire'. The old Sumerian temple evolved into a religious establishment more familiar to us through Judaic and then Christian tradition. In his later notion of 'the temple' Abraham of the Old Testament created a religious institution, not a commercial institution, when he and his tribe emigrated to the Levant.

Large commercial establishments such as the Sumerian 'temple' were to become commonplace feature of the ancient world. When Sir Arthur Evans unearthed what he determined to be the palace in the previously unknown Minoan civilisation of Crete, the building proved to have a large number of storerooms. However else a king in such a palace chose to spend his time, his counting-house evidently occupied much of it.

The Minoan palace probably served a similar function to the Sumerian of temple of half a millennium earlier as a central strategic reserve, especially of cereals. Concerns about the uncertainty of the next harvest never change all that much; kings who ignored it were likely to be usurped.

As the third millennium BC dawned in Sumer, the rôle of debt-rememberer had been transformed. No longer the wise old men in a Neolithic village with a good memory, their successors now had themselves evolved into the chief creditor as well. Temple records survive in profusion, and as noted they give a clear impression that Sumer's economy was a bureaucracy and nothing else. Although archaeological evidence is now interpreted to show that the bureaucratic economy came first, that is not to say there was never a free market of any kind. Permanent records of everyday market transactions are rarely kept even today : ask any street market vegetable stall-holder. It was probably little different over 4000 years ago. Informal business activity certainly existed as well, but who would ever bother to record its transactions for the benefit of future archaeologists? And how was it done without a common coinage? Perhaps customers ran a tally, an accountancy technique which fell out of fashion only with the beginning of the Industrial Revolution. Tally sticks were well-known to Adam Smith; there is ample evidence that much more recent societies have used tally sticks for that same purpose.[19]

SUMER'S TEMPLE ECONOMY may well have invented silver certificates. Some clay artefacts, showing a record contained within another breakable clay seal, appear to have represented a stated quantity of silver. In today's terminology, it was an official IOU. The metal itself was too precious, and never left the Temple, but clay was not.

So long as holders of such clay devices were confident the local temple would freely honour its debt in some way, and provided the current holder could expect to find someone else sharing that confidence, then the clay tablet proxy for silver might circulate as a rough and ready predecessor of money.

Crucially, the legend on such a piece of clay would need to make it plain that the Temple promised to pay in silver. More likely it would make the promise to any 'bearer' - no matter who happened to be holding such Temple markers at any given time. Since the temple remained the unique, identified debtor however, these clay

19. *See Chapter Four*

devices could function as 'money' only as far as the probity of Sumer's temple was recognised by creditors - not much further than the city limits.

The final step to devising money in its true modern full sense was still far into the future. Sumer's international merchants were distinguished citizens of society. Further large quantities of clay records, in inscribed tablet form, have been found in the ruins of Sumer's trading colony at Kanesh. near Kayseri in present-day Turkey (see p 71). Its aristocratic merchants were probably trading with the mysterious Hatti on the far bank of the river The Hatti in turn were about to be overrun by the expansionist Hittites who then adopted their name. Kanesh itself was the site of a major battle.

Cuneiform tablets translated so far show Sumer's creditary system at Kanesh was strictly reserved for deals among members of its exclusive Sumerian trading fraternity. Although creditary activity within the 'guild' was clearly extensive, it is quite evident that none of its commercial privileges extended to the ruffians on the other bank of the river.[20] By a long chalk, Sumer's clay tablet creditary system was not yet any kind of international money. Although financially sophisticated, it was creditary system strictly for the benefit of 'the locals' only.

Detail mechanisms of Sumerian economic life will remain a rich source of discoveries for archaeologists for many years yet. Now they know what they are looking for it will be all the more interesting doing so. One vital lesson for economists is already

---

20. *A point made very clearly in discussion with Christopher Walker of the British Museum, see above.*

apparent. Transactions which we would nowadays call derivatives, were commonplace. Some deals were so sophisticated they would probably have been illegal in commercial London before the mid-nineteenth century. The law of commercial contract was highly advanced.[21] The principle of charging interest was well-established.

SUMER IS ALSO THE EARLIEST known society to have set great store by precious metals. Records show that eventually silver was used as a unit of account. The 'mina' of silver, roughly one pound in weight, was certainly used as a valuation for other commodities. It is perplexing to some historians that precious metal seems to have been an exclusive property of the Temple, and there it remained. For many centuries, it was simply hoarded by the state, and never became a coinage.

Historical records show that a true circulating coinage did not appear in Mesopotamia until almost two millennia later along with the conquests of Alexander the Great. He introduced money into the region by the rudimentary method of requisitioning the bullion stored in the palace or temple treasury and then minting it. It was a quick way to get rich.

Although it marked a huge step forward in mankind's creditary expertise, the limitations of Sumer's clay debt records were considerable. It could only be used by recognised traders who were members of a regulated guild, and to deals with the temple itself. It

---

21. *A point made by banking expert Ned Swan, see bibliography.*

was never a system for the common man. Clearly any transgressor, could be thrown out of the guild and denied his livelihood, no doubt a powerful deterrent to any dishonesty.

Nor could the system extend beyond the writ of the temple. Sumer's creditary records and 'licensed' transactions were confined to a single city state. An enforceable regulatory system would have been necessary to punish malpractices, or canny Sumerian traders would never have agreed to become creditors in the first place.

Cylinder seals would be an essential element in any creditary system based on easy to copy clay tablets. They uniquely identified a specific debtor. Should anyone seek to deny what he owed, his seal soon showed the truth. However a signed deal might depend on some Official Registry which could both trace and authenticate the mark made by a particular seal. So far, no such cylinder seal registry has been reported, yet the function would be as necessary as the master examples of customers' signatures held by a modern bank in our own day.

THIS CHAPTER HAS INTRODUCED the Creditary principle as a technique to help construct a fresh architecture of economics. Although credit in some form has been recognised by many economists since Adam Smith, it has not generally been viewed in an ethical light. The pages above have sought that fresh perspective, not by re-examining existing treatises of economic thought, but by looking further afield. Archaeology, anthropology and history between them can deliver a far more systematic and convincing picture.

As the book progresses, other disciplines come into the mix. The next chapter looks at the origins of coinage; the experts on that are the numismatists. After that, chapter four draws heavily on experts familiar with the history of banking, and there are more relevant disciplines besides.

Rather than being some Aristotelian division of knowledge, experts 'knowing more and more about less and less', what follows is an attempted exercise in being holistic, in fusion. Perhaps so doing will help change the confusion which the author believes has dogged the conventional teaching of economics for too long. In contrast to those who work in the commercial sphere, academics draw much comfort from specialising in their own small patch, with scant interest in what lies beyond.

That has been a further purpose, noted earlier in this chapter, in delving into the intriguing story of Stonehenge. As is also suggested on p.77, by drawing on the varied disciplines of geology, geography, astronomy, arithmetic and economics a different picture of its origins emerges. The standard fall-back explanation of archaeologists - that something they cannot interpret must have been 'religious' - is rather more pervasive than it is persuasive.

More generally it emerges that early economic thinking which revolved around the specialist principle and the operation of markets alone was at best incomplete. Creditary economics is based on another version of the double helix, this time comprising two interdependent forces, the specialist and creditary principles, which between them make economic development possible. Giving credit the importance it deserves paints a different picture of economies, and not just of their origin. Meanwhile the dismal science devised in the wake of nineteenth century economists can be abandoned at last. Their academic successors have clung on to antiquated insights for too long. Far from being some amoral calculus, the essence of economics is now shown to have moral and indeed profound religious components. One imagines that 'Opium of the People' Karl Marx would definitely have objected to that.

Economists since have followed his example by seeking to explain economies with mathematical equations. It will not work. Beneath all that, a deeper economic reality was concealed in the earth beneath their feet.   It is time for today's convention-driven economists to extend their intellectual curiosity and learn from archaeology. They may then join William Shakespeare's Hamlet and discover that there are more things in heaven, and definitely more in earth, than have so far been dreamt of in their philosophies.

Chapter Three

1500BC to 100AD

*Money is none of the wheels of trade: it is the oil which
renders the motion of the wheels more smooth and easy.*
                                    DAVID HUME, 1742

WERE TODAY'S mainstream economists to pay
economic origins the attention they deserve, one
ancient civilisation would surely give them much
cause for thought. Sumer should ring alarm bells
for anyone who automatically assumes money will always occupy
centre stage in a serious economy. That is not necessarily so.

Mankind's creditary skills made their appearance long
before money, as we would recognise it as notes and coins. In
the saga of devising ways to organise credit and debt, money is
little more than a johnnie-come-lately. Any such notion might
have astonished primitive economists, especially Karl Marx.

He firmly believed that debt - and therefore credit - was
impossible without money. Marx was out by at least seven
thousand years. There is much to be learnt from finding out what
had really been happening in the world before the 18th century
gave rise to the Industrial Revolution in Britain. Even today's
conventional economists would have much difficulty explaining
how the economy of ancient Sumer worked. Where was all its

money? Any money? Where were all its banks? If a team of investigators from the International Monetary Fund had arrived in ancient Sumer four thousand or so years ago, they would have stared about themselves in utter bewilderment.

The early economists would be equally bewildered. Long before their first inklings of economic theory inspired by 18th century agricultural lore and a division of labour used in pin factories, a factory economy had already been devised in ancient Mesopotamia by the pioneering civilisation of Sumer. Had such knowledge of history been available to primitive economists, they might have taken a very different view as they formulated their thoughts. Discovering fundamental mechanisms of most systems by searching back for their origins can be a salutory experience. As the saying goes, history is the window through which we understand the present.

One could fairly draw a comparison between uncovering the mechanisms of economies and mechanisms of the human body. William Harvey's fundamental realisation in the 16th century that blood circulated was to transform medicine, moving it forward from mere quackery to insight.   In its current atrophied state, economics - still a fairly new discipline - is surely overdue for a broadly comparable transformation. Some contemporary economists take that more enlightened view.

T HE PURPOSE OF THIS book is to investigate the original systems of economic activity and see where that leads. A clear understanding credit is crucial : it was a key ingredient from the very beginning. If the purpose of the previous chapter was to show how the creditary wheels were set in motion, the purpose of the chapter which follows is to examine the origins and consequences of money. Its invention was entirely pragmatic, as almost all economic origins have proven to be down the ages. It is nearly always necessity, and sometimes just happenstance, which is the mother of economic invention. It is hardly ever a matter of premeditated contrivance.

The further characteristic of all economic origins is that they are unrepeatable. There was never a script or blueprint to follow; all the pioneers could do was make it up as they went along, working from basic needs to devise solutions. If they worked then the basic principles later emerged. None of those involved in devising what became 'money' had any knowledge of where their invention would lead. At least those who devise new technology, the foundation of progress in the specialist principle, do have some inkling [1] of the likely consequences.

Only now can we see that money was probably the greatest single step forward ever in creditary technique. Such major successes are acknowledged centuries later, when people perceive their broader consequences. In contrast, many derivative advances in technology have immediate and startling impact. That explains why historians of economics have been more absorbed by chronicling advances in technology, the readily accessible saga of mankind's successive economic inventions.

As already noted the explanation of economies pursued here takes a different course. This book seeks the unobtrusive, the unremarked, the things that had already happened long before people started to take any notice. As it unfolded the story of creditary invention, that other essential twin component of specialist technical invention in mankind's economic progress has

---

1. *The point has been made many times, and with many inventions other than coinage. When asked the eventual use of his or her invention, the honest inventor typically replies 'I don't know yet.' It was certainly true of the original computers. Again, Benjamin Franklin and Michael Faraday are both fabled to have replied 'Madam, what use is a new-born baby?' to questions about the purpose of hot-air balloons and discovering electricity. The eventual uses of money would have been far less obvious - at the time of its original devising - than either. In our own time, the same lack of predictability is true of graphene.*

almost always been like that. Of importance to fathoming economies is working how what came first and how it was achieved. The lessons so learnt should have a ready application in our own era for backward countries seeking that elusive path to economic wealth. Those who would bring their economies into the modern world of prosperity for most would benefit from understanding how it all first evolved. There are no short cuts.

Peoples of Sumer would never have regarded their remarkable new expertise recording debt and credit in writing as the launch of some splendid new chapter in the annals of economics. There was no official fanfare. Ceremonial perspective is an exclusive view of subsequent historians, who enjoy the pleasure of hindsight from their much superior vantage point. At the time the makers and traders of Sumer simply got on with it, one step at a time. The future could take care of itself.

SUMER WAS AN ECONOMIC FIRST. Without anything comparable elsewhere to copy it developed a fully-functioning craft factory system, a rudimentary welfare state, absentee landlords, implicit rates of interest, understanding and use of derivatives, international merchants and later a unit of account.

Bringing such economic ingenuity to fruition took Sumer a thousand years and more, four times as long as our own Industrial Revolution has lasted so far. No-one should be much surprised by that. How each next step was achieved could only have been a matter of trial and error, and that takes time. With no extant syllabus explaining 'how it should be done' everything had to be original and experimental.

Writing was almost exclusively used for recording credit deals, not for publishing instruction manuals. Unsurprisingly Sumer's pace of economic development was fairly slow by more recent standards : the impressive aspect is that it ever happened at all. To fathom mankind's next advance, his invention of money, attention must turn to a region a thousand miles north-west of early civilisations around the Indus and Euphrates. It happened in ancient Greece. Money was to become the next great creditary step forward - maybe only a temporary one - in man's unassuming creditary progress. In our 21st century some people believe that money is already on its way out again, having served its purpose. It could soon be totally replaced by simplified debit and credit cards - note the vocabulary. A younger generation is rapidly heading in that direction.

If so, coinage would have served as a creditary medium for around two and a half thousand years. For some purposes, such as bus fares, it has almost disappeared already. Technology tailored to that task has long been available, yet untapped for almost half a century.[2]   A version has been adopted for pay-as-you-go phone cards; is that a glimpse of our creditary future? Is PayPal the future for everyday retail banking? Who knows?

Whatever happens to metallic coins in years to come, whether they survive or not, advancing economies will always require a creditary system in some form, the more trouble-free the better. Credit will probably outlive the monetary era. Spores of our creditary future are among us now. Yet who can tell if they are a glimpse of what comes next - or just a dead end?

Money, metal coinage, traces back to a common paradox, one to be observed not only in economies. Simplicity is a finale, never the overture. People too often overlook a near-universal truth about human innovation. Systems of all kinds normally develop by beginning with a complicated version which gradually

2. *In 1971 the author organised an item for BBC Television's* Tomorrow's World. *It demonstrated a stand-alone development of a debit/ credit card designed for handling small payments (invented by a Luton company, Revenue Systems Ltd) which would not require any connection with a bank's central computer. In a retrospective review of his years with the programme, Raymond Baxter recalled it had been one of the most intriguing items he had ever introduced.*

retreats toward its barest essentials. If the logic perhaps sounds inverted, the experience is not. Down the ages most landmark innovations have been greeted with a familiar cry: *"It's just so simple, it's amazing no-one ever thought of it before."* That is probably more true of money than almost anything else.

MONEY IN THE SENSE of coinage was still a thousand years into the future when Sumer's factory economy was already in decline. Banks which generated credit were still two thousand years more distant than that. Sumer's complicated creditary system was just one step along the road from complexity to simplicity. A coinage depended on further sophistication beyond anything achieved in Sumer, despite its remarkable innovation.

A precise yet cumbersome creditary system like that of Sumer can only evolve into money, in the strict sense adopted in this book, once basic debt tokens have passed through three further stages of development. First they become transferable, then they become generalised and eventually they are also re-usable; the identity of an original debtor is forgotten.

The key to understanding is transferability. Money as we would recognise it does not identify a specific creditor, nor does it denominate what it should be used to pay for. Transforming single-use debt records of Sumer into de-personalised money that can circulate - for that is its essential feature - required all three of those upgrades. It took a long time, but that is what happened. In essence, money is just a very sophisticated, very simple, transferable debt token.

The first of these three advances was to dispense with the identity of the creditor. Sumer's clay debt tokens could be traded around, in a commercial version of 'pass the parcel'. Whoever happened to be holding a debtor's token at any one moment became the current creditor. No longer were creditary instruments being tied throughout their active existence to an original debtor and his original creditor. It is fairly evident from their shape and size that Sumerian clay tablets were designed to be handed around; their cuneiform writing was microscopic. As noted above (footnote, page 100) even reading them is a demanding skill for today's archaeologists

They have been erroneously described by museums in the past as ill-defined 'trade records', for want of a better explanation. The logic of that is implausible; in labelling their exhibits, curators were taking an unhelpful short cut. If tablets had simply been a retrospective, passive record of completed trade deals it would have been much less awkward had they been made larger. The orthography would have been less demanding; there was hardly a shortage of clay as the raw material. Had they been an active, but non-transferable record of debts it would have been in everyone's interest to build them large, and make them difficult to tamper with. That didn't happen either.

There can be only one reason why Sumer's debt tokens were quite so small. Qualifying merchants carried them around on their person for safe keeping. It might all sound tame stuff today, but 5,000 years ago it was all very adventurous. Accepting a fragment of clay with its tiny markings as full title to someone else's debt, no matter how detailed the cuneiform inscription, was a notable act of faith among a community of merchants.

Sumer's revolutionary clay tablets each recorded a whole variety of different goods. Netting off such convoluted mixed debts must have been quite a palaver. No matter how tortuous, such procedures do endure in business and commerce, as systems pursue their course of evolution from perplexingly complicated to astonishingly simple. Sumer's creditary complexity was no more convoluted than the work of Britain's Railway Clearing House in the nineteenth century.

That now-forgotten institution precisely allocated the revenue earned by each individual wagon to the numerous railway companies whose tracks it had travelled, each journey painstakingly measured mile by mile. Even by Sumer's standards it was a huge exercise in clerical bureaucracy.

Despite all its complexities unfamiliar to us, the Sumerian system worked. The pace of Sumerian commerce speeded up; its economy grew many times over. The basic tenet of creditary economics held good : the more credit agreements an economy can sustain, the greater the division of labour it may attain.

S UMER'S NEXT ADVANCE was to dispense with the specification of the commodities which were owed. A debt incurred in one set of products might ultimately be redeemed by handing over something different. Only adoption of a standard unit of account, typically a notional weight of silver, made the advance possible. Notional quantities of barley were similarly used for such accounting purposes.

In the process, Sumer eventually drew up a complicated schedule of silver valuations. It was a pricing system, yet there was still no 'money'. Settlement transactions at the temple are well-documented. They were enumerated in, but not actively paid in, quantities of silver.

Although this might all sound straightforward to us, at the time it was another sophisticated step forward in understanding debt. No longer did a debtor necessarily owe something material, fixed and specific. Already in Sumer by 2000BC, indebtedness was understood, and circulated, as something in the abstract. The debtor was in effect affirming that *"I definitely owe someone something, but no-one has quite decided yet what exactly it will eventually be."*

Once a separate, standard unit of account was widely used, so the prospect of inflation - or deflation - loomed and has been with us ever since. Inflation can only arise once goods and services are no longer valued in terms of themselves, but priced by reference to a standard something else. The success of these two upgrades in Sumer's creditary techniques had an intriguing consequence. It probably delayed eventual emergence of recognisable money, the coinage, by as much as a millennium. As a creditary system, the regular use of clay tablets to record one-off debts and credits had become just too embedded in Sumer's economic architecture.

More than that. Clay tablets could circulate freely because they had little or no intrinsic value. Yet the less their intrinsic value, the more the debt's validity depended on locating the original debtor. In effect it was a portable entry in a ledger. None of the worth of the debt was embedded in the token, it was just a record of a debt owed between people somewhere else. So the creditor, whoever that was at any one moment, still needed to keep within hailing distance of the original debtor.

It was a vital constraint which prevented Sumer's clay tablet creditary system extending beyond the jurisdiction of a single city state. The creditary system, though evolving rapidly, still had to remain under the aegis of a single controlling guild, and probably that of the Sumerian temple as well.

Accumulating quantities of silver bullion seems to have had a contrary effect. The greater its assumed intrinsic value, the less anyone was prepared to allow it to circulate freely. It was hoarded instead. For centuries the Sumerian temple, and later the palace, served primarily as a depository of bullion. America's Fort Knox has a four thousand-year old antecedent. The consequence was that Sumer's temple became, not a bank, but a silver warehouse. The idea of circulating precious metal may seem wholly unremarkable to us, but in ancient times it was almost beyond comprehension.

Given the burgeoning scale of Sumer's economy, it is unlikely that anything like sufficient silver was in stock to let it circulate throughout the commercial community. Instead it was hoarded. Such private bullion hoarding is still with us. One can observe that same Sumerian mentality in our own era, with the popularity of the Krugerrand. Although South Africa's solid gold Krugerrands have been deliberately minted to look like coins and even show a nominal monetary value, they are hardly money. People who collect them (or collect the variants minted by other gold-producing countries in imitation) prefer to hoard them for safe-keeping rather than spend them on purchases.

Such people effectively become a gold warehouse - not unlike the original silver warehouse temple of Sumer. Their treasured possessions serve, not as circulating coins, but as a fluctuating and unreliable store of value. Although today's manufacturers of Krugerrands go out of their way to emphasise what a safe refuge for savings their product provides, the facts show otherwise [3]. In the decade to January 2015, for example, Krugerrands rose in value from $400 to $2,000, before falling back to $1,200. Reliable store of value they were not.

It would be interesting to know how many, if any, of the forty-six million Krugerrands minted so far have ever been spent in a shop, or indeed used to settle any kind of impersonal debt other, perhaps, than among close friends. The answer is almost certainly none. Rather a Krugerrand would first be sold for conventional cash and that in turn would be handed over. The creditor would want something he could spend, not something he must also squirrel away in his attic.

In terms of economics and finance, Krugerrands are effectively a kind of jewellery, in much the same sense that 'diamonds are a girl's best friend'. Both are hidden away somewhere safe. Gold coin enthusiasts are pursuing a concept of 'finance' which is over four thousand years old, one which was already outmoded almost three thousand years ago.

---

3. It was part of the duties of the present writer, when he worked on the Commodities page of the Financial Times in the 1960s, to ensure the gold price at its daily Fixing appeared without fail. It did not take many months of doing so to realise how poor a 'store of value' gold can be - and it never pays any interest.

Keynes's renowned observation, that practical men are usually the slaves of some defunct economist, holds better than ever as one considers the slavish admiration of gold. One may wonder how long it will be before the 'gold bugs' realise they are being taken for a ride exploiting their insecurity by mine owners only too keen to find fresh customers for their decreasingly useful product : gold is no longer used in dental fillings, for example.

Its excellent electrical conductivity makes gold useful in expensive electronic circuits, and we may assume there will be a market for wedding rings in the foreseeable future. Otherwise its weight and softness , quite apart from the cost of extracting it from the ground, rather circumscribe gold's practicality. No wonder gold mine owners are so keen to encourage gold bugs to hang onto it for its own sake. Under Chancellor Gordon Brown the British Treasury at long last realised the futility of doing so and offloaded a large proportion of it gold "reserves".

S UMER'S NON-MONETARY written creditary system may have been cumbersome, yet versions of it spread around the eastern Mediterranean and probably beyond.
The civilisation of ancient Egypt developed later than Sumer, but it was not far behind and clearly the two shared many economic practices, including their reverence for stored gold.

Precise records survive of a most illuminating Egyptian lawsuit, dating from around 1300BC. It well illustrates the practical difficulties of using silver as a numeraire only, in the absence of an effective coinage. The lawsuit recounts[4] how a merchant went from house to house offering a Syrian slave-girl for sale, until finally the wife of an Egyptian official bought her. A price was agreed in terms of silver, the numeraire, but payment was actually made in various cloths, garments and bronze vessels,

---

4. Cited by Professor H W F Saggs in his 'Civilisation before Greece and Rome'; see bibliography.

each item being separately rated against a standard valuation. The recorded text of the lawsuit specifies that bronze vessels were obtained from the purchaser's neighbours.

It readily demonstrates how prosperous middle-class Egyptians were well accustomed to lending and borrowing among neighbours who trusted one another - a basic creditary principle. As they did so they kept a neighbourhood record of debits and credits, rather like village debt-rememberers of nine thousand years previously When eventually it became necessary for someone to make a larger purchase, a creditor could call in goods from neighbours who owed them something.

Professor Saggs' valuable Egyptian example also points to avenues for future creditary historians to explore. How were such local debts generally recorded? Did local society impose a collective moral or legal obligation comparable to that of a mercantile guild? Were debts written in some manner on an Egyptian successor to Sumerian clay tablets, or in hieroglyphics?

Or did the sophisticated peoples of ancient Egyptians use tally sticks? Belgian bakers were still using tally sticks to record door-to-door deliveries of bread in the 19th century, only about a century ago. In Egypt it was about the same time that the abacus was first developed. So people had a way of doing arithmetic, and they must have had a way of recording their debts, yet money was still nowhere to be seen.

The creditary practices of early Greeks, the Achaeans, followed a similar path to that set by Sumer and Egypt. Homer's Iliad, dated in its earliest oral versions to a few centuries after the Egyptian lawsuit, refers to a bronze cauldron 'worth twelve oxen' used as a sporting prize. So familiar objects, and not just precious metals or measures of barley were used as numeraires. Greece apparently used cows and bulls.

Homer also describes how the Achaeans had traded a variety of commodities by valuing them in terms of an amphora of wine. In no sense were they an early form of money. Full amphorae each held an equivalent of fifty modern bottles of wine, plus the weight of the pot. Amphorae stayed where they were; circulating such heavy objects as 'money' would have been unthinkable.

Resorting to such numeraries was the normal practice for centuries, long before portable money itself emerged. Nurtured on a diet of these heroic tales, yet unaware of economic activity which preceded and surrounded them, too many people have jumped to the mistaken conclusion that immediately before money, there was barter. It was simply not so; as noted in the previous chapter, the evolution of creditary technique was more complex than that, while barter cannot encapsulate debt.

CREDITARY HISTORIANS and economists, by contrast, should be diligent in filling in many historical and logical steps, as they analyse how economic expertise grew. History is the window through which we can understand the present. Part of the story is noting how a new understanding of creditary technique had spread well beyond its origins among an exclusive merchant community originating in Sumer along the Fertile Crescent and beyond.

Debt was now recorded : it was no longer a matter solely of consulting tribal debt-rememberers. It spread geographically, probably from port to port around the Mediterranean. It also spread socially from the merchant community to be shared by their customers; the example from Egypt of 1300BC well illustrates that, while its date is educative too.

The community in Egypt had grown in population far beyond anything which could be served by a tribal debt-rememberer.   It was not merely barter but something rather more sophisticated; the sub-contractors who built Egypt's pyramids had a system of written agreements for their work. As observed at the start of Chapter Two "jumping in half-way through the story inevitably means missing fundamentals which have long since been obscured from view".

Even if Homer's Iliad can be somewhat misleading on exactly how money came about, it is remarkably close on where it happened - probably accidentally so. The Troy of his classic fable was less than a hundred miles from the ancient kingdom of Lydia in that same region of western Anatolia around the modern port of Izmir. The birthplace of further creditary innovation had moved about a thousand miles west from its origins in Iraq.

T HE WORLD'S EARLIEST KNOWN examples of proto-coins have been dated to some time around 700 BC in the reign of Lydia's King Gyges. Inscribing dates on them at the time was wholly unknown : it would of course have been quite challenging to date them 700BC.

So it is largely conjectural at what stage ordinary chunks of metal came to treated as circulating tokens of recognised debt. No-one was keeping notes, or a record of the event. The practice just emerged, imperceptibly. Unsurprisingly there has been no shortage of academic adrenalin lavished on the issue.

It is probably best to follow the judgement of coin collectors, numismatists, people who invest their own money in what they consider to be collectable. The proto-coins of Lydia are the earliest yet found, an origin in economies. Non-ferrous metals do not rust away, they survive; so there is by now not much likelihood anything will be found in sufficient quantity to suggest coinage was actually invented elsewhere.

The first coins recognised as such by numismatists are called 'staters' a word which like 'shekel' means 'weighing'. They were of more or less uniform weight, at least, if not of shape. Their weight gradually settled down to approximately 12 grammes, the same weight as a modern British £2 coin.

They were originally made from an unusual alloy of gold and silver nowadays called electrum. The Aegean Sea and the region around it sit on a fault zone between two tectonic plates. That typically gives rise to geological formations which favour concentrations of distinctive minerals and unusual metals. The basin of the river Pactolus in Lydia seems to have provided deposits of both gold and silver, and in sufficient proximity for electrum to be produced by smelting them together.

It is uncommon for gold and silver to occur in such proximity; however such metallurgical coincidences have already been noted in the last chapter. The proximity of deposits of copper and tin in Cornwall almost two thousand years previously were probably an origin of the Bronze Age. And if Cornwall's tin did find its way to Sumer as suggested above, that ancient trade would have passed within two hundred miles of Lydia and its attendant merchants. That may be a further link.

Unfamiliar as coins to our eyes, the earliest examples of proto-coins were more like a jelly bean in size and shape. Crucially, however, they bore a 'royal' mark, in effect a hallmark. There are fine examples of early Lydian staters to be seen in several museums. Their official branding gave them a distinctive status, and that has been the signature of coins ever since.

Without such branding they were merely anonymous chunks of metal, much like the metal blanks to be seen pouring in their millions from presses at Britain's Royal Mint in South Wales. The Mint then feeds the blanks into a stamping mill and thus they become coins, exactly the same principle that had been originally adopted in Lydia over 2,500 years previously.

So it is quite feasible that Lydia's pioneering 'money' was also the world's pioneer branded product. In passing it is also important to observe that the word 'money' itself was still well into the future - let alone the word 'coin'. Many people keen to promote their own explanation of the origins of money, and typically jumping in half-way through the narrative, overlook that awkward reality. No-one then had a clue what 'money' meant; that common acceptance around the Mediterranean civilisation was still several hundred years into the future.

THE KINGDOM OF LYDIA nevertheless grew very prosperous on the proceeds. One might well ask whether its royal status actually grew from that. Was being 'a kingdom' the consequence of, rather than the cause of, the family's wealth? There were to be several more instances of that process in the millennia to come.

In the absence of written records, a lot of archaeological guesswork must necessarily be spent in fathoming the metallic activities of what became the royal house of Lydia. Troves have been unearthed with both stamped and blank metal lumps. Numismatists regard them as the original transition to coinage.

Two centuries after Gyges, the last king of Lydia was Croesus, fabled even today as the very embodiment of opulence. In both the popular vernacular and in precise creditary logic, Croesus really was coining it. It is reckoned he devised a means to manufacture coins separately out of either gold or silver, thus putting an end to any debate about the actual metallic composition of those made by mixing them in electrum alloy. It was a very astute move which won many adherents. In the pre-Classical period the gold piece of the Mediterranean was known, inter alia, as a 'croesid'.

So how did the branded nuggets devised in Lydia gradually evolve into circulated money? Again the archaeological record shows it began in a small way, it was not instantaneous, rather it occupied up to two centuries. At some juncture a merchant customer of Lydia, originally trading to obtain an electrum nugget for its familiar metallic content, then thought the better of it. Instead he offered it to a colleague to settle some mutual debt. That was how it all began, as unexcitingly as that.

Lydia had stumbled on a clever wheeze. By making its electrum chunks match in weight and branding them, they became interchangeable and reliably so. One they started to circulate among merchants in the eastern Mediterranean, they became an accepted debt token of commerce. The value of those early staters was certainly not a currency for the ordinary man. One estimate is that a single coin would to buy twelve sheep, roughly £600-700 in terms of British values today.

Among a progressive merchant class, the staters became a common currency, a shared convention or custom. Yet only that, nothing more. No merchant could be obliged to accept them to settle a debt - there was no concept of legal tender. He might have no interest in rare metals. As the diligent research work of numismatists shows the new system nevertheless worked, far better than any creditary technique had done before. Along the way the original purpose of Lydia's nuggets, as a source of precious metal, was steadily forgotten.

In modern jargon, the utility of Lydian staters as a system of debt and credit grew more important than their utility as a source of raw metal. Other archaeological evidence shows quite clearly (see later, shipwrecks) the number of merchants expanded many times over, largely because the new technique for denoting and transferring debt was so simple.

Regular use of coinage originated among sophisticated merchants, competitive businessmen always on the lookout for a new, cleverer and more profitable way to pursue their commerce. Money started life, not at the retail level for small purchases, but with high-level transactions among professional traders, much as the original debt tokens had first been used in the Sumerian economy by professional traders some two millennia previously.

The precise research of numismatists clearly shows the spread of coinage in time, worth and region. The geography alone makes it apparent their original function was to facilitate trade among merchants of the Aegean islands and the early communities which evolved into Greek city states.

Familiarity with coinage steadily gained ground. Branded royal nuggets enjoyed less and less significance as precious metal, more and more relevance as money. Their shape adapted to their new function. Over a period of about a century from around 600BC onwards they looked less like jelly beans, steadily becoming the flattened (if not yet quite circular) discs we have known ever since, and invariably with some imprint to brand them. The system was clearly becoming a great success which others now wanted to share.

From the time of Croesus onwards - the mid sixth century BC - the number of active mints increased rapidly [5]. Lydia did not enjoy its coining monopoly for very long. Supply of acceptable coins increased rapidly as more mints were set up to meet burgeoning demand. Those early mints - no more than craft workshops - each had to win their credentials, gaining a public reputation that they produced reliable coins. Numismatists have also plotted that growth with precision.

The region over which coins became an acceptable way to circulate debts expanded steadily, as new merchants decided to join in. The idea they were exchanging chunks of metal gave way to a more subtle notion they were exchanging debt. The 'money illusion' took hold. Gradually the actual metal content became less and less significant - but that took several centuries.

In the meantime it was realised that silver, on its own, was much more widely available than electrum alloy. Any suggestion that minting coins should be a state monopoly was still several hundred years in the future; apart from Athens, all those early mints were strictly private enterprise operations.

---

5. *As attested by the price paid for ancient coins in the modern numismatic market. That provides an accurate index of how many have survived, and thus a rough idea of how many were minted originally.*

That lends further support to the notion that 'King' Gyges and his successors in Lydia were much more mine-owners than kings. Any new mint had to earn its reputation among the merchant community. There would have been many substandard forgeries which failed that test - there still are [6]. As commercial use of metal coins became established and familiar, so the precise metal from which they were made waned in importance. The widespread recognition of coinage as tokens of debt was taking another step forward.

B Y THE LATE FIFTH century BC, three hundred years after electrum staters first made their appearance, the earliest Mediterranean bronze coins emerged. They were introduced originally by a Greek mint in Sicily. Once again, we may hazard a guess that innovation originally had much to do with finding new ways to sell a raw material.

The first bronze tokens were cast in all sorts of unusual and intentionally attractive shapes, and only subsequently settled down to imitate the more or less circular disc by then familiar in silver coinage. The pattern does not suggest the mint set out to popularise a cheap substitute for silver, but rather it was seeking a more attractive and profitable market for its own output of bronze. Their idiosyncratic shapes turned out to be yet another would-be creditary innovation which was a dead end.

The advent of bronze coinage in smaller denominations enabled the money habit, now more widely understood, to reach beyond sophisticated wealthy merchants and into the populace at large. No longer was a basic coin worth as much as twelve sheep. The creditary logic and widespread use of coinage as we

---

6. *As recently as 2017 it was necessary to introduce a much more sophisticated British one pound coin, incorporating two different metals in a shape which was harder to copy; a kind of "post-Croesid" perhaps. Even the Royal Mint had been forced to admit that over three per cent of previous, simpler one pound coins were forgeries, and we may rest assured that was a politic underestimate.*

understand it was, by 400BC, familiar around the Mediterranean and beyond. It had taken about two centuries from invention to public acceptance. From then onwards in recorded history, the evolution of coinage is a more or less continuous story, fully documented by the numismatic record right up to our own time.

General acceptance of the new creditary system in the centuries after 400BC coincided with the golden age of Greek prosperity, culture and achievement.   It was not just a coincidence; the new creditary system made that 'golden' age possible. The wealth of Athens in particular generated a leisured, intellectual class for whom writing was the norm. That was new.

MEANTIME THE STATER BECAME the single Mediterranean currency. Although the term 'Greek' is generally used to describe them, such classical coins were in practice minted as far afield as Russia, Egypt and Spain. While Alexander the Great helped extend their popularity eastwards, Greek maritime merchants were busily doing the same in the West, throughout the Mediterranean region and places beyond.

Macedonian staters, or more frequently regional copies of Macedonian staters, circulated throughout the known world. Coins reached Britain, a far corner of the classical world, during the 2nd century BC, about half a millennium after they were first devised. The earliest coins found in the British Isles came with overseas trade, and through migration of Belgic peoples from continental Europe. Once it arrived, the idea caught on quickly enough.   Good copies of gold Macedonian staters were already being minted in Britain even before the visit of Julius Caesar.

Once again the numismatic record is revealing. First foreign coins were used, then local metalworkers manufactured good native copies. Later as the money habit took hold, they invented designs of their own. That progression required no more than a century or so. The popular notion that Julius Caesar was greeted by savages leaping up and down atop the White Cliffs of Dover could not be further from the truth.

To begin with money, the metallic coinage, had evolved slowly. It was certainly not invented overnight, least of all by primitive tribesmen who had lately grown bored with barter. According to the song money makes the world go round. Its astrophysical influence is probably not quite as potent as that, but with classical civilisation and especially the Roman Empire it changed just about everything, the most important such being economic geography. A single change in the creditary system had a far-reaching effect. Routine trade over long distances now became feasible for the first time ever. It became the economic foundation of the Mediterranean's classical civilisation.

A division of labour was no longer restricted to different crafts within a single city state. Whole countries now became specialists in specific products, their economies linked by international trade on a scale inconceivable before money was invented [7]; all because a mercantile debt no longer need be traced back to an original debtor in a single neighbourhood. The debt could now be owed by anyone, anywhere. The three-stage upgrade from one-time clay tokens to a full coinage had finally been achieved.

The new creditary technique turned debts into something universal. In the process it was too easily forgotten that despite its anonymity, money - the coinage - continues to represent someone's debt of something to someone else. We may note that, once again, another fundamental origin of economies too easily faded into forgotten history. Neither rulers, nor merchants nor mine owners had any prior inkling of the eventual

---

7. *Dacia, the modern Roumania, became the granary of the Roman empire. Never before would it have been commercially feasible to ship a commodity as cheap as wheat or barley over such long distances.*

significance of their creditary technique. They had to work out its mechanics, its potentials and its pitfalls as they went along. In the early days of coinage, some merchants would refuse to have any truck with the system. They would still want to know who the original debtor was. Some would dispute the quality of the coins. Others were stung by disagreements over the metallic valuation of their goods.

Others were simply robbed; that was another new phenomenon. Where Sumer's creditary system of individual debt tokens had been vulnerable to fraud, the Greek creditary system of universal debt tokens was now vulnerable to theft.

Why, when Sumer's pioneering civilisation had developed one clever method for recording and transferring its debts and credits, did early Greek civilisation build its economic foundations on quite another? So far there is no archaeological evidence the proto-Greeks had ever made any use of clay tablets.

On the face of it, the Greeks leapfrogged two millennia of creditary evolution, apparently starting from nowhere, moving directly to a sophisticated creditary technique of universal money. It was to remain the creditary norm for the next two thousand years. How did the Greeks manage that? The literary and archaeological records are unhelpful in providing an answer.

THERE IS A PLAUSIBLE explanation for the Greeks' remarkable advance and it is in the best tradition of Occam's Razor. It is provided by geology. Early civilisations, just like more recent times, made use of whatever materials came readily to hand. On the alluvial plains of Mesopotamia, that abundant material was quite evidently clay.

In Asia Minor and all around the Aegean, which is a region of hard rock, there were convenient deposits of precious metals. Those metal deposits, particularly of silver, were the crucial resource driving Greece's pioneering creditary system. The growing prominence of Athens was built on its publicly-owned silver mines at Laurium in Attica. It was not the first nor last occasion a basic shift in mankind's culture, power structure and economic geography was driven by what was in the earth.

The communities which flowered into Greek civilisation were doubly fortunate. First they inherited from Sumer - and Egypt - the high esteem, reverence even, in which gold and silver were by then held. They were the precious metals which did not tarnish with age, gold even less so than silver.

That rare attribute was attractive to anyone who wanted their rule to appear immortal. Look no further than the funerary relics found in the pyramids of Egypt, or the rare gold relics of kingship unearthed in ancient British sites and elsewhere. Or for that matter go to the Tower of London and admire the generous quantities of gold used in Britain's crown jewels. The gold crown used at the Coronation - the crowning - even more than the person wearing it is still the permanent symbol of Britain's monarchy and sovereignty. It is all part of the same story.

That ineffable aura of scarcity and desirability of the precious metals rubbed off on the Greeks. It was their accidental inheritance, and made them some of history's most conspicuous nouveau riche. Previous civilisations had built their economic success using more convoluted creditary techniques, yet grew prosperous enough to covet precious metal, acquire and store it in their temples and treasuries. Bullion had always been rare stuff to them, much too scarce to hand around as a token of debt.

Another stroke of good fortune for the Greeks was the providential quantity of precious metal discovered in their lands. For a coinage of precious metal to succeed, a steady supply of silver, and then the rate at which it was extracted and minted, were both critical. Too much at any one time and it would have flooded the market, rather as the conquistadors were to do some two millennia later with their gold booty from South America. Too little, and there would have been insufficient to manufacture an everyday currency. It would have remained a cherished rarity, squirrelled away and reserved for sumptuary uses such as temple treasures or jewellery. The good fortune of the Greeks was that precious metal, silver in particular, was available in their territories in just the right quantity to mint a coinage.

THE ENIGMA OF "Who were the Greeks?" seems to have perplexed historians for generations. Where did their remarkable civilisation spring from, seemingly out of nowhere? Did they perhaps arrive from some unrecorded exotic paradise of intellect? No, they didn't. Creditary insight now offers a much more down-to-earth answer to that enduring conundrum.

The 'early Greeks' were just local tribes who discovered they were suddenly rich, simply by living in their particular geological region. Their cultural brilliance did not arise from unprecedented philosophical ingenuity - it was far more a matter of geological serendipity and the leisured opportunities that wealth created. One might say much the same of the House of Saud, little-known tribal sheep herdsmen of Arabia - until oil was discovered on their lands.

There was a clear affinity between royal houses, mine-owning and great wealth stretching back at least as far as the Bible's King Solomon and his legendary mines. Croesus was one of the first. As with the silver mines of Athens at Laurium, so also the Holy Roman Empire. In 968AD silver deposits were found near Goslar, in the northern Harz mountains of Germany. That was enough to persuade Emperor Henry II (1002-1024) to build his first imperial palace in the town.

Half a millennium later, Queen Elizabeth I of England moved quickly to confiscate mining rights from the Earl of Northumberland, on whose lands metal deposits had recently been found. In 1568 a compliant panel of twelve judges determined on her behalf that '*all mines of gold and silver within the realm, whether they be in the lands of the Queen or of her subjects, belong to the Queen by prerogative.'* Her decree was the antithesis of democracy; it was ruthless expropriation condoned by her courts - no doubt Elizabeth's judges knew what was in store for them if they incautiously decreed otherwise.

Ten years before that, as she succeeded to the throne, Elizabeth had taken full advantage of the new-fangled idea of a joint stock company. Two of the very first such, the Company of Mines Royal, and the Mineral and Battery Company, were both created in 1558. A decade later they were to provide a handy legal formula by which the queen could confiscate valuable mineral rights from her noble subjects. The proponents of Magna Carta 352 years earlier might well have taken a dim view of Elizabeth's legalised theft. Once again might was right, and the inheritance rights of the meek, or even the aristocratic Percy's, had precious little say in the matter.

The striking connection between thriving royal dynasties and profitable mining businesses has an enduring pedigree, and surely merits further examination. In a way, the link still persists. Royal wedding rings are traditionally made out of a nugget of gold found in Britain. The ancient gold mines in central Wales at Dolaucothi, about halfway between Lampeter and Llandovery, were well-known to the Romans[8]. They also knew of the copper mine in North Wales on the Great Orme at Llandudno.

The Greek invention of a metallic coinage was just one episode in a long, and too-easily overlooked, economic and political tradition. By 400BC the 'money illusion' had established itself throughout the Mediterranean civilisation and was also doing so in China - see later. An interesting question for creditary historians is what system did Greek coinage replace? What

---

8. *The mines are outside Pumpsant ('Five Saints') and open to visitors. It appears the Romans approached the gold mines from the east. The nearest remnants of a Roman castle are to be found near Brecon, about one day's march away. The mines were a clear attraction to the conquering Romans.*

creditary technique was previously used,   until that historic
juncture, among enterprising   merchants of Asia Minor?   It
could have been tally sticks, it is unlikely to have been verbal. The
answer may once again lie in simple geography.

The Lydian capital of Sardis was three hundred miles
west of modern Kayseri, site of ancient Kanesh. We know a
Sumerian merchant community there was using transferable debt
successfully over a thousand years before the Šfard, as the
Lydians were to call themselves, emerged into the spotlight of
history. If the Greek merchants who eventually devised a
coinage had used something like the clay tokens of over a
millennium previously in much the same region, there is so far no
archaeological evidence of their doing so. Maybe someone
should go and take a look.

T HE VITAL DIFFERENCE between Lydia and
previous regimes was that bullion was now constantly
available from a mine-owning 'king'.   In marked
contrast to the wealthy temple hierarchy in Sumer or to
the magnificent pharaohs of ancient Egypt, the kings of Lydia
wished to sell gold and silver profitably, not acquire yet more.
Producing it was their local industry, and astute Lydians
monarchs almost certainly realised it was not in their best
interests to flood the market. Quite likely they restricted their
output of branded staters in much the same way that the modern
de Beers restricts the output of gem diamonds. Lydia needed to
preserve their market value.

The creditary practices of Greek merchants would only
take hold once they felt assured supplies of staters would be
forthcoming at a rate which maintained their essential scarcity.
Alternatively, if there had been insufficient quantities to go
round to make their novel creditary system popular, the metal
would have disappeared from sight, just as bullion around the

eastern Mediterranean had disappeared into hoards over the previous two millennia. As it does still when times are turbulent. Putting all this creditary jigsaw puzzle together it becomes evident that the particular circumstances which made possible the first successful coinage were finely balanced - perhaps reminiscent of the exceptional circumstances which originally gave birth to successful farming.

The origin of money required a far-sighted mine owner who saw the advantage of standardising and certifying his product. First Gyges then Croesus needed to regulate both the quality and the quantity of their staters as dependable debt tokens to encourage circulation. Success also required a sophisticated merchant class who trusted one another sufficiently to settle their debts in the new way, with nothing written down, merchants who trusted the mine-owning king to ensure that further staters would retain their quality and value.

No-one wished to be left with a pile of staters if the market was suddenly awash with them and creditors no longer saw them as worthy tokens of vital debts. The risk was a triple one, of quality and of either glut or insufficiency. Above all it required a confident mercantile outlook which did not cause nervous traders to squirrel away their staters, but to continue circulating them to settle debts.

As with farming, the conditions for the origins of coinage add up to a formidable list of requirements, one which could have been met on very few occasions. Just because money seems such an obvious concept today does not mean that was the case around 600BC. It was more than just a novelty, it was exploring totally unfamiliar and risky territory.

When merchants first risked using branded Lydian metal to settle their debts they had no idea, as we now all do, what would happen next. It could so easily have collapsed into a costly miscalculation. For close on two thousand years previously, merchants had been accustomed to knowing the precise identity of their debtor whenever they held a debt token. From now on that fundamental source of security disappeared. Debtors were no longer identified individually. If creditors simply refused to accept the proffered 'money' (not that any such word was yet used) then the new creditary system would not have survived. It was not, after all, copying recognised conventions from anywhere else; rather it was a true origin of economies.

Even now, when almost all societies are conditioned to agree that uniform chunks of metal are tokens of debt, the system can and will collapse anyway. When it does so, the debt tokens become worthless, and the creditor left with a pile of them becomes everyone else's fall guy. In our own era, that exact same fate befalls hapless creditors in times of hyper-inflation.

NOWADAYS, THE FOLKLORE of economics is teeming with pet theories to explain the origins of coinage, some less logical than others. Most fall into the simplistic trap of assuming that people already understood 'money' before it had actually been invented. In reality those pioneers could, at best, only understood basic debt. What happened after that was experimental and accidental, never deliberate or preconceived; there was no instruction manual.

A couple of examples of such 'explanations' should suffice. Some theorists maintain coins were originally 'invented' to pay taxes. Their logic is bizarre. Would potentates set about distributing new-fangled bits of non-explained metal, totally unfamiliar to everyone, simply to collect them all back in again as 'taxation'? It beggars imagination. When taxation did later latch onto the coinage, both debtors and creditors alike had long grown accustomed to its utility and value. Only when coins had been used for generations could that familiarisation unfold and that took generations. Eventually many people understood what 'money' could now do; some early version of shops would have existed, merchants accepted coins as a matter of course. Then, and only then, would it have made sense to demand citizens surrender some of the now familiar debt tokens in the form of taxation. Before that people typically handed over tithes of their produce; the records show the Temple in Sumer was demanding that. It was probably how the pharaohs of Egypt had also generated their wealth. Such wealth-accumulating ideas as tithes or sharecropping were doubtless passed around - that was much easier than inventing new ways to grow rich.

Through overseas trade, Greek coins progressively found their way into distant communities which neither paid Greek taxes nor faced the unwelcome attention of an invading Greek army. The remote and mysterious former 'Tin Islands' were one such. Neither Greek taxes nor Greek soldiers ever came within six hundred miles of the south coast of England, but Greek coins certainly did.

Despite that, another fanciful notion has been that money was invented to enable leaders to pay their soldiers. It is another anachronism. Soldiers would never suffer the rigours of military service, an unpleasant existence in their day, face the imminent prospect of incurable disease, losing limbs or even death, in exchange for meaningless chunks of metal they had never seen before - which is what 'invention' must necessarily involve.

Only when they, too, were well accustomed to the availability of shops and the less salubrious services soldiers desire, would they ever agree to be paid in coin. The people who originally 'invented' money could, at most, only comprehend debt. The rest was accidental. By definition they could not possibly comprehend money beforehand because only after that point in history did any such things as coins even exist.

Yet for all its hazards we know the coinage system caught on. By the time Alexander the Great (356-323BC) was mounting his military campaigns, it was generally known that scarce metal was much better used for coinage than merely stored as bullion.

He seized the temple hoards of gold and silver in conquered Mesopotamia and minted them for his soldiers' benefit. Alexander was hardly inventing coinage when he did so; it had been familiar for about 200 years. In short, coins were already something about as old to him as railways are to us.

The essential creditary foundation of coinage was already firmly in place. Neither for the first time nor for the last, a popular creditary technique had grown out an entrepreneurial, innovative merchant class. So who were those merchants knocking at Lydia's door for electrum? Judging by the dates of the earliest coins, it happened around 700BC. At about the same time the Phoenicians of the Levant started importing tin from Cornwall, and founded their prosperous trading colonies in the western Mediterranean at Carthage in North Africa and 'New Carthage', Cartagena on Mediterranean coast of Spain. It is a fair guess that Gyges' unknown original customers for his electrum nuggets were the same Phoenician merchants.

They were becoming experts in maritime trade in metals. Quantities were not large, supplies of such rare commodities were insufficient for that. Maybe it was a captain's private perk, a bag of portable nuggets he kept safely in his locker. The Phoenicians had a ready market for gold and silver in Egypt as well as one for tin, its ultimate purpose being to make bronze. In the seventh century BC they were onto a good thing, just the kind of enterprise which businessmen with the nous would devise, and in due course develop as a new creditary system.

THREE REMARKABLE PHASES in the creditary story, as we trace the origins of economies, now become manifest. It all began with mental recording of specific trade debts in the Neolithic Revolution when the debt-rememberer came into his own. Sumer then devised a way to write debts down. In the process they devised ways to dispense with the identity of a creditor and then with the precise nature of a commodity owed. The Greeks then found a way to dispense with the identity of the debtor. In all, it had taken around eight thousand years. That need to locate specific debtors still survives in many places. Even in our own time, local trade debts are still assured when a creditor says to his debtor *"that's okay; we know where you live."* Until quite recently shopkeepers asked people to write their home address on the back of their cheques. It was all very Mesopotamian, indebtedness being locally controlled within an identifiable community

With the emergence of true coinage, creditors no longer needed to trace an original debtor to redeem a debt. So the creditary system was no longer confined to a local community of traders. A universal debt-credit system could now operate over much greater distances. Creditors no longer required the reassuring umbrella of a single city's legislative structure, as they had done in Mesopotamia. No longer was some legalistic Code of Hammurabi labouriously carved on a pillar to spell out the rights of those owed debts.

Creditors and debtors were now left to work it all out for themselves. Provided the coinage itself was trustworthy and its supply wisely managed, they were free to determine prices without any supervision. No longer was it necessary, as it had been in Sumer, to draw up a complicated schedule of silver valuations. Money had made debt, credit and pricing far more democratic than that.

Money, the coinage, marked a fundamental shift in the understanding of debt. Until then, value had always been vested in the debtor; the creditary system was merely a way of tracking him down. With the advent of coinage, however, all that changed. Value was now vested in the debt token itself. It meant anyone could trade with anyone, and do so without reference to a third party - be it a tribal debt-rememberer or a merchant's guild. When Aristotle wrote that "money exists not by nature, but by law" he was mistaken. It exists by mutual consent, by application of the creditary principle. Perhaps surprisingly for a Greek, Aristotle's attempted explanation was far more Sumerian than Athenian. The economist's habit of comforting retrospection proves to have a venerable pedigree.

G REEK COINAGE SPREAD around their network of city states, linking Asia Minor with Cyprus, islands of the Aegean, to mainland Greece and beyond.
Sicily provided a convenient staging post into the western Mediterranean. Greek colonists arrived in Massilia, modern Marseilles, from about 600BC onwards. Their timing is surely no surprise to a creditary economist.

Coinage encouraged 'international' trade over much greater distances; after eight millennia of advancing creditary techniques commerce could now move far beyond the confines of an individual village or city. It no longer mattered who the original debtor was, and as a result long-distance 'foreign' trade became a free-for-all; it no longer needed supervision.

In the ancient world of Mesopotamia, foreign trade had been bureaucratic and regimented. It was conducted by state-authorised merchants with all the aplomb of diplomats, and primarily involved luxury goods, strategic raw materials such as metals, and probably salt. It was an exceptional activity. Using the donkey caravans and camel trains available at the time, long distance bulk transport of everyday commodities for the ordinary people would have been prohibitively expensive.

A creditary system based on a metallic coinage permitted an entirely different economic order to emerge in Classical civilisation; and that economy it was its cultural foundation. If geology did the Greeks one great favour by supplying a judicious quantity of precious metals, then geography did them another. The Aegean archipelago was their navigators' academy. Greek trade enjoyed the cheapest of all modes of transport, the sea, while making reassuringly coastal and mainly short voyages.

Only rarely had they to risk sailing out of sight of land.   Amid this cultural maelstrom emerged the Phoenicians;   under Hannibal they were to become the sworn enemies of Rome. Although the term 'Greek' is typically used, many Mediterranean traders would have been Phoenicians - although as far as the Bible was concerned, the commercial distinction between those maritime Canaanites and the mainland Greeks was minimal.

So who were the Phoenicians? They did not move into an empty wilderness when they arrived in the Levant. Correspondence has survived between the pre-Phoenician mayor of Tyre, and the contemporary Egyptian pharaoh Akhenaten, and is dated to around 1350BC.   Significantly it is written on clay tablets in old style Akkadian cuneiform, which suggests outposts of successive Mesopotamian civilisations had reached the coast of the Levant in the second Millennium BC.

The later Phoenicians who colonised those lands may perhaps owe their original writing to that Mesopotamian tradition, but if so they changed it a lot; they had wholly different ideas of their own. Phoenician writing was long way removed from the complicated pictography of the ancient world.

Their distinctive alphabet first appears on the sarcophagus of Ahiram, king of Byblos, and is dated to some time more recent than 1000BC. The writing was phonetic, no longer pictorial. It was a technique next adopted by the Greeks who augmented it with vowels, something the Phoenicians had not devised. By that route the original Phoenician concept became the ancestor of almost all our modern alphabets.

The greatest era of Phoenician - or Punic - power and influence followed the invention of coinage. They were a society of accomplished sailors who built their network of trading centres round the Mediterranean.   In some accounts they developed as many as three hundred 'cities', more probably trading stations, but the most famous and largest of them was Carthage. Its earliest traces go back to 800BC.

They built Carthage in a natural strategic location close to modern Tunis. It commanded the narrow straits between Africa and Sicily, roughly 75 miles across, which almost divided the Mediterranean in two.   Carthage was a perpetual thorn in the side of the emerging Roman empire, which finally sacked the city in 146BC, demolished it and ploughed it over.

The earliest Phoenician trade specialised in Tyrian purple, a rare and exclusive dye made from the murex shellfish. As already noted, the Greeks named the Levantine traders after the colour. The dye had the unusual property of becoming brighter rather than fading in strong sunlight, and was for many centuries the prized symbol of wealthy Mediterranean aristocracies.

In the west purple is still colour of nobility. Not so in the Far East, where yellow enjoys similar status. Or in desert states of the Middle East where green is, understandably, the most cherished colour of all.

THE COMMERCIAL ADVANTAGE of seagoing trade to the Greeks and Phoenicians made a great impression on Adam Smith. Writing in his *Wealth of Nations* he observed of the Mediterranean : '*That sea, having no tides, nor consequently any waves except such as are caused by wind only, was, by smoothness of its surface, as well as by the multitude of its islands, and the proximity of its neighbouring shores, extremely favourable to the infant navigation of the world; when from their ignorance of the compass, men were afraid to quit the view of the coast, and from the imperfection of the art of shipbuilding, to abandon themselves to the boisterous waves of the ocean*'.

Such sentences of 84 words may seem somewhat prolix nowadays, but no-one can say fairer than that. Better yet, Adam Smith was clearly acknowledging that mode of transport is another fundamental driving force of economies. No method of land transport could ever compete with the low-cost commerce made possible by Mediterranean navigation. Faced with a choice between easy sea routes in one direction, and awkward land routes in the other, it is hardly surprising that Greek merchant venturers preferred to head west with their trade. By contrast a Greek military adventurer like Alexander the Great, needing to move an entire army, preferred marching along land routes to the East. Greek merchants, seeking fresh profitable enterprise rather than victory over former foes, were eventually to wield the greater historical influence.

The expansion in seagoing trade in Classical times was immense. Not until in the late twentieth century did a telling indicator of the scale of that trade become available.

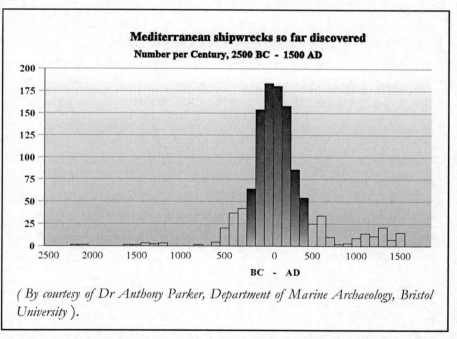

Mediterranean shipwrecks so far discovered
Number per Century, 2500 BC - 1500 AD

(By courtesy of Dr Anthony Parker, Department of Marine Archaeology, Bristol University).

The number of wrecks serves as a fine indicator of the volume of successful trade in general; it is most unlikely sea captains had jointly lost all their skills of seamanship, and were suddenly wrecking their ships in unprecedented numbers. Effectively the sunken record reveals a massive increase in trade during the

Classical period. Adam Smith would surely have found it fascinating, for the evidence chimes well with his own understanding of navigating the Mediterranean. Of course no such data was ever available to him. Like so much evidence on which to build a fresh architecture of economics, it was unavailable until the twentieth century.

Wrecks beneath the Mediterranean only came to light with the growing fashion for recreational scuba diving from the 1950s onwards. Thousands of amateur and professional divers explored the congenial waters of the Mediterranean; there can be few things of greater fascination to investigate than ancient shipwrecks beneath its surface. Since many such ships came to grief around rocky or hazardous coasts, they typically lie in shallow waters. That in turn makes their discovery even easier.

They were almost exclusively cargo boats : passengers hitched a ride when and where they could. So their cargoes of new goods may be precisely dated, often to within a few decades by pottery types, other distinctive relics and even coins. The design of ship often gives further clues. Thanks to the marine archaeology unit at Bristol University, the collated wreck information provides a vivid and excellently calibrated index of maritime commercial activity, and by extension of merchant activity generally, around the Mediterranean in the Classical era.

THE RESULTING SHIPWRECK chart covers four millennia, beginning just a few centuries after the invention of writing in ancient Sumer, and runs as far as the invention of printing in mediaeval Germany. The record illustrates three great eras of creditary and economic innovation, starting in the earliest city state economies, chronicling the rise and fall of Classical civilisation in Greece and Rome, and reaches as far as the Renaissance; see next Chapter. Its peak in the first century BC and first century AD, coincides almost exactly with the zenith of the Roman empire.

The extent of shipping and maritime trade in the early empire, during the unsurpassed dynasty of the Antonines, appears not to have been matched again for a further thousand years. The oldest wreck found so far in the Mediterranean has been dated, quite remarkably, to 2200 BC. It is impressive that anything recognisable can still survive from a wooden ship which sank more than four millennia ago.

Quite possibly other wrecks of that period, or even earlier, have left no traces whatever for today's scuba divers. The wreck chart shows scant evidence of maritime trading activity in the ancient, pre-Classical world of clay tablets, omnipotent temples and aristocratic merchant houses. That pioneering economy of Sumer was focussed on communities 600 miles inland to the East, far from the Mediterranean sea. Maritime navigation was low on their list of priorities. Any such trade with the primitive West was on the outermost ring of the Mesopotamian sphere of interest. Not until tin became a strategic raw material was there any practical reason for such trade.

Sumer's trading outpost at Kanesh, in what is now central Turkey and dated to around 2000BC, suggests that land routes through Asia Minor gave its merchants greater security than entrusting their wares to Adam Smith's "boisterous waves of the ocean". Had they been capable seafarers, their aristocratic trading post would have been built not in the heart of Anatolia, but on the coast of the Levant.

That said, there must have been some seagoing trade in ancient times. Copper mining on the island of Cyprus dates back to around 2300 BC, producing one of the two crucial raw materials of the Bronze Age. Copper was originally named after the island. Long-distance overseas trade in those earlier, ancient times was however confined to luxury items, and to strategic raw materials such as metal. It was too expensive for anything else. The expansive era of Mediterranean sea transport coincides with both the rise of the Phoenicians and the propagation of coinage as an increasingly familiar means of transferring debts. Neither should come as any surprise to a creditary economist.

As ever, the more credit agreements an economy can sustain, then the greater the division of labour it may attain. The rise of Classical civilisation, built increasingly on its economical, international sea transport, provides a vivid illustration of the basic creditary principle at work.

The increasingly frequent shipwrecks revealed by the chart testify to the human cost of economic expansion. From the historical record we know of at least one of those shipwrecks individually - that involving St Paul on the coast of Malta. It is dated, by the Maltese, to 60AD. Conceivably it is among those wrecks which have since been found by modern scuba divers.

The seafarers who suffered the 504 shipwrecks ascribed to the period 650 BC - 1 AD were discovering hazards the hard way. The Pharos of Alexandria, most recent of the Seven Wonders of the World, was built in 280BC. In the Classical era it was easily the most impressive, but surely not the only navigational aid built to safeguard ships at sea.

MEDITERRANEAN SHIPS OF 500BC, and for centuries later, were dependent on the whim of the wind, sluggish in movement and incapable of rapid manoeuvre. Unsurprisingly such vessels account for the majority of wrecks found by modern divers. It was a risky business; Adam Smith was right about those 'boisterous waves.' The shipwreck record shows little evidence of the militaristic Egyptians who, according to hieroglyphic records, were sailing the coast of the Levant from the earliest era of the chart.

However those pioneering Egyptian voyages were sponsored by successive pharaohs as state foraging expeditions, conducted under ideal conditions with military precision. The golden wine made from grapes growing wild on the Golan heights is said to be one of their favourites. However they did not naturally consider themselves 'peoples of the sea'. Nor were they venturing abroad with the same commercial outlook as the business-minded sea captains of later centuries, who cut corners and costs to the bone in the hope of turning a reasonable profit from their seagoing commerce.

The rapid reduction in wreck numbers from the first century AD onwards has several causes, not just diminishing levels of maritime commerce as Rome went steadily into decline. The lore and accumulated expertise of seafaring improved greatly while, from around 200 AD, ship design also advanced. The earliest ancestors of the English 'tub' or 'round ship', and of the French 'vaisseau rond' began to make an appearance.

The design was almost certainly derived from Mediterranean expertise: the masterly Viking long ship was still several hundred years into the future. Those proto-English and French vessels were much more seaworthy than any of their predecessors, and therefore less likely to founder. The exact picture of progress in ship design is unclear. "They were imprecisely documented, and only after a gap of 1,000 years to the early 13th century did the city seals of seaports begin to record the appearance of sailing ships." [9]

The revival in wreck numbers from the 11th century reveals a resurgence in Mediterranean trade, much augmented by the need to supply the Crusades. Then over the following few centuries, the picture changed once more. Other historical sources confirm the massive expansion of maritime activity in the Renaissance, yet that expansion is not at all evident in the record of Mediterranean wrecks.

The seeming anomaly is surely explained by further improvements in ships and in maritime expertise. The 15th century enjoyed another revolution in ship design, with advances

9. *Douglas Lobley in* Ships through the Ages, *p.*14.

in hull shape, superstructure, rigging and sailing ability. The dangers of sailing the Mediterranean had largely been tamed. By then, seafarers were beginning to develop the skills which by 1492, and probably even earlier, enabled them to brave the even more boisterous waves of the Atlantic.

The shipwreck chart also illustrates, indirectly, something of far wider significance to the origin of economies. Information from unexpected sources which should be of interest to economists is expanding all the time. Much of it is still beyond the central argument of this book. One such source is provided by metallurgy, which can nowadays reveal the geographical source of ancient metal by reading the exact isotope signature of its trace elements.

Haematologists can now explain and even quantify the extensive migration of past peoples by mapping the distribution of blood groups. Some of the results are surprising. The future economic wisdom of the 21st century will be able to draw on many new kinds of knowledge, and the discipline needs a much broader canvas on which to assemble this expanding wisdom.

As this book was originally being written, the first full draft of the human genome was announced. In addition to its medical benefits and its ethical dilemmas, it is already providing entirely fresh insight into the distribution of genes in history and geography. That should revolutionise our understanding of peoples past and present, their relationships, their movement, their way of life and therefore their economic behaviour.

From what we now know, the use of sea transport, rather than costly donkey trains or camel caravans, at last brought the delivered price of imports, even of staple commodities, within reach of the ordinary man.

It was all far removed from the ancient world, in which every community would still require to be virtually self-sufficient in all but the most exotic, expensive goods. The new economic order made possible a cosmopolitan division of labour, and with it an international market economy. Freed from the restrictions of clay tablets whose worth depended entirely on tracing an original debtor, the more flexible use of coinage now enabled sea-going merchants to trade bulk commodities between communities spread across parts of three continents.

THE CLASSICAL ECONOMY marked a major shift in the broader structure of debt. In the ancient world, the Sumerian temple had been everyone else's creditor. Later the palace, like the Pharaoh in Egypt, accumulated wealth in much the same way. In the classical world, in marked contrast, the state could and gradually did become the great debtor. Where a simple debt and credit agreement between two individuals is fairly easy enough for us to grasp, the notion of an entire society having a vast collective debt at its centre is far more difficult to comprehend, even now.

So it helps to remember that every debt must by definition have a balancing credit somewhere. In creditary logic some such dividing line between centres of debtors and creditors is essential if debt tokens are to exist; you cannot have money without debt. Much later in this book, it is a debate which is essential to fathoming the seemingly daunting problems of the early twenty-first century, many people cannot fathom what they see. But for the time being let us be patient.

The largely self-sufficient city states of the ancient world, in which a central institution such as the Sumerian temple controlled the whole economy, were now obsolete. It was not just an economic change but one which went to the very foundations of civilisation. The economic decline of the temple took with it an unyielding autocratic wisdom, one which brooked no philosophical dissent. The Temple and its cultural descendants, like the pharaohs of Egypt, imposed a unilateral and monolithic understanding of the world. In the Classical world that exclusive philosophy eventually gave way to the bilateral dialogues, the discussions and discourses of Plato and Aristotle. It became two-fold argument. In turn that became the basis of our modern philosophical outlook and one of the fundamental reasons that Classical civilisation is so justifiably admired. Intellectually there had been nothing like it before.

So who brought this intellectual transformation about, and how? In the civilisation of the West it can be traced back to Pythagoras (582 - 500 BC), the son of a rich merchant of Samos. The island is about fifty miles from the modern port of Izmir: back in 600BC it was at the very epicentre of the birth of coinage. Samos would have been one of the first places whose merchants adopted and grew accustomed to metal coins as the new, much improved, international creditary system. Pythagoras was born into that world. The timing is significant.

Unlike the inflexible-minded priests of Sumer and Egypt who had preceded him, Pythagoras travelled round the communities and civilisations of the eastern Mediterranean, and learn about different cultures and kinds of wisdom. That was very new. A purse of the very latest debt tokens could have paid for his hotel and restaurant bills in places far from home. That was even more recent; it was probably a convenient creditary device learnt from his merchant father.

Men of the same generation as Pythagoras' grandfather, even, no matter how brilliant their powers of philosophical observation might have been, would never have been able to undertake such a grand tour. Sumerian clay debt tokens of local values only, or indeed any other debt trading system which depended on institutionalised trust through a regulated guild, would have been quite useless.

The cultural Grand Tour, which became a obligatory rite of passage for nineteenth century wealthy young men once Europe's railways had been built, was a recreation devised by Pythagoras almost 2,500 years previously. No-one had been able travel as freely as he appears to have done. It would be interesting to know just how closely his travels match modern archaeological evidence which reveals geographically the early use of coinage. Before Pythagoras' day, such civilian tourism was impossible anywhere. The only way to travel and see the world was to lead or join a conquering army.

S MALL WONDER THE insights of Pythagoras were so revolutionary. He is said to have visited Egypt, and surely the mercantile crossroads around the Phoenician Levant. That end of the Fertile Crescent would provide a conduit to the mathematical and ancient wisdom of Mesopotamia at the other end. Pythagoras of Samos eventually settled at Croton in the far south of Italy, where he established a teaching centre of philosophy, laid the foundations of western mathematics and, in the formidable opinion of Bertrand Russell, was intellectually one of the most important men who has ever lived.[10]

It was Pythagoras's unprecedented ability to travel around and learn about differing cultures which made feasible his towering importance in Western philosophy. He was not the only one of his contemporaries in a position to do that. Far to the east, Confucius (551-479 BC) was meanwhile emerging as the founding father of another great intellectual and cultural tradition.

At almost exactly the same time as Pythagoras's travels, he too was travelling round and learning from the different states and fiefdoms of China. Creditary economists would argue it was no coincidence, for Confucius was travelling through his country in the pioneering days of Chinese coinage. It does look as if a novel creditary method based on metal and the anonymity which that brought to the system was an essential catalyst.

Money not only makes the world go round, it makes distant travel possible, as local credit tokens could never have done. The new system of money enabled both these men, two

10. *Bertrand Russell writing in his* 'History of Western Philosophy'.

of the most influential ever in human history, to bring together
entirely new factual knowledge, insight and wisdom simply by
touring around in a way only made possible by coinage.

David Hume was pointing in the right direction when he
wrote that money is the oil which renders the motion of the
wheels more smooth and easy. It did the same to the motion of
people as well. However creditary economics can demonstrate
its consequences were infinitely more far-reaching than that.
Major steps in creditary ability might be unobtrusive, but
eventually they prove to have a momentous effect on the whole
progress of civilisation.

Before this saga moves on, this is a useful juncture to note
the creditary advances of contemporary China. The great valleys
of the Yellow and the Yangtze rivers gave birth to a remarkable
civilisation, although nothing like so early as people often believe.
Along the Yellow River the earliest signs of agriculture, as distinct
from hunter-gathering, date from about 5000 BC. That is four
millennia more recent than the traceable beginnings of agriculture
in the Fertile Crescent.

WESTERN INSIGHT INTO China's pioneering
economic techniques is not great, although creditary
logic would strongly suggest there was of necessity
some effective system for recording agricultural
debts. Did Chinese village clans also have a debt-rememberer?
Not until around 1200BC is there any evidence of writing in
China. Perhaps some new generation of Chinese creditary
economists will try to find out.

China's first recorded dynasty, the Shang, began to
impose itself on the neighbours from around 1700 BC. By then
the successive civilisations of Mesopotamia had already known
about writing, number and elaborate commerce for something
like 1500 years.   The very earliest emergence of Chinese

civilisation is contemporary with, and no older than, Stonehenge. Its impressive feature is not its great age, but rather its speed of adaptation. The same jet-propelled pragmatism has been apparent in the China of our own day, as a massive economy labelled 'capitalism with Chinese characteristics' has swept away the debris of Maoist inertia at a speed which has impressed the world, no-one more than the Americans.

There are creditary mysteries about early China which are little understood in the West. It was quick off the mark to devise a coinage of its own. The pioneer was the kingdom of Zhou in north China which began to cast miniature hoes in bronze specifically as a token of debt. They are dated to around 580BC. Each hoe was inscribed with a serial number of the particular craftsman's name as a guarantee of correct value. The word 'jin' used on the coins to mean a hoe is still used in modern China to mean a pound weight.

Other states in north China adapted the system, devising knife shapes for their tokens or in some cases copying the shape of cowries. Gradually the items diminished in size. As in the classical Mediterranean, their success as debt tokens steadily made their actual metal content less and less significant.

China stuck to its own distinctive manufacturing process. Unlike coins manufactured in the West from Lydia onwards, whose impression was almost always struck onto a metal blank using a die, China was still casting its coins in moulds as recently as the 19th century. The European technology for minting coins from blanks, with dies under pressure, was not adopted in China until as recently as1890.

China's cultural ascendancy traces from before Confucius but accelerated greatly thereafter. By 200 BC the Ch'in dynasty had completed the Great Wall to exclude central Asians and protect China's agricultural society. Nineteenth century pioneers in the expansionist United State of America encountered much the same fractious relationship between settling farmers and the

indigenous population.   Attritional warfare between cowboys
and Indians was not a new phenomenon. It was much the same
in China's Wild West some two millennia previously, which
makes the much earlier Neolithic Revolution from one society to
the other in Mesopotamia even more remarkable.

Walls to separate cultures may have begun in China, but
have several more recent descendants. In Britain alone, the
Roman emperor Hadrian built a wall between modern Carlisle
and Newcastle to keep out the Scots. In the Antonine dynasty
another wall serving the same purpose was built further north in
the lowlands of Scotland between Glasgow and Edinburgh.

KING OFFA OF ENGLAND dug a 140 mile ditch
from Chepstow to Prestatyn to keep out the Welsh. In
the twentieth century East Berlin built a ruthlessly
guarded wall to keep in the East Germans. The
imperial British built a hedge across India to separate its peoples
which was over two thousand miles long.

So the excitable controversy over an American president's
proposal to build a wall to keep out the Mexicans does have an
air of contrived indignation about it.   The idea has a recent
ancestry going back at least three presidents before that. The
tradition of building such strategic walls to separate peoples dates
back well over two thousand years.

The difference has been that the United States of America
at least had the coast of th Pacific to delineate a natural frontier.
China enjoyed no such clear-cut demarcation. Where Americans
could forge ahead to the very end of their continent with their
railways, facing only brave, warlike but primitively equipped
native 'Indians', the much earlier Chinese confronted much
more powerful opposition and perforce had to draw a physical
line somewhere en route.

The ever-pragmatic Chinese built that line in stone. Like the pyramids of Egypt, the Ziggurat of Ur, the cities, roads and aqueducts of the Roman empire and Britain's Stonehenge, the Great Wall of China would never have been built without an economy which could assemble and provision a substantial workforce. That is another intriguing set of historical events for inquisitive creditary economists to investigate.

In many cases there is ample archaeological evidence to suggest that such great projects were not built by slaves in a command economy, but rather by commercial contractors and sub-contractors much more familiar to our own era; the roads of the Roman empire, by and large, were built by soldiers of the Roman army but that was unusual. Any commercial workforce would require a substantial creditary structure. There is much still to be explored by future generations of inquisitive creditary historians and archaeologists.

Chapter Four

100 AD to 1600 AD

It is well enough that the people of the nation do not understand
our banking and monetary system for, if they did, I believe
there would be a revolution before tomorrow morning.
HENRY FORD

FOR MANY YEARS, conventional economics has taken the view that money may be explained simply by observing its superficial behaviour. Such economists simply catalogue what it appears to do - 'a unit of account, a medium of exchange and a store of value'. Traceable back to the 1870s, this 'definition' of money steadily became a mantra of twentieth century economics, but no matter how many times it has been recited, it has never become a constructive explanation.

Consider a handy academic equivalent. In much the same frame of mind, physicists might explain lightning simply by observing its superficial behaviour: 'brilliant flashes in the sky frequently accompanied by heavy rain and loud bangs.' Few people nowadays, physicists least of all, would consider that to be a constructive explanation of lightning.

A proper explanation of money, so prominent in mankind's succession of debt-credit techniques, is key to fathoming much of economics. A half-baked explanation can throw anyone off the scent. That three-part mantra about money may be superficial but it would not do much damage, were it at least enlightening. Unfortunately it is not.

Money is clearly a unit of account but, as shown by the various numeraires listed in the previous chapter, that is scarcely a defining feature of money alone. 'Medium of exchange' is better. To the extent it means something more than simple swapping, then 'medium of exchange' does perhaps hint at the continuous debt circulation, the creditary principle, which is the cardio-vascular system of an economy. Thus it comes close to David Hume's definition at the start of Chapter Three.

It is the third observation, that money is some kind of 'store of value', which has become so distracting. Not many people would confidently regard an assorted pile of IOU's as a reliable 'store of value', come what may. Yet as the previous Chapter has been at pains to demonstrate, money is no more than that. Personal chits such as IOU's are only as good as, and never any better than, the willingness of their debtor to co-operate. Just the same goes for money.

To creditary economists, money - that is notes and coinage - marks just one phase in the development of debt-credit techniques. As mankind's creditary expertise continues to evolve, money may once again disappear completely. The creditary element, in some manifestation, will be with us in perpetuity. The monetary phase could well have only a finite life span. That is the enduring lesson, and huge significance, of the economy of Sumer from over four thousand years ago. Nor is money, as some might have us believe, a tangible commodity in its own right, as David Hume pointed out in 1742. Unwieldy principles of supply and demand have a tenuous relationship with the creditary system - because debt is not a commodity which consumes resources to produce. Creating more debt does not mean tapping into increasingly scarce raw material. On the contrary debt and credit can be conjured continuously out of thin air. Any theory of economics which seeks to apply the friable 'laws' of supply and demand to money runs into intellectual sand.

OBSERVED FROM OUR favoured vantage point of the twenty first century, the misleading view of money as a commodity was the graveyard of much twentieth century economics. Early though David Hume's writing figures in the genesis of the subject, his observation comparing money with oil comes closer to the truth than many economists have achieved since. The half century and more before 2010 was not a distinguished period for economic theorising. David Hume's basic rule was too easily overlooked: money, rather like oil, helps the machinery go round, but is not a discernible machine in itself.

Even though it is just one of many debt-credit systems down the creditary ages, money is much the most ingenious so far. It is a debt token of great sophistication, one stripped to the barest essentials. Coinage is so simple because it denotes a debt without any need to specify a commodity, or be tied to an original creditor, or maintain contact with an original debtor. The debts which fully-fledged money represents are thus abstract, anonymous and universal - quite unlike those embodied in any IOU, a cheque or in a Sumerian clay tablet; or for that matter, credit card transactions. An economist who grasped the essential point was Adam Smith, who wrote *'a guinea may be considered as a bill for a certain quantity of necessaries and conveniences upon all the tradesmen in the neighbourhood.'* No mention of a specific commodity, no specific creditor, no specific debtor, no essential use of metal either.

If we replace Smith's guineas with the pioneer coins of the classical Mediterranean, we may extend his geography considerably. Already by 100 BC the Macedonian stater - direct descendant of the original staters devised in Lydia half a millennium earlier - was already accepted by Adam Smith's tradesmen in a commercial 'neighbourhood' extending from the Welsh marches to the frontiers of Afghanistan.

The commercial success of coinage in the centuries after its invention around 600 BC was phenomenal and it did two things. First, it drove economic expansion on which Classical civilisation was built. Second, that success nurtured malpractices with money which helped bring about the collapse of Classical civilisation. Such is the potency of just one phase in mankind's creditary progress. Some of the malpractices with money were condemned by early Christianity and even more so, five hundred years later, in the Koran.

Those malpractices and misconceptions, and some of their consequences, haunt us to this day. By far the most damaging of these misconceptions is the store of value variant of the 'money illusion'. It will persist so long as money is extensively regarded as some sort of commodity in its own right, a near-indelible belief that money must have some intrinsic value of its own. It is thus imbued with a more palpable existence than David Hume's metaphorical oil.

It is not. At last we can and should abandon the clumsy twentieth century mantra that money is a unit of account, a medium of exchange and a store of value. Just as a meteorologist explains that lightning is an electrical discharge rather than a spectacular display of flashes and bangs, so a creditary economist explains that money is fully transferable, non-specific debt. As Oliver Wendell Holmes once declared, do not put your trust in money, but put your money in trust.

CREDITARY REASONING EXPOSES the damage caused by the notion of 'store of value'. Sometimes the illusion is just economically debilitating. At other times it is intellectually distracting, which can often prove worse. The latter manifests itself in the craze for declaring a discovery of primitive 'money' in all kinds of exotic locations.

Such proclamations have been the stock in trade of promoters of tourism for more than a century. Inhabitants of the South Pacific island of Yap collect massive stone wheels which they display in front of their houses. They thereby reckon themselves wealthy. Significantly their discs are made from limestone, which does not occur locally, but is imported with much effort, heroism even, from over the sea.

The shape of these cumbersome treasures suggests they originated in some other society which actually understood and valued large millstones. On Yap, however, any such practical application is unknown. The artefacts are just a conspicuous and rather grotesque symbol of 'wealth'. They have nothing to do with debt and they are no more money than is jewellery - in fact less so. This has not inhibited enthusiastic promoters of tourism from describing Yap's unwieldy chunks of limestone as an exotic form of money. Illusion indeed. The reality is that the shops on Yap accept American dollars, not massive chunks of limestone. Just try spending a stone 'coin' which is several feet across and see what happens. Tokens of 'wealth' are highly subjective; true money has to be objective to be anything at all.

ANOTHER, MORE ELEGANT, variant of much the same Yap money illusion survives in the central banks of advanced countries. Vast quantities of gold have been accumulated in a mistaken belief that they 'protect' the value of a currency. Yet for all the gold squirrelled away in the vaults of Fort Knox or the Bank of England, neither the dollar, nor the pound nor other currencies were ever protected from the gross inflation of the 1970s and 1980s.

For all the supposed awe, those redundant stockpiles of bullion are evidence of a deep flaw then, and still, in conventional economic thinking. Such gold ingots are Yap's stone millstones, only shinier. The fallacies of the 'store of value' are enduring, and they trace as far back as imperial Rome. They have been discussed and rejected many times.

Yet gold is still presented as something precious; the world's gold mining corporations persist with their sales endeavours in order to preserve their very profitable market. Too often that means extracting gold from one hole in the ground, casting it into ingots which are then entombed in another hole in the ground. It is an arcane pursuit which might well strike many people as a futile application of time and effort.

The pace of economic growth in the classical world, culminating in the Roman empire, is readily illustrated by the chart of Mediterranean shipwrecks shown in the previous Chapter. It is an index of a revolution in man's creditary expertise and commercial success. Those records from the deep also reveal how in all things economic, matters rarely stay the same for very long. They are almost always getting better or getting worse, often quite rapidly. It is a salutory lesson for those who too willingly assume that things are always getting better. That is not necessarily the case; note the observation from John Kenneth Galbraith at the start of this book.

It was the invention of money, specifically of coinage, which transformed the pace of economic expansion. The slow-moving Ancient world gave way to the much faster-moving economy of the Classical world. The new creditary device made trade possible between the merchants of many different states even if, politically, their governments were barely on speaking terms. That was new, and a unified 'international' economy became possible for the first time in mankind's history. In turn that built a market so vast it enabled entire communities to specialise in supplying just a few products.

A continent-wide division of labour emerged which was unimaginable among the largely self-sufficient city states of the ancient world. Countless thousands of Adam Smith's 'tradesmen' now became part of a single inter-related economic machine. The low-cost commercial shipping of the Mediterranean, as he correctly noted, meant that bulk commodities such as grain, oil or wine could now be transported over long distances but still at a profit.

International trade was no longer restricted to rarities and sumptuary goods. Money made that trade feasible, shipping made it practicable. The granaries of classical Rome were not just

down the local valley. They were in North Africa or the eastern
province of Dacia, now called Romania; note the name.

For centuries the simple creditary device of coinage even
lacked its modern name. Not until the Roman era was the word
'money' itself invented. The Roman mint, or one of them, was
located on the Capitoline hill. The new name was probably a
simple matter of geographical proximity; the temple of Juno
Moneta, dedicated to the goddess Hera, was also on the
Capitoline hill. And that is how the word 'money' arose. The
word in the temple's name probably derived in turn from the
Latin monera, meaning to remind, warn or instruct, the root of
modern English words such as admonish. So all those words
through classical Latin link up; in short they are cognate.

B Y THE TIME OF CHRIST, economic growth in the
classical world had created an international trading
economy so large that the city of Rome abandoned
most productive activities to become a specialist
financial centre - a prototype for London and New York in our
own era. In classical Rome, however, the development attracted
somewhat less than boundless praise. Writers as early as Cato, not
long after 100BC, had expressed their disapproval at the growing
throng of moneylenders so conspicuous in the capital city.

The literati may have objected, but the citizenry were
having a whale of a time. Columnella complained that *'instead of
using our hands to dig up fallow fields, we would rather use them to applaud
at the theatre and the circus.'* The capital city of that great empire
became Swinging Rome. Life during the first century was
undoubtedly attractive; there was bustle and enjoyment, endless
argument and discussion, entertainment in plenty and even a

modicum of work. Fresh overseas conquests sent more and more wealth back to Rome in triumph, while the smart thing to do among its wealthy citizens was to become an absentee landlord. Principal cities of the Roman empire evolved as centres of consumption rather than production.

It was nowhere near being a sustainable position. Once further imperial expansion ground to a halt, the cities became centres, not of prosperity, but of impoverishment for the empire as a whole. The creditary system was being abused. Financial ingenuity was no longer applied to oil the wheels of legitimate trade, as in David Hume's apt metaphor. Debt now became a tactical weapon instead, deployed by acquisitive financiers as a battering ram.

A vicious cycle was devised by moneylenders to ensnare farmers who were once free men into becoming impoverished debtors. First they were granted loans at exorbitant rates of interest. The uncertainties of the harvest offered plentiful opportunities to do that. Sooner or later a handy excuse would be found to foreclose on the debt, so transforming former yeomen farmers first into tenants and eventually into slaves.

The vogue among the plutocracy of Rome was to amass land. Some Roman estates grew so vast that - reputedly - their owners could not even ride around them. In the lands of Latium around Rome, the once staple crop of corn was steadily replaced with more profitable vines, before easy to manage pasturage supplanted both. Formerly productive arable land was turned over to sheep, the work done by slaves chained together.

The yeoman farmer was a dying breed. In the Roman province of Africa during the first century AD, the younger Pliny calculated that just six overbearing landlords came to own half that vast stretch of territory.   Gradually the absentee-owned, inefficiently run estates of the later Roman empire reverted to waste. No one with a financial interest was there to take care of them. Swathes of north Africa, a fertile grain province in the days of the Republic and the Empire's heyday, never recovered. They became a permanent extension to the Sahara desert, arguably the planet's first ever man-made dust bowl.

The landowners no longer looked to the commercial productivity of their real estate, merely rejoiced in its notional selling price. They were not seeking a productive dividend : they simply wanted capital appreciation. There, too, a discomforting parallel may be drawn with financial preoccupations of more recent times. In a modern financial capital such as London, and as the twentieth century became the twenty first, people increasingly regarded domestic properties as an investment, seeking capital appreciation, rather than something just to live in. It is all very Roman, and if that weakening civilisation is anything to go by, it does not augur well for our own economic future.,

Dispossessed peasant farmers, reduced to lowly tenants and even worse, were disinclined to join an army.   They no longer had anything of their own to defend. By the first century, thoughtful Romans already looked back to the time when small landowners were both ploughmen and part-time soldiers as a bygone golden age. The empire was now obliged to hire foreign mercenaries to defend its frontiers instead. The cost of paying, feeding and supplying 300,000 men became a nightmare.

The Roman had inherited from the Greek a disdain for trade. Commercial centres of the empire had workshops where craftsmen plied their skills, but their pursuits were not held in much regard by the rest of society. Slaves were considered appropriate for such pursuits. Only one form of manual labour was respected - work on the land - and the fashionable citizenry had even abandoned that.   If they needed to make money, people lacking vast estates became moneylenders or took up tax farming, thereby joining that unpopular platoon known to the New Testament as 'publicans'.

EMPIRES CANNOT EXPAND for ever.   As the inflow of easy wealth to be plundered from newly-conquered lands dried up, successive emperors were driven to seek reforms to plug the gap.   Unable to distinguish between economic causes and effects, emperors repeatedly reformed the currency rather than attempted to reform the economy itself.

Not for the last time in history, too many people believed that currency innovation alone would resolve all economic problems and bring lasting prosperity. Shunting money around, rather than raising economic output, was assumed to be the solution. Emperors and their advisers took refuge in the money illusion, seeking that store of value, rather than in any real insight into how an economy functions. One cannot manufacture 'value' simply by manufacturing money willy-nilly, which is why that 'store of value' mantra is so crippling.

One easy target for reform was the moneyers themselves. In the early years of the Roman empire, coins were manufactured by specialist slaves. By the third century, enterprising guilds of freemen and freed slaves had taken over the business and were making large profits.   The emperor Aurelian moved to close down their workshops. When this led to bloody revolt, he reformed the guilds instead. Henceforth they were made collectively responsible for taxes owed by their members and for any counterfeiting by their employees.

Gradually the moneyers' guilds were taken over by the state. In the Theodosian Code of 400 AD, it was decreed that coinage was no longer a free market facility, but now became an official instrument of exchange. The coinage had been nationalised. From that time on, the notion that running a mint should be the exclusive perk of the state took deep root. In one sense, things had come full circle since the first coins of the kings of Lydia over 1100 years previously, but now the notion was backed by the force of law.

The state control of coinage may be traced thereafter through the Carolingians of France into our modern era. From the time of St Louis in the thirteenth century onwards, the French royal house required that the public conduct their transactions using royal coinage alone, and should reject any coins minted by a legion of only-too-willing provincial seigneurs.

Diocletian, who became Rome's emperor in 293 AD, repeatedly struggled with doomed reforms of the imperial coinage. He and his administrators promptly ran up against a snag which is intrinsic to all bullion currencies, a result of the 'Krugerrand effect' noted in the previous Chapter. In times of strife, people prefer to hoard bullion-based coins for their supposed metallic value rather than allow them to circulate.

To achieve his monetary reform, Diocletian first had to pacify military anarchy, mutiny triggered by disputes over soldier's wages. Once that quietened down, gold which had previously vanished into private hoards re-emerged for use. His laudable aim was a coinage of full weight and metallic purity. Imperial mints struck the gold solidus weighing a little under six grammes, and he replaced the debased and plated antonius with a solid silver denarius weighing 3.4 grammes. The names of the new coins were to survive far longer than their currency, becoming original forerunners of the **'s'** and **'d'** in the United Kingdom's £.s.d. notation until decimalisation in 1971.

For everyday small purchases, Diocletian also created a copper coinage, thinly plated with silver. At the same time as reforming imperial coinage, he tried to tackle the closely related problem of inflation. In 301AD Diocletian issued an Edict on Prices which sought among other things to control workmen's wages. Its preamble states *'to put a stop to the dishonest practices of merchants who were forcing up unduly the price of provisions and other commodities, thereby doing serious harm to the entire country, especially in places where troops were garrisoned and wherever soldiers were obliged to buy the necessities of life out of their army pay'.*

DIOCLETIAN'S DECREE SET official prices in the currency of the common people, the denarius, which because of continual debasement was extremely unstable. His pioneering attempts at price control were a failure, of course: price-controlled commodities simply disappeared from the open market, so that his edict had to be repealed. Inevitably, perhaps, when a money-driven economy was still a relatively novel phenomenon, the easy attractions of the money illusion were mingled with a profound misunderstanding of inflation. The pattern of economic mismanagement is quite evident by modern standards. However it is no purpose of this book to compete with Edward Gibbon in tracking the decline and fall of the Roman empire. An epidemic of malaria around the Mediterranean probably hastened it.

Clearly some of the economic factors listed were central to its decay, but in broad terms the Roman civilisation had not been an era of great creditary innovation anyway. Rather it was an epoch in which the creditary ingenuity of the Greeks was first adopted, the exploited, and eventually debauched.

One resulting legacy was a widespread distrust of coinage, and a decline in its use. Another legacy was the amalgamation of small land holdings into great estates, or sometimes into whole villages of free farmers. This was in part the outcome of a form of land tenure in Roman law called the *precarium,* a contract by which a small landowner in distress made over his land to a financier in exchange for its use - a kind of sale-and-leaseback.

The legal device of the *precarium* gave rise to the villa, in turn a vital factor in the economic evolution of the early Middle Ages. Out of it grew serfdom. It created a new aristocracy attached to the land, in an economy which could revert to isolated pockets of subsistence. These communities were generally left alone by the invaders who ultimately overran the western Roman empire. The same economic unit evolved into the ville of medieval France. The word survives also in the villages of England and in the word villein.

The collapse of the Roman empire in the West caused European civilisation to shrivel into what we now call the Dark Ages. Flawed attempts to restore economic vitality by meddling with the coinage had simply served to dismember the creditary system. Inevitably the mercantile economy based on a division of labour was disrupted and largely disappeared. The empire and its trading economy were to shrink to a tiny fraction of former greatness, as the Mediterranean shipwreck chart well illustrates.

A T ITS ZENITH, THE CIVILISATION of Rome had supported its poor with free handouts of bread, oil and meat. In the third century free distribution of wine, salt and even clothing were added to the largesse. Such are the economic possibilities created by an extensive division of labour and the resulting level of prosperity.

In Europe's dark ages poor people, the overwhelming majority, were once again reduced to subsistence living. Nothing better was any longer possible, while any surplus the agricultural system could generate was minute. The prospect of municipal largesse being distributed to the poor, for free, disappeared.

To any local European warlord in 500 AD, Rome's achievements in extensive social welfare three centuries earlier would have been beyond his most daring imagination. In four centuries western Europe, by comparison with classical Rome or ancient Sumer, had regressed by forty centuries. The basic rule of creditary economics states that the more debt and credit agreements a society can sustain, the greater division of labour it may attain. The denuded creditary system, and the absence of division of labour prosperity in the Dark Ages, together reveal how that process can equally go into reverse.

The progress of a civilisation is calibrated by the rise and fall of its cities, and they are the product of creditary expertise. City states in Mesopotamia, the first ever, would have been unsustainable without their novel creditary system based on clay tablets, backed by the economic authority of the Temple. Exploiting the brilliant creditary system devised by the Greeks made the Roman world go round. It removed any need for an economic bureaucracy, the mainstay of ancient Sumer. With a healthy creditary system, villages could grow into towns, while in classical times the population of Rome itself reached a million.

Yet when their creditary system dissolves, so must large communities. That cat's cradle of interwoven urban debts, developed from the debt-rememberers and ancient Jericho onwards, is no longer feasible. Denied any creditary means to sustain an intricate division of labour, former large and prosperous stone-built cities can no longer function. They are the first to go, inevitably so given the creditary principle. As likely as not, they reverted to being quarries.

Departing Roman legions in 406AD left behind them an economically advanced Britain[1] with some fine stone-built cities. With the collapse of a viable creditary system those cities fell into disuse and decay. Londinium, which had been one of the greatest cities of the Roman Empire, was simply abandoned. It was eventually succeeded by a modest Saxon hamlet of wood and thatch called Londenwic, a mile or so to the West in what has since become Covent Garden.

The numismatic record shows that after the Romans left, no more coins were minted in Britain for the next two centuries or more. Civilisation was going backwards. Widespread illiteracy inevitably meant that nothing equivalent to Sumer's written clay tablets, able to sustain the economy of a single city state, would have been feasible either. Civic and economic decline accompanied creditary decline; the two basic forces are inseparable. With the collapse or sacking of so many of its once

---

1. *As attested by the remains of the Roman palace at Fishbourne near Chichester. Complete with underfloor heating, it is the largest of its kind to be seen north of the Alps and could well have been the country mansion of the Roman governor of the province of Britannia.*

great cities, Europe as a whole relinquished any global importance. As it did so, a new centre of civilisation was about to emerge into prominence. It was the culture, and the empire, of Islam, and it sprang from the wealth of an avowedly mercantile society, one which still used coinage.

THE ADVANCES OF ISLAM may trace their roots, as may Classical civilisation, to the distinctive geography of the eastern Mediterranean. On its southern coast the Suez isthmus was a barrier of strategic importance. It separated important trading regions, one being the surviving components of the Byzantine empire based on Constantinople.

The need to unload and reload ships, then haul goods overland between the two seas, created important merchant centres. These towns grew into the crossroads of trade routes. The coast of the Red Sea was a natural place for mercantile communities to congregate, exchange their wares and, like merchants down the ages, prosper. They created a network of ports.

One of them was Mecca, where the prophet Mohammed was born in 570AD. His business-minded upbringing, in a poor family, meant he shared none of the snobbery about 'trade' which had so afflicted Greece and Rome. His mercantile outlook, naturally inquisitive, was influential in guiding the early phases of Islam to investigate and value knowledge from anywhere and everywhere.

Intellectually, early Islam was far ahead of contemporary Western Europe. Its academics established the first universities, rediscovered and rescued the classical philosophy of Greece from the dark ages and imported the philosophical and practical

achievements of India and China.   From its beginnings in
Baghdad the Moslem empire reached out in many directions. Its
cultural influence eventually stretched across southern Asia as far
as Indonesia; it does still.   Westward, it reached along the coasts
of Africa and through the islands of the Mediterranean into
continental Europe.

T HE MOSLEM PROVINCE of Andalus in Iberia,
today's Spain and Portugal, became a prominent focus
of Islamic culture. Its capital at Cordoba was, for about
two hundred years, the cultural centre of the west, and
in the process far outshone its Islamic starting point in Baghdad.
With an estimated population of half a million in the tenth
century, it became the largest and most powerful city in Europe.

Its enlightened Islam attracted intellectual and creative
individuals from many other societies, and they became
accomplished scientists, astronomers and navigators.   The
academics of Cordoba included both Christians and Jews. Their
intellectual and academic attainments were substantially ahead of
the modest cultural achievements of contemporary Christendom
That was notable mainly for its ignorance and introversion.

Around the superstitious rest of Europe the knowledge
and science radiating from Cordoba were regarded, with awe, as
'magic' - the works of magi. With Mohammed's death in 632AD
the Arab armies then embarked on an extensive campaign of
military conquest which built their empire. When Charles Martel,
grandfather of Charlemagne, finally halted the Moslem advance
northwards in 732AD, its Arab army had penetrated to within
200 miles of Paris.

So far as one can tell, theirs was one of the first societies to use the Chinese invention of paper for economic and military administration. Arab soldiers in Umayyad times were paid in written scrip. The chits entitled each recipient to a specified quantity of grain from state granaries following the harvest.

These, the world's earliest-known luncheon vouchers, were evidently transferable as well. Troops quickly discovered they could sell their future grain vouchers for cash to camp-following speculators who, despite Islam's strictures on usury, created a thriving secondary market. In the 1970s, canny clerks in the City of London did exactly the same, selling forward their Luncheon Voucher entitlements for months at a time. Islam's soldiers had invented derivatives trading in an embryo form.

Surviving manuscripts reveal how Arab traders developed ways to transmit payment instructions which were then carried out on their behalf by other merchants and money changers. For all that, the Arabs never transformed their written payment techniques into a banking system, largely because Islam condemned the charging of interest

Mohammed had disavowed the wealthy and corrupt merchants of his youth, their materialist excesses and their sharp practices. His religious teaching rejected them with some anger. Indeed the final sixteen years of his life had been spent, intermittently, waging war on them. His strictures live on to this day; orthodox Islamic banking still prohibits the payment of interest. Its restrictive code was devised in a bygone era when bankers did not yet have customers, but rather moneylenders still had victims. That no longer applies, banks could no longer survive with such commercial crudity, but religiously observant banks in the Gulf have to cope, still, with the impediment.

In one of the ironic twists of economic history and geography, the Islamic civilisation of Baghdad thrived in the very region where the rate of interest had originally been devised. Almost three millennia previously, the Sumerian civilisation of the Tigris and Euphrates had employed interest rate techniques so sophisticated they would have been prohibited in Britain's financial circles until Victorian times. They did so without any coinage, long before Rome exploited that potent creditary device to build a great empire.

Yet by the time of Mohammed, coinage had existed for at least a thousand years. Before his emergence it had given rise to financial practices so debauched that he deliberately threw creditary evolution into reverse. Had he not forbidden the payment of interest, the very system which was eventually to prove the key to economic prosperity, by encouraging fair rates of interest instead, there would have been little to prevent the emergence of a sophisticated Islamic banking industry. Instead he threw not one, but all the economic toys out of the pram.

Islam's mathematicians and clerks had all the requisite expertise in abundance. With more enlightened creditary underpinning the Industrial Revolution could well have taken hold in the Moslem world around 1200 AD, not in Western Europe over half a millennium later. In virtually every aspect apart from its creditary system, the civilisation which Mohammed set in motion was on the verge of such advance.

It was the construct of minds from many cultures and religions and it developed much of the expertise on which Europe's industrial revolution was later to depend. The technology for wind and water-powered factories was more or less in place by 1000AD. Despite this commercial opportunity, large-scale industry never emerged in Islam and the reason for that was, as much as anything, its draconian embargo on creditary expertise. The financial rules laid down by Mohammed in the Koran in effect prevented a division of labour and the prosperity to which that, alone, can lead. That gaping hole in Islam's economic armoury is of major relevance still, for it applies in other countries as well. As economists seek answers to the shortcomings of today's Third World, they really need to look first at their creditary systems, or too often lack of them.

WITH ISLAM FIRMLY shackled by its reactionary attitude to finance, creditary evolution found a different breeding ground.   It revived in Western Europe as the continent gradually re-emerged from its dark ages. One of the great culture transfers in history was about to emerge from invasions the Europeans chose to call the Crusades. In seeking to expel Moslems from the Holy Land, the agents of medieval Popes came face to face with the commercial expertise of Islam and copied it.

The Pope's front-line troops in those Levantine adventures were the Knights Templar. Founded at the Council of Troyes in 1128 - and despite their supposed penury - the Knights Templar soon became the rich financial agents of the Crusades as well as their military professionals.

They supposedly embodied the quite recent notion of a 'perfect Christian knight' - in some ways a throwback to the professional armies of Rome, and a far cry from the part-time rustic pugilists of the more recent past. Did encountering men like the urbane Saladin play a part in that? Such was the respect for the Knights Templar, King Alfonso of Aragon bequeathed them a third of his kingdom.

With their financial head start the Templar Order grew almost inordinately wealthy. The Templar knights were regularly endowed with numerous estates of farms and 'granges', not unlike the Sumerian temple of three thousand years earlier. However the Templars were now an exclusive and separate brethren, whereas Sumer's 'temple' had really been the central economic bureaucracy which supervised society as a whole.

Another key difference was one of geographical extent. Templar possessions were not confined to the immediate neighbourhood of an ancient Mesopotamian city state, but were scattered the length and breadth of Western Europe.

Many small English towns and villages, to this day, are still called 'Temple' this or 'Temple' that. Evidence of those wealthy medieval knights is to be found in some large cities too, in familiar locations such as Bristol's main Temple Meads station, or in London's Temple district now inhabited by comparably wealthy barristers. It all traces back around nine hundred years.

A large organisation was needed, partly to recruit and train new members for the Templar Order, but also to manage its huge revenue and to transmit money and supplies to the Holy Land. Achieving that built international financial expertise the world had not seen before. The primitive moneychangers of the classical world had never been able to achieve anything like the same level of far-reaching organisation. Then Mohammed's strictures had prevented anything remotely like it in Islam.

The financial services developed by the Knights Templar were revolutionary. The seeds of the next great creditary advance were being sown. Under Pope Alexander III in the late twelfth century the Templars became papal chamberlains and almoners: they also collected crusading taxes. By the thirteenth century their Temple in Paris had grown to become the largest financial institution in the known world. It had taken just a hundred years for 'crusading poor knights' to achieve such mastery and wealth.

At the outset they had no competition from banks, of which there were none. For most of that century the Temple served, in effect, as treasurers to the French crown. Then in 1295 a separate royal treasury was established - ominously the Templars had grown too powerful for the comfort of the French king and his state machine. By then, too, there were some alternative sources of creditary expertise.

THE ROYAL TREASURY OF contemporary England was never quite so dependent on Templar financiers. A Templar brother did however serve Henry III (1216-72) as head of his Wardrobe, the office which managed the finances of the royal household.

In their financial prime, the Knights Templar gained the expertise and confidence to issue and honour letters of credit which could traverse Europe from one temple to another. This facility proved a very attractive alternative to the awkward and vulnerable business of shipping large quantities of physical coin. It was clerical-based banking in embryo form, simple but able to span long distances, work with large numbers, and was of course extremely profitable.

The Templars also devised virtual credit cards. People making pilgrimages across Europe to Rome or to Santiago de Compostela could obtain a Templar document entitling them to board and lodging at recognised hospices along the way. Once their pilgrimage was accomplished, they received a bill from the Templars for the completed adventure. It was a very convenient creditary technique which effectively anticipated Diner's Club by about nine hundred years.

FOR OVER A CENTURY the financial prowess of the Templars grew and became legendary. Ultimately it was also their downfall. They grew arrogant and, perhaps inevitably, their great wealth incurred the wrath and envy of kings. King Philip of France (1268-1314) was already heavily in debt to the Templars when he asked for a further loan. They naturally refused. During the early hours of Friday 13 February 1307 agents of the king arrested, on suspicion of heresy, every known member of the Templar Order.[2]   King Philip 'The Fair' seized their lands and treasuries.

After several years of legal wrangling with the king and the Pope, their case was lost. Some fifty-four Templars were burned alive in May 1310. Four years later the leader of the Order, Jacques de Molay, was executed in public by burning. That cruel incineration put a dramatic and sudden end to medieval Europe's first-known success story in creating a continent-wide, paper-driven financial network.

Before their grisly demise, the Knights Templar had achieved remarkable creditary progress. International banking albeit in embryo form had been tried, tested and taken hold. By the time the Templars were murdered, their innovation was already being developed by Italian merchants. Once again the

2. *In the centuries ever since, any Friday 13th has been regarded as an omen of bad luck in Western countries.*

springboard for invention was the Crusades. As the banking historian Edwin Green remarks in his book Banking: An Illustrated History: 'The events of this period did not produce a banking tradition by accident or magic. Their real importance in financial history was the creation of customers for banking services.'

Yet if the Knights Templar helped create a prototype for Europe's eventual banking industry, they were not its only inspiration. The birth of proper banking needed more than one parent. It was now the turn of Italy's merchants to move forward. They drew on a variety of known techniques in the steady evolution towards the accomplished banks of the Renaissance. One of them was tally sticks, a creditary device which rarely figures nowadays in conventional explanations of economics. That is a pity, for a proper understanding of tally sticks brings with it a much more penetrating insight into the origin of economies and banking.

No-one seems to know how far wooden tallies go back in history, but they most likely emerged in a small way to record IOU's in a private circle of traders. There is some evidence to suggest they could have been the creditary system used to build the pyramids of Egypt. As observed in the previous Chapter, something along those lines may well have been used by ancient merchants trading with Lydia, before they engineered the crucial switch to a metallic coinage.

As a calculating system, tallies mesh very conveniently with the abacus. Both avoid any demanding arithmetic, and may yet prove to have some shared ancestry. Tally debts are recorded on shaped wooden sticks each uniquely notched crossways to represent details of the transaction. Debtor and creditor then need to identify themselves by making their mark in some mutually acceptable way. The stick is split lengthways. The longer half, the stock, is retained by the creditor and the shorter half, the stub, is retained by the debtor.

Neither party can tamper with the tally record without it becoming readily apparent when the two halves are again put side by side. In our own day the terminology of mediaeval tally sticks survives in that familiar institution, the Stock Market.

Unlike coinage, it was a creditary system which had no capacity for anonymous debtors, and to that extent it was a throwback to Sumer's clay tablets. So merchants who became debtors using tally sticks once again needed to belong to some guild or fraternity which supervised and enforced the system. It could only survive among traders who respected one another and acknowledged without question the commercial obligations implied by making their mark.

BY THE TWELFTH CENTURY, the tally stick was familiar in England; the timing suggests it arrived from continental Europe in the wake of William the Conqueror. England's Court of the Exchequer was originally known as the 'Court of the Tallies' and was the place used to match pairs of stocks and stubs once again to redeem royal debt. English kings used tally sticks to furnish themselves with funds, a process known as 'raising a tally'.

Provided they enjoyed a bond of trust with known merchants, it was a convenient alternative to the considerable expense of obtaining metal to mint coins. Typically, royal tally sticks were spent at one of the four great English fairs, then settled up at the next. Instead of receiving coin straight away, merchants would receive from the king's officials a creditor's half of a tally, the stock, while the royal household retained the stub. The Court of the Exchequer travelled around the country and set up shop in each major market town.

Provided the king restricted his tally spending to his anticipated levels of tax revenue, it was a simple creditary cycle without obvious drawbacks, other than the cumbersome woodworking of the tally itself. Even if the debtor, the king, was the same person throughout the life of the tally, the other half of the stick could and did change hands among selected creditors - very much as Sumer's mercantile clay tablets had done.

Tally sticks were not an effective creditary method for general circulation, but they did develop into a convenient method for organising taxes. At one time or another they have been used throughout much of the known world. The Chinese ideogram for 'contract' is composed of two simpler signs signifying 'notched stick' and 'knife'. In Arabic, the verb-root *farada* means both 'to make a notch' and 'to assign one's share of a contract or inheritance to someone'. Article 1333 of the Code Napoleon refers explicitly to tally sticks as a way to ensure that delivery of goods has been made.

The tally stick was familiar enough to Adam Smith. In *Wealth of Nations* he notes how the Bank of England had instigated a long overdue recoining of England's worn and heavily-clipped silver currency in 1696. In the meantime it stopped selling bullion and as Smith points out, 'tallies had been at 40, 50 and 60 per cent discount'. [3] Tally sticks were not finally abandoned by Britain's Exchequer until the early days of the Industrial Revolution. In effect the tally stick system had survived about seven hundred years in England.

---

3. *Adam Smith* 'Wealth of Nations' *Book II, Chapter ii.*

Throughout history, the physical recording of debts seems to have made use of whatever raw materials came to hand. Unlike the archaeologists's conventional sequence of Old Stone, New Stone, Bronze and Iron ages, the creditary sequence is memory, clay, metal, wood and paper. And eventually electronic.

THE KNIGHTS TEMPLAR, along with tally sticks, were both to play a vital part in the eventual emergence of banking, one of the key components of the Italian Renaissance. It was a long time coming. Merchants of various cultures had teetered on the edge of being bankers for three millennia. The sanctuary at Delphi in Greece, like the Sumerian temple before it, had been used for safe keeping of bullion and valuables.

Within 400 years of the first coins, the practicality of lending and borrowing them was so commonplace that the Greek general and historian Xenophon advocated a public safe custody institution in fourth century Athens. Profits from its lending business would have been shared by all citizens. Yet even the wisdom and acumen of Athens in its golden age was unable to bring this visionary proposal to fruition.

We may guess that the rough practices of real-life moneylenders were too far removed from the ethical standards required. The moneyed citizenry remained unconvinced. Had it ever materialized, Xenophon's institution would have been a major step toward the joint stock bank, or at least the mutual savings society of modern times. There may however have been another practical difficulty : the problem of calculating and accountancy using the numerical system of the day.

The money shops of Rome, two hundred years after Xenophon remarked on the prospect, also went some of the way to becoming banks. They were able to carry out customer's orders to deal with tax payments and to settle accounts with their creditors. It was not all that different in principle from a system using the banker's draft or cheque. The Roman dealers, known as *argentari* or silversmiths, paid interest on money deposits and provided money-changing facilities

Yet these Roman achievements, like those of the Greeks, all depended ultimately on using physical coin. This book adopts a strict creditary definition of banking which is free of such limitations, and for that the world had to wait a further 1200 years. An institution which generated its own supplies of fresh coin, and did not just re-lend those which had been deposited with it, would be a mint, not a bank.

The Greeks and Romans, like the Knights Templar, went a long way towards fully-fledged credit banking, but never quite reached it. Of continuing interest to creditary economists, therefore, is why the thirteenth century merchants of Lombardy succeeded. We may identify some immediate ancestors to Italy's banking success, but there is more to it than that. A central theme in this book is the close link between religious structures and ethics, and the powerful morality necessary to sustain credit agreements. It is a fundamental principle.

The events which were to unfold in Italy depended on bringing religious and commercial morality back into harmony with one another. Mutual trust among the early Italian bankers was a far cry from the amoral usurers and destructive entrepreneurs who contributed to the downfall of Rome - or from the unscrupulous moneylenders condemned by early

Christianity or the Koran. The cultural shifts which steadily led
to the Italian Renaissance moved a very long way beyond any of
that usurious dishonesty.

Tally sticks had helped build a level of international
expertise which was necessary for banking to emerge. Merchants
in medieval Italy extended their use far beyond the more localised
business of kings collecting taxes.

Well before they developed into bankers, Italian
merchants were making the arduous journey over the Alps to
trade in the great fairs of northern Europe. Merchants of
Piacenza and Tuscany originally visited those northern fairs to
buy cloth and sell alum. Wooden tallies were the creditary system
which enable the travelling merchants of medieval Europe to
organise themselves.

Their advancing skills and growing trustworthiness won
the confidence of the princes of Christendom, who recruited the
Italian merchants to ship coin and bullion to the Holy Land -
there was no way to do that using tallies - in exchange for credit
granted at the royal treasuries of Europe. This generated
commercial wealth on a grand scale, with the added bonus of
Papal approval and even encouragement. That was very new.

WEALTHY LOMBARDY merchants of the
thirteenth century gave financial and military
support to the Crusades. It was a far cry from the
Christian condemnation of moneylending and
financiers which had shaped economic thinking in the Middle
Ages. Perhaps for the first time in its history, Christianity now
found itself on the same side as the money men.

In gratitude, or more likely as a *quid pro quo*, Popes rewarded merchants with commercial privileges throughout the recently re-conquered eastern Mediterranean. The resources available for commerce received a great fillip with a large influx of gold from Constantinople when it was looted in 1215. Minted into coinage, it helped augment the creditary base just when business opportunities were blossoming. The earliest Italian banks date from exactly that time.

The ensuing mercantile activity enabled the ports of Venice and Genoa to famous generate prosperity which spread inland to Pisa, Florence, Sienna and Milan. Like the city states of Greece 1700 years earlier, the cities of northern Italy competed with one another for economic and cultural prestige. Civic beauty and elegance became the latest craze.

By the thirteenth century the competitiveness of Venice had fathered a large public debt, funded by its wealthy citizens. That debt needed to circulate. The Genoese were using the term *bancherius* to describe money-lenders who took deposits, re-lent them and settled debts. The term was derived from the Italian word bancha, the table at which mediaeval money changers did their business.

The concept was next adopted by Venetians to describe merchants who went one critical step further. They were called *banchi di scritta*. The practicalities of the tally stick, the trail-blazing of the Templars, the mercantile opportunities generated by the Crusades, the new-found ethical behaviour of money men, the indebtedness of glamorous cities and the resulting wealth of their citizenry were, in combination, giving birth to the pioneering Renaissance bank. There was one more essential element. Arabic (or more accurately Indian) arithmetic was introduced into the West. The cumbersome Roman counting system of I, V, X, L, C, D, M was swept aside. Zero at last made its appearance, and with it the prospect of efficient and accurate book-keeping.

A key figure in this education process was Leonardo of Pisa, son of Bonacci and so known to mathematicians ever since as Fi'bonacci. In 1202 he published a tract explaining the exotic arithmetic of the East which he called *Liber Abacci* - the book of the abacus. Even amid all the religious enmities and ravages of the Crusades, Leonardo had visited Islamic centres and universities around the Mediterranean, and in them studied how the Arabs did their sums.

Leonardo's father was a public scribe in the town of Bejaia, now in Algeria, where he worked in its customs service - the word tariff is after all one of Arabic origin. He was protecting the interests of Pisan merchants. *'My father made me learn how to use the abacus when I was still a child because he saw how I would benefit from this in later life. In this way I learnt the art of counting using the nine Indian figures 9 8 7 6 5 4 3 2 1. With these nine numerals, and with the sign 0 called zephirum in Arabic, one writes all the numbers one wishes.'* [4]

ADOPTION OF INDIAN-ARABIC arithmetic was crucial, and it marks a fundamental difference between the commercial achievements of the Classical world and those of the European Renaissance. For all their brilliance in other branches of philosophy, the Greeks never quite came to terms with arithmetic. The word, like alchemy, algebra, astronomy, astrology or algorithm, has an Arabic, not classical root. The Greeks even debated whether one, the monad, was actually a number. The very idea that zero could be a workable

4. *Leonardo of Pisa, or Fibonacci, in* Liber Abacci.

number as well would surely have thrown them into paroxysms. It was a simple, peerless insight, essential to the workings of a modern computer, which escaped them completely.

Some European academics had translated Arabic texts on Indian arithmetic in the previous century, including Robert of Chester, Bishop Raimundo of Toledo and Adelard of Bath. However their influence was small. In the minds of Europe's erudite Christian clergy,   the little-remarked yet brilliant arithmetical achievements of India, embraced by Islam's scientists and exploited by Italy's merchants, were merely a quaint Oriental curiosity. The merchant community took a different view.

While Leonardo's book and teaching were gaining ground in the classrooms of northern Italy, and in transactions between merchants, the universities of Oxford and Cambridge were both founded in England. but such arithmetical insight passed them by. Their avowed purpose was to train clerks for the church, not clerks for the world of commerce.

Fibonacci, by contrast, was looking ahead. *'Leonardo's stated purpose in writing Liber Abacci was to introduce Arabic numerals and methods of arithmetic into Italy. He deemed them vastly superior to the Roman numerals then in use in business and accounting.'* [5]

Thus it required a scion of Italy's merchant class, first to recognise the practical advantages of India's decimal system, and then to broadcast them to the world at large. Once again, necessity rather than ability was the mother of invention. The earliest-known English arithmetical tract, the *Crafte of Nombrynge,* dates from as recently as 1350, more than two centuries after Adelard of Bath had translated the *Algoritmi de numero Indorum.*

5. *L E Sigler's translation of Leonardo Pisano Fibonacci's* 'The Book of Squares', *page xviii.*

The revolution in arithmetic stands alongside printing as two technical advances which made the Renaissance feasible. It would be hard to identify any other basic attainment which comes anywhere near either in importance. Decimal numbering, and even more the realisation that zero was also a number, meant people with an ordinary school education could now calculate faster and more adroitly than even renowned philosophers had been able to do in the Classical era.

It was to transform how the West thought. *"The unknown man who devised the new system was from the world's point of view, after the Buddha, the most important son of India. His achievement, though easily taken for granted, was the work of an analytical mind of the first order, and he deserves much more honour than he has so far received."* [6]

Pioneering bankers of Italy made good use of the new arithmetic. It enabled their clerks to do complex calculations, previously the secret of philosophers and magicians. The sums could now be undertaken by those with a basic school education. Better still, such normal folk would be prepared to calculate for everyday wages, something which famous philosophers or magicians would never have been willing to do.

So bankers could afford to pay them everyday wages out of a moderate level of interest income. They had no need to resort to the exorbitant interest rates of the old, pernicious moneylenders. The church could now tolerate this new era of banking, where it had been a stringent critic and unwilling to tolerate the usury of previous centuries.

The new bankers had customers, not prey. Their loans were designed to be repaid, not to become an excuse for foreclosing. The working capital of the banchi di scritta grew, as

6. *Professor A L Basham in* The Wonder that was India, *Appendix IV*

did their profits, and they soon abandoned the other mercantile business from which they had originally sprung.

They now became financial clearing houses, their arithmetical ledgers replacing the former traffic in tally sticks. Banking clearances, *giro di partita,* developed to settle transactions negotiated in remote markets. It was essential that banks could deal among themselves as well with their own customers.

By 1257, a merchant from Lucca was able to buy Chinese silk in Genoa by arranging for a colleague based in Piacenza to make payment at the Champagne fairs. With transactions like that, banking had already come of age. In the centuries since, a confusing mystique has grown around banking which obscures some basic truths. A bank even in the twenty first century can do only one of five things with money : receive and store it, lend it, move it, exchange it for another currency and pay it out. It really is an area of economics where one needs to keep it simple.

WE CAN USEFULLY IMAGINE some early *banchi di scritta* in Venice, *circa* 1250 AD. One day a ship captain and a silk merchant called on the banker and asked him for loans. They knew that his strongroom contained a large heap of gold ducats. But instead of receiving a bagful as they had done in the past, the banker checked out their creditworthiness, then offered them an entry in his latest arithmetical ledger instead: *"you now have a loan of 1,000 ducats apiece, money you did not have previously, but on one condition. We all agree the ducats remain in my strongroom for safe keeping. You will avoid the risk of robbery. Just send me a note each time you wish to make a payment, and I will adjust your heap of ducats accordingly."* A *banchi di scritta* was one which wrote new loans, rather than re-lent old coins. The next day a builder and wine merchant each made similar loan requests, and they received the same response. They now received an entry in a ledger, rather than a bag of recycled gold coins.

The banker's pile of ducats in the strongroom remained untouched, while the number of loans in his ledger grew prodigiously. Provided everyone trusted his arithmetic, and provided most honoured their IOU's, there was nothing to stop one single banker providing commercial Venice with all the credit it required. A new creditary era had dawned and like most others, it did so by accident rather than by design.

Eventually it would no longer occur to landowners, navigators or merchants to go and stare at the glistening heap of ducats in wonderment, just to reassure themselves. Physical money was now redundant. Their creditary reassurance lay the honesty of the banker's arithmetic and ledgers, not in the size of his pile of gold ducats. The banker might just as well have melted down his obsolete bullion or sold it to make wedding rings.

CREDIT BANKING HAD ARRIVED. Yet as with all previous leaps in creditary skill it began by happenstance and was for centuries restricted to a merchant community.   As ever there were the ones with a professional reputation to protect. Such potent finance for the ordinary man was still a long way into the future. It was a matter of balancing trustworthiness and risk.   In the basic principles of creditary economics, it is credit that absorbs business risk and the two must always balance.

Merchants who owned stocks of valuable goods which might be seized, and were meanwhile jealously guarding their commercial reputation, were a much safer bet for a loan than ordinary citizens who might simply squander the proceeds. The same profligacy with loans made purely for consumer spending helps explain creditary problems of the early twenty-first century. There really is very little that is new under the sun.

So long as the money illusion persists, it remains difficult to grasp how a bank actually works. It most certainly does not apportion loans from some finite stockpile of accumulated 'wealth' in its strongroom, as many folk still fondly imagine. Were that how a bank works, it would then be difficult to explain why some early Sumerian bank could not go into profitable business creating loans from clay shovelled from a nearby pit, or some medieval bank do the same using a bundle of blank tally sticks harvested in a convenient woodland.

It was the creditary principle, the two-sided recognition of the debt which was important - not the physical material with which the debt was recorded. Credit is not some scarce commodity, like gold, which must therefore be rationed. Nor is the physical material used to denote a bank's lending of any real significance. From the mid-thirteenth century it was already being replaced by an arithmetical process.

When making loans, banks do something quite different from distributing dollops from a heap of 'stored wealth'. The inner secret of a bank is not some jealously-guarded stockpile of debt tokens, but its clerical ability to transform one kind of abstract debt into another kind of abstract debt using competent book-keeping. To be precise, in making a loan, a bank first accepts a new debt from a trusted customer, their personal IOU which has one-to-one acceptability only. That individual's IOU is then exchanged by the bank for a bundle of freshly-created

IOU's of a kind which many more people will find acceptable. Effectively, creditary expansion was being conjured out of thin air, but it works. The bank now has both a fresh asset on its books (the customer's original IOU) and a fresh liability - the new common use IOUs it has handed over. So its books balance as soon as the twofold transaction has been completed.

When they are 'making a loan', all banks do in practice is convert one kind of private IOU into another, more generally acceptable kind of IOU. Two qualities of debt have been exchanged. And like that pioneering Venetian banker, any bank can keep manufacturing credit by such means without limit, or at least until some central authority lays down external rules to regulate the process.

In the minds of numerous economists even in the twentieth century, the origins and function of banks remained hazy if not completely incomprehensible. Many of them even assumed a central bank was essential to creating credit, when in fact such an institution was to not see the light of day for a further 450 years. One of the most successful financial centres of all, Hong Kong, has never had a separate central bank.[7]

In our modern era, internationally-agreed regulations alone limit the number of times a bank may generate fresh credit. That is the purpose of the successive Basel Accords, which individual governments then impose.

Until the early 1990s the banks of Japan were lending with little regard to the prudent limits observed in other countries.

7. *As the author had to explain on regular occasions in his job as principal spokesman for the Hongkong and Shanghai Banking Corporation at its global headquarters in the 1980s. HSBC was not only the largest commercial bank in the territory, it also doubled up as the central bank as well.*

When the rules were changed they came down to earth with a thump. Free market economists may find the notion irksome, but banking is one economic activity which must always be regulated. That old truth re-emerged with a dreadful dawn of realism in the global financial crises of Summer 2007.

FROM THE RENAISSANCE ONWARDS, banks have deliberately propagated a seductive myth about their own solidity. In reality, banks take something which is nothing, use many zeroes in its manufacture, and sell it for a profit. They then seek to present this gossamer-like activity as solid and substantial; read Henry Ford on the subject at the start of this chapter. Their headquarters are deliberately built as temples of mammon. They adopt all kinds of architectural devices, from lofty pillared halls to sumptuous detail in marble, polished metal and wood, all to create that reassuring impression.

The twentieth century skyscraper was the banker's godsend. And all to good effect. Despite the effortless ease with which banks can crash, the general public and many economists have long been seduced into believing they possess some innate solidity. They most certainly do not, as those unfortunates in the early 21st century who believed they were getting a really good deal in Iceland rapidly learnt to their cost.

The banking mechanisms of the Renaissance were different from what went before in another way too. Unlike all previous methods of plain moneylending, they no longer depended on physical use of coinage. Gold and silver went back to being numeraires only. This change had an important consequence, one which has been quite invisible to generations of economists, banking administrators, central bankers and 'practical men' right up to our present day. The quantity of credit generated by bankers was no longer dictated by the availability of precious metal. That finite pile of ducats in the vaults had become irrelevant. The era of undiluted monetarism had already come, and gone again, by 1300AD.

Although many people may draw some sense of reassurance from the idea that their bank owns a big pile of metal, they are deceiving themselves. An ancient system which had used metal for betokening debt has been wholly replaced by a new system which uses arithmetic instead. After its previous ages built around a variety of different commodities, the creditary system entered its arithmetical age shortly after 1200 AD.

The stability of a bank is not built on the size of the ducat pile, or the bullion pile, or the pile of anything else in its strongroom, but on the creditworthiness of its loan portfolio and on the honesty of its managers. That reality became all too cruelly apparent to the many customers who lost out in 1991 with the collapse of BCCI, or with the collapse of Northern Rock in 2007, or RBS, or with America's sub-prime mortgage crisis at the same time, or in the collapses of scores of other banks in the centuries before. In every case it has been the loan book, not the security of the strong room, which has gone astray.

The creditary realities of banking and money were lost on an entire generation of monetary economists who honestly, but mistakenly, believe the creation of money, more specifically credit, to be a sole prerogative of governments. From that misconception emerged a witch-hunt for public borrowing and debt, and the ferocity surrounding of the 'PSBR'. [8] In reality the birth process of credit is nowhere near so exclusive. Any loan-

8. *The 'Public Sector Borrowing Requirement'.*

granting bank can do it. Not for the first time in twentieth century economics, a misleading edifice of conventional wisdom was built on an inability to comprehend the basic principles of credit creation and management, insight which must be central to any appreciation of creditary economics.

THE ITALIAN BANKING INDUSTRY was an invention of the thirteenth century, and it was already strong enough to survive the vicissitudes of the fourteenth. Foremost among those setbacks was the Black Death in 1347-48, which killed perhaps as many as half Europe's inhabitants.

Originating in central Asia, it had travelled along the Silk Road and first reached the Crimea in 1346. From there it probably travelled around Western Europe on merchant ships. The devastation was greatest in port cities such as Genoa, Hamburg and Bremen, hitting the mercantile sector at least as hard as anyone. The effect on the mainstream economy was disastrous too, partly through loss of manpower, partly from the collapse in demand.

The loss of manpower was felt very strongly in the agricultural economy, where labour became more expensive. That in turn helped hasten the demise of the feudal system, as local lords now had to hire labour where previously they could rely on the days of work owed by their villeins. Despite the death of so many millions in the Black Death, the banks survived. It was never natural calamities which defeated the bankers, but weakness in their loan portfolio - whether they had chosen customers wisely enough when accepting those personal IOU's.

Throughout the Middle Ages there was no shortage of financial failure. Banks could, and did, grow too ambitious in their desire to expand, accepting as customers those whom others had more prudently rejected. Bankruptcies were one of the fledgling industry's more visible characteristics. The House of Buonsignori in Sienna had already collapsed by 1295.

In the following century the banks which carefully avoided such calamities prospered and grew. Lessons were learnt steadily. It is in the nature of prudent banking to spread risks by building a widely diversified portfolio of borrowers, and to do that a bank needed geographical reach. Such expansion across the breadth of Europe persuaded the bankers of the Renaissance to work through associates, rather than directly. Long-distance travel was slow, arduous and expensive.

RATHER THAN TRUDGE ACROSS the Alps to distant fairs, a Renaissance bank's chief executive remained comfortably at his headquarters. His deal-making and the vital business of gathering commercial intelligence was put in the hands of distant agents. Gradually this spread of the business developed into fully-fledged branch banking. The Bardi house of Florence, for example, soon operated over 30 branches in Italy and several others abroad, as far afield as Bruges, Spain, Moorish Africa and the Levant.

Another Bardi branch was established in London, where its leading customer was King Edward III. He was engrossed in wars with France and ran up astronomical debts, for those days, totalling 1.5 million florins. Sadly for the Italian bankers, England was still well beyond the Pale, and its king had yet to come to terms with the peculiar notion that bank loans should be honoured eventually. England's royal default forced the Bardi, along with fellow bankers the Peruzzi and the Acciajoli, to suspend payments from 1339 to 1343.

English kings were still taking Italian bankers for a ride over a hundred years later. The mighty Medici, no less, were forced to close their London branch when Edward IV welshed on loans he had raised to fight the Wars of the Roses. The idea of needing to repay loans one day escaped his attention. Such were the manifold risks, then and now, of sovereign lending.

The incautious optimism of international bankers in the early 1980s, that sovereign lending was somehow a risk-free way of making large profits, betrayed an alarming ignorance of the history of their own industry. It was never so; sovereign borrowers can frequently be the worst of all

Despite its altercation with Edward IV of England, the house of Medici rose to eminence among Florentine bankers and stayed there. The fabled wealth of successive generations of the Medicis in turn became a mainspring of the cultural flowering of the Italian Renaissance. Just like the wealth and cultural magnificence of Classical Athens brought about by the invention of coinage, the invention of banking had a comparable effect in Italy 1700 years later.

The name of Medici has since been enshrined in history as the very essence of Renaissance banking and great wealth, although the word itself means doctor. Established in 1397, the bank expanded under the inspired direction of first Cosimo, then Lorenzo Medici to achieve great economic distinction and, in Florence, great political power: *Technically the most advanced financial institution before the late 16ᵗʰ century and possibly the late 17ᵗʰ century, it was definitely surpassed only in the 19th century.'* [9] Much like the evolution of money, the evolution of banking was not achieved in a single leap. The financial sophistication of the Medicis, and others, required great skills in company management and commercial intelligence.

For two hundred years Italian bankers struggled with accounting rules of thumb of their own devising. Then in 1494 the Italian Luca Pacioli set out the principles of double-entry book-keeping in his first book, *Summa de arithmetica, geometria, proportioni et proportionalita.* Banks no longer needed to rely on rule of thumb. Pacioli went on to become housemate of, and mathematical tutor to, Leonardo da Vinci.

Luca Pacioli was codifying the hard-learnt practices of Italian merchants, yet some historians think they have detected signs of those techniques as early as the accounting methods of Sumerian clay tablets. Pacioli, however, now provided an instruction manual setting out the irreducible logic of double-entry book-keeping. With that semi-obscure insight, the accountancy profession embarked on its own relentless and highly remunerative march to ascendancy.

The Italian Renaissance names of Fibonacci, Medici and Pacioli deserve an honoured place in the pantheon of creditary heroes. For almost half a millennium from the twelfth century onwards, Italy and its merchants stood at the centre of creditary invention. Their financial strengths made possible voyages which explored the globe and established colonial enterprises in five continents. Their own networks reached far north, and they were copied in great trading communities beyond the Alps. The march of creditary innovation moves ever westward. Henry

---

9. *Raymond Goldsmith quoted by Edwin Green, op cit.*

Tudor's victory at Bosworth Field in 1485 proved to be a watershed for England and its economic sophistication. Just a few decades earlier, Edward IV displayed a Plantagenet contempt for banking in his treatment of loans from the Medicis. Under the Tudors all that was to change.

While England had been absorbed by its Wars of the Roses, the great centres of fairs and markets in continental Europe had prospered. Foremost among these was Antwerp, whose innkeepers had long been in the business of putting its merchants in contact with one another, providing a commercial service which was the forerunner of a stock exchange. Today the central square of Antwerp bears testimony to its success.

T HE SIXTEENTH CENTURY saw such financial broking become a separate profession in its own right, and the continental bourse emerged as an established focus for commerce. Observing this competition from across the Channel, England's Tudor monarchs inched their way toward a variety of their fiscal and creditary techniques.

Between 1539 and 1546, Henry VIII lowered customs duties levied on foreign merchants to match those levied on English merchants. An Act of Parliament in 1545 legalised the charging of interest up to a rate of 10 per cent. Such 'usury' had previously been an indictable offence in the church courts of England. As with many creditary advances, the freedom was initially short-lived. In 1552, charging interest once again became illegal in England.

If Henry VIII's fumbling with the legitimacy of interest rates looked indecisive, his dissolution of the monasteries was anything but. The ownership and management of England's major economic assets changed forever, and on a nationwide scale. That triggered an economic boom, for the reactionary policies of the monasteries had inhibited progress.

The Black Friars, for example, had claimed ownership of the banks of the River Thames. Along the river they prohibited, not only commercial development, but even fishing. Once their authority was abolished, wharves and docks were built. Maritime development downstream from the city created a centre of trade, shipbuilding and manufacturing.

London was set fair to become the world's leading port, a position it was to hold until the middle of the twentieth century. Land was released and developed on which, among other developments, Shakespeare's Globe Theatre was built. Tudor, then Stuart London generated the same wealth which provided his audiences. If they were willing to pay, he and his associates were willing to write.

CONFRONTATION WITH entrenched catholic interests in mainland Europe served England in another way too. The Crown Agent, Sir Thomas Gresham was based in Flanders, in Antwerp, between 1551 and 1566. His was a perennial quest for state funds. Queen Elizabeth the First, as already noted in her ruthless treatment of mineral rights, was anything but low maintenance.

In March 1566 Gresham witnessed at first hand the first revolts by the protestant Flemings against the catholic king of Spain. Over the next twenty years, Spanish troops twice sacked Antwerp to crush the rebels, killed many thousands of its citizens, and in the process wrecked the city's international reputation as a centre of commerce. Merchants cannot thrive amid that, and hastily shifted their activities to Amsterdam, which in turn became the new "Venice of the North".

Amid all this turmoil Thomas Gresham spotted an opportunity for England. His father Sir Richard, merchant and Lord Mayor of London, had wanted a bourse for merchants in the city to match those on the Continent. Twice his requests to establish one had been rejected by King Henry VIII.

The spendthrift Queen Elizabeth and her courtiers took a more enlightened view. On 7 June 1566, just three months after Antwerp's first Protestant uprising, Sir Thomas laid the foundation stone in the City of London for what became the Royal Exchange. Trading on Gresham's 'bourse' was conducted mainly in commodities and credit. Sadly Gresham's original building was engulfed in the Great Fire of London in 1666, and a new building opened in 1669.

The mercantile revolution made feasible by the arrival of true banking transformed Europe, and pushed it into the van of progress worldwide. The continent now swept past all the material and intellectual achievements of China, India and even Islam at the zenith of its Caliphate. The same mercantile culture played a vital rôle underpinning great voyages of discovery, most notably those which opened up the Americas.

With the emergence of merchant banking a new level of creditary expertise grew out of northern Italy. It was accompanied by other advances, notably improvements in ship design and navigation. Once again the creditary principle and the specialist principle were marching hand in hand. The seeds of the Industrial Revolution had been sown.

Chapter Five

1600 AD to 1800 AD

The radical of one century is the conservative of the next.
MARK TWAIN

ANKIND'S PIONEER creditary advances, from 9000BC onwards arose in quite small, close-knit communities. Inevitably so. Memorised debt was devised among tribes of Neolithic farmers; written debt, then money and banking were each devised among groups of clear-minded and progressive merchants in city states. Belief and trust, the original Latin meaning of credit, started small.

Those origins of economies were also few and far between, and each arose in exceptional circumstances. Such advances are wholly unlike those in technology which are, by and large, continual. The economic mechanism embraces those one at a time and, if advantageous, they steadily advance human capabilities; the ever-improving specialist principle at work.

So advancing technology and advances in creditary skill are very different. One is more of a steady graph; the other is invariably a dramatic step function. The reason is simple. Usually an advance in technology is the achievement of an individual inventor following a unique train of inspiration in isolation. His - or her - thought processes are not reliant on the agreement of others Many have an individual's name attached to them, from Croesus to Archimedes to Marie Curie and beyond. Many more such are to be found in the last two chapters.

Creditary advances, in contrast, are typically anonymous and initially imperceptible.   No-one knows the name of the first Sumerian merchant to accept a clay tablet, the first to use a Lydian stater as a coin, the first Italian businessman to negotiate a credit-based loan from a Renaissance bank. None of them at the time had any notion they were triggering one of the origins of economies. That realisation only came many years later.

The occasion had a different essence from pioneering technology, one which was much more demanding. Rather than and individual flash of inspiration, it required willing co-operation around a community of competing merchants. They agreed to move forward together in concert, simultaneously adopting a mutual understanding. There was no grand announcement, or fanfare, nor even acknowledgement of its eventual consequences.

No matter how inspired a genius, someone who concocts a new way of handling debt and credit has achieved nothing until others join in. It is a paradox, a mutuality which explains the bashfulness of the creditary principle. Perhaps standing out from the rest one individual discovery which made credit banking possible, the introduction of zero was also anonymous.

It was made by a Indian in the remarkable Gupta dynasty, yet no-one knows his name either; they may yet find it. As Professor Basham concludes (see p.196) he was nevertheless one of the two most important sons of India. Everyone knows the name of the other great son of India - the Buddha. No-one forgets the name of those who establish new religions. Yet everyone seems to forget, with rare exceptions, the name of those who establish new advances in creditary skill. Those events almost always taken for granted. As noted in Chapter one, everyday occurrences are always the least remarked. Is there any wonder the general creditary principle has managed to evade the awareness of so many economists for quite so long?

WHEN SOME MAJOR creditary thresh-hold is first surmounted, even then people at large are unaware anything historic or momentous is taking place. There is nothing to shout *Eureka* about; no-one even knows if it is going to work. As noted in Chapter Two, the Creditary principle is the unassertive twin of the far more conspicuous Specialist principle, the one remarked upon by Adam Smith in 1776.

Previous creditary advances had arisen in close-knit communities, typically in village or city states. In the seventeenth century that would cease to be the case. Progress was very different from a small group of hunter-gatherers agreeing to take up farming as a novelty. It now emerged within entire nations. Yet in one respect they would all share a key characteristic. Be it early farmers, or Sumerians with their clay tablets, or merchants (who were probably Phoenicians) with their shiny new staters, in each case just a single step function in creditary technique was sufficient to trigger a new kind of civilisation.

The last built commerce around the Mediterranean, giving rise to Classical civilisation in all its majesty. The fourth creditary step built the European Renaissance, taking civilisation

214   CHAPTER FIVE : 1600AD TO 1800AD

to new heights and sponsoring voyages of exploration which opened up the globe. Yet we cannot name anyone who opened the first *banchi di scritta*. Devising new debt and credit methods may not sound thrilling, but they have unequalled power.

Each creditary flowering in turn produced some seeds of what was to follow, some vital elements for the future, but lacked any capacity to bring them to fruition. Sumerians certainly venerated silver bullion, as did the ancient Egyptians, but they never devised a circulating metallic coinage. In Athens there was a first hint of banking. Some kind of public institution offering safe custody for money and provide loans was once proposed by Xenophon, yet it did not see the light of day for a further two millennia. Creditary advances have in the past been inclined to take their time. That was about to change too.

Seeds of a further, fundamental creditary step forward had already been sown well before the sixteenth century. When true credit banking eventually emerged it did so in northern Italy, and for over three centuries it grew in sophistication and influence. Europe's first public bank, as distinct from a private merchant bank, was the Banco de Rialto, established by Acts of the Venetian Senate in 1584 and 1587. The Republic set up a second public bank thirty years later. It was originally called the Banco del Giro but for many generations subsequently was better known as the Bank of Venice.

It embodied a new understanding of finance, and its influence was to spread far in the seventeenth century, most notably into northern Europe. That does seem to be the creditary gestation period, give or take ten generations. Roughly two thousand years previously it needed roughly three hundred years from the first proto-coins in Lydia to a fully-fledged coinage circulating among the citizenry of the Roman empire in the Classical era. It had taken about that time for Sumer to discover the commercial potential of its remarkable methods for writing, recording and transferring debt.

The landlocked Mediterranean, its geography of handy inhabitable islands ideal for sea-borne trade, became a nursery of creditary innovation. Merchants of many different states, in political terms, nonetheless co-operated. It was an economic advantage in the West which found no handy equivalent in the East. Apart from the fabled Silk Road across open steppe where pack animal caravans could pass unhindered, Chinese trade with the West, or anywhere, was decidedly limited.

WITHIN THE MAINLY self-contained, self-defensive attitude of the Middle Kingdom there was no justification for any such cultural pollution. Quite the opposite. The most important economy of the Orient, then as now, developed in virtual isolation, complete with its own distinctive form of inward-looking feudalism, one with Chinese characteristics.

That said, a Venetian merchant's son, Marco Polo, did report a distinctive Chinese creditary technique invented within the country itself. In 1271 he allegedly left his home city for the long overland trip to the Orient and explained he stayed there for seventeen years, becoming a diplomatic agent. While working in China, Polo claimed he saw the use of 'paper money' [1].

---

1. *Paper was first invented in China in the Han dynasty (206 BC – 220 AD); an earliest date of 105AD is frequently cited. The technology spread slowly to the West along the Silk Road. European manufacture of paper began with the Muslims in Andalus - today's Portugal and Spain - and Sicily in the 10th century. It slowly spread to the rest of Italy and then southern France, reaching Germany by 1400.*

Given the remarkable advances in Venice's creditary skills in the decades before he left, one might wonder why, and whether, Marco Polo could really have been quite so awestruck as he would have his readers believe. Nor was paper a novelty either. By the time he set off on his supposed trip of discovery, banks and paper had already been known in Venice for decades.

Marco Polo's merchant family upbringing would have been at the very heart of Venice's creditary innovation, and his astonishment does seem distinctly contrived.[2] Nowadays there are doubts whether he ever went to China at all, but instead merely cobbled together marketable Oriental stories he acquired secondhand from others. Whatever the truth of his travels, there can be no denying his enduring expertise at public relations, exploited successfully over a century before printing became a reality in the West.

Although some even claim that Chinese 'paper money' was in use as early as 650 AD, during Europe's dark ages, it is profoundly unhelpful that no actual examples from that early era have survived. The earliest surviving Chinese paper money dates from the much more recent Ming dynasty (1368-1694) by which time banking, if not yet the banknote, had long been familiar around western Europe.

China's paper money was not a banknote at all, although over-enthusiastic historians often use the word to describe it. China had no banks. Those oriental debt devices were most probably promissory notes issued by the emperor and his treasury to deliver a specified quantity of silver. He would have distributed them to purchase his needs. One wonders how far

---

2. *Mark Chicken, the direct English translation, could very easily be read as the chosen stage name of some highly entertaining, income-seeking charlatan.*

afield imperial creditworthiness was recognised in order for such financial instruments to circulate. Nor was there anything particularly original in the system. Silver devices along similar lines, albeit manufactured in clay rather than written on paper, had been issued by the Sumerian temple over three thousand years previously.

The same principle of a silver certificate still survives in the world's largest economy. A promissory note for a quantity of silver supposedly held by the US Treasury has always been the commercial logic of an American dollar bill. Strictly speaking, American paper currency is not a banknote at all. That is an important distinction lost on generations of economists - the underlying rationale of British and American paper money is fundamentally different. A British banknote does not depend on, nor require, backing with stored bullion.

O VER A PERIOD OF FOUR centuries Marco Polo's home city of Venice and its fellow Italian city states made unrivalled advances in creditary expertise. As always, such advance generated unprecedented wealth when compared with anything known before: the more credit agreements an economy can sustain, the greater the division of labour it may attain. The city's prosperity became legendary and for once it was not the exclusive preserve of a privileged few, but spread much more widely among its citizens. Previously there had only been one palace in a typical city state, that of the king. Venice had over two hundred of them.

Building work began in 1340 on its Doge's Palace on the Rialto, as the centre of the republic's government. From the thirteenth century onwards prosperous Venetians built around

170 palazzos along the banks of the Grand Canal alone. Nowhere else in the world could even start to match that. Yet for all its commercial and cultural achievements, Venice was just one more staging post on the creditary principle's everlasting journey. It now moved north and west, out of the Mediterranean region which had been its cradle for two thousand years.

A tectonic shift in the Christian religion drove creditary innovation elsewhere, into the emerging nation states of Europe's Atlantic littoral. Not only Italy's merchants had benefited from the bonanza of the Renaissance. So had the priests, and particularly the Vatican and the Papal States. The sumptuary excesses of the Catholic church were its greatest miscalculation, to be eclipsed by a far more abstemious version of Christianity.

It is also now possible for the first time to identify some of the individuals who hatched the original ideas. Often enough the true creditary innovators have been more than a little disreputable. However the man who helped start the next phase of innovation was probity itself. In 1517 the German priest Martin Luther sent ninety-five theses to the Bishop of Mainz objecting strongly to the self-indulgence of the Catholic church. There is much dispute nowadays that he ever nailed his thoughts to the door of a church in Wittenburg, as kind mythology has long maintained. Luther and his friends in fact resorted to the recently-invented printing press to propagate their views.

As the protestant reformation took hold it stimulated a wave of political and economic self-confidence throughout north western Europe. The uxorious Henry VIII of England broke with the Catholic Church in 1533, and promptly confiscated and sold off all its domineering monasteries. The change in asset ownership triggered an economic boom in Tudor England.

Thirty years later, Prince William of Orange headed a protestant rebellion against much-resented Catholic hegemony in the low countries. They had long been an oppressed province of Spain, provoked by its cruel Inquisition. Successive stretches of the country were regained by rebels and in 1579 seven northern provinces united to form a protestant federation.

Finally an Act of Abandonment in 1581 declared independence of all the low countries from Spain. Enjoying their new-found independence the confident Dutch moved ahead rapidly, expanding their overseas shipping and trade. With its extensive network of canals their commercial capital of Amsterdam could justifiably claim to be the new Venice of the north. Dutch sea captains were willing to venture further afield than their Venetian predecessors; the stormy North Sea and the Atlantic were a much tougher navigational training ground than the benign Mediterranean.

HOLLAND'S MERCHANTS SET about poaching the highly lucrative Indonesian spice trade from catholic Portugal. To that end, the Dutch East India Company was formed in 1602 by wealthy Amsterdam traders. A British East India Company had been launched two years earlier. Unlike the Dutch enterprise, however Britain's motive had been not so much merchant venture, more a case of replenishing royal revenues by sale of an enticing monopoly.

The joint stock structure of the Dutch spread the heavy risks which the distant spice trade involved, and the ambitious enterprise is sometimes hailed as the world's first multinational company. Another new method had been evolved for absorbing business risk, just as the first credit agreement between farmer had done over ten thousand years previously. Like its creditary predecessors, it was another origin of economies.

In 1608 a Dutch commercial fleet seized the Spice Islands, the Moluccas, in Indonesia. In 1641 they took control of Malacca, in today's Malaysian peninsula, and in 1656 control of Ceylon. The company also looked west. The Dutch set up the first colonial settlement on Manhattan in 1624, just a few years after England's Pilgrim Fathers had arrived in New England. Only in 1664 did the invading British capture Holland's pioneering New Amsterdam and rename it New York.

WHILE DUTCH COMMERCIAL enterprise radiating from Amsterdam was awakening protestant Europe, the most adventurous step in creditary invention was the work of an ambitious Dutchman operating further north. He found a willing test bed in Sweden for his revolutionary ideas but it had taken almost fifty years to prepare the ground.

Three Swedish monarchs, beginning with King Gustavus Adolphus, shouldered the task of modernising their country. Once again, and with no deliberate planning, another major pioneering step in the origins of economies was about to emerge. Succeeding his father in 1611, Gustavus was determined his country should move beyond its medieval ways. The new monarch was just fourteen, but after a period of enlightened regency, he revealed a deft military and diplomatic expertise. In the Thirty Years War, Sweden successfully attacked Prussia and Poland, sweeping through modern Germany. Adroit treaties were signed and Sweden's national ambition grew apace.

At home, Sweden's legal system and its Treasury were modernised, modelled on Dutch practice. Uppsala university was given royal funding to improve training for government officials, the church was reformed, new towns were built and given charters. Such enlightened reform could scarcely bear fruit overnight, or even in the space of twenty years. When Gustavus Adolphus died in 1632 at the still youthful age of 35, Sweden's Council of State refused to allow foreign visitors to attend his funeral 'lest they witness our poverty'.

Upon his death, his six-year old daughter Christina became queen, and under another regency and then her own rule continued Sweden's drive for modernisation. However her regal extravagance, and the continuing cost of fighting wars, further impoverished the Treasury. Then in her twenties, Queen Christina manoeuvred her cousin Charles Casimir first into the post of commander-in-chief of the Swedish army, and then to be her heir-apparent. She then surprised Europe by becoming a Catholic, abdicating in 1654 and departed to Rome.

In his brief six year reign, the new Charles X continued Sweden's military adventures. He attacked Poland in 1655 crushing its forces in Warsaw the following year, then turned his warlike attentions to Denmark. Military adventure on that scale never comes cheap. As often happens in economic history, the heavy cost of war became a springboard for financial innovation.

With adroit timing a young Dutch nobleman called Johan Palmstruch, leaving behind a dubious career in Amsterdam, persuaded the Swedes that what they really needed was a government-sponsored bank. Palmstruch's proposal was very broadly modelled on the public banks Venice had established some seventy years earlier. His version, however, was to be underwritten financially by the state and that was wholly new. Under King Charles X, the Bank of Stockholm opened for business in 1657. Palmstruch received royal Letters of Appointment as its director and even the promise of an annual salary from the state. Some 400 years after the pioneering merchant bankers of Italy had fathered the Renaissance, their craft had now evolved into a profession considered suitable for state-employed bureaucrats.

In 1661 the emerging Bank of Stockholm began issuing standardised official printed notes, *kreditivsedlar,* which circulated among prominent members of Stockholm society. As they did so each holder in turn became due a payment from the bank. They were the world's first true banknotes, claims on the account of a bank itself, rather than cheques drawn on the accounts of its individual customers.

PALMSTRUCH MODESTLY disowned any such originality, perhaps for the sensible purpose of reassuring customers that holding his *kreditivsedlar* was not all that revolutionary and should give them no cause for anxiety. He maintained that his notes were simply derived from the *kopparsedlar* which Sweden's great copper mining concern, the Bergslaget, had paid to its miners as receipts for raw copper. Johan Palmstruch found it simpler to take refuge in the money illusion than to explain what was actually happening. His *kreditivsedlar* were not connected to any supplies of valuable metal. It might all seem a tad pedantic today, but as economics wisdom unfolded that distinction between true banknotes and metal certificates, even now, provides a vital if somewhat elusive key to understanding banking and finance.

Banknotes are simply a claim, much like any other cheque, on an intangible deposit in the banking system. By contrast nation's treasuries, which are not strictly banks, issue certificates which are claims on precious metal, and they do ultimately depend on backing with bullion. As noted earlier, that still distinguishes British banknotes from American dollar bills.

There has never been much creditary logic in seeking to back any of Britain's banknotes with reserves of gold. Large chunks of the stuff gathered dust in the vaults of the Bank of England, yet they served no constructive economic purpose whatever. As noted earlier, they are no more significant in creditary logic than the large chunks of limestone gathering dust in front gardens on the island of Yap.

In seventeenth century Stockholm, Palmstruch's pioneering banknote venture soon ran out of control, so much so that it was suspended in 1664 after just three years. Dishing out state-backed IOU's is the easiest thing in the world for a bank to do, controlling them is far less so. His powerful financial weapon proved impossible to manage and a commission of enquiry declared Palmstruch personally responsible for the bank's losses. It reported that his book-keeping had been slapdash.

Even if Renaissance banking had made the journey north, the clerical finesse of Luca Pacioli evidently had yet to do so. Sweden may have been in the throes of civic modernisation but its legal penalties were still medieval. Johan Palmstruch was at first sentenced to death for his financial misdeeds, although the draconian sentence was later commuted to one of imprisonment. An improved second issue of notes, often called Palmstruchers, appeared in 1666. These required no fewer than eight handwritten signatures on each note, together with individual seal impressions. They were the world's first banknotes to have a specific watermark; forgery was already a concern. Like the notes which appeared in England thirty years later, they specified neither a depositor nor interest payment, and were simply payable to 'bearer', the same as making a cheque out to 'cash'.

Controlling this second issue also proved too much for the Bank of Stockholm, which was still unfamiliar with the challenges of credit management. The enterprise had first become insolvent in 1664, ran into trouble again and was eventually liquidated in 1668. Its pioneering banknotes had simply been ahead of their time.

Though the circulation of Palmstruch's banknotes was blamed for the eventual collapse, even so Sweden's parliament still welcomed the notion of an official bank. In September 1668 the Sveriges Riksbank, the Bank of Sweden, was founded and placed under guarantee and administration of the legislature. It had no truck with the new-fangled banknotes, using instead a more restrictive official document which was not legal tender.

Sweden waited a century and a half before attempting such a risk-laden technique again. Its first modern banknotes were not issued until 1803, but already by the 17th century Sweden had pioneered the next great step in creditary evolution.

Whatever Palmstruch's setbacks, nevertheless state-run central banking had made its first and permanent appearance, even if its inventor died in disgrace. Palmstruch became just one of the numerous economic pioneers whose reputations were to perish in pursuit of innovation. As is so often the case in the origin of economies, the inventors themselves were anything but paragons of virtue. The man who was to devise the Bank of England, a little less than thirty years after the Sveriges Riksbank, was no paragon of virtue either. Creditary advance rarely comes easily, and Sweden's experience was all too typical.

Although the birth of central banking in Sweden proved painful, the underlying notion had been gestating for about a hundred years. Spanish bankers had made a similar suggestion to King Philip as early as 1583, while a Banque de France had been proposed to King Henri IV in 1604. Overtures for nationally-supervised banks had been playing around Europe for almost a century, but they never quite reached the point where the fat lady sang. The one who eventually did sing was the Old Lady of Threadneedle Street.

D URING THE SEVENTEENTH century another north European nation state was about to make its important pioneering steps in creditary progress. Again, it was now whole nations, rather than single city states, which were taking the creditary lead. Only two hundred years previously, Plantagenet England had still floundered well beyond the Pale in financial improbity. Under its Tudor monarchs however, a much better understanding of disciplined financial management came into vogue.

An important profession which benefited from England's financial enlightenment was that of scrivener. In the Elizabethan era they were the professionals who provided all variety of legal services, from handwriting and title searches to conveyancing and mortgage-broking. In London, scriveners also accepted cash deposits from provincial merchants and ran private accounts for them. By the 17th century specialist 'money-scriveners' were adapting their expertise in property to handle complicated financial transactions.

One such firm, Clayton and Morris, was founded in 1658, a year after the Bank of Stockholm. The firm was to enjoy considerable prominence for the next thirty years and its accounts have survived. Its business was established quickly and developed with aplomb. The earliest-surviving English cheque, for the very substantial sum of £400 [3], was drawn on Clayton and Morris on 16 February 1659. The firm's surviving account books for 1677 reveal its total deposits had already topped £1.8 million [4].

England's commercial acumen set in motion by Sir Thomas Gresham a hundred years earlier was beginning to bear fruit. Once again the economic stimulus was the cost of war. While Europe was embroiled in its regional conflicts, England under the Stuarts inflicted much the same burdens on itself.

The Civil War, the Commonwealth, Cromwell's ventures in Ireland and then the Restoration all put government finances under great strain. Although the merchant sector was proceeding apace, the way in which Stuart monarchs restored their depleted Government coffers was still far from enlightened. '*Traditionally the shortage was made up by an unedifying combination of selling land, confiscation and dishonouring debts.*' [5] Such unbecoming financial etiquette was to have one final fling.

From the early 1600s, London goldsmiths were a linchpin in its financial expertise. Like the scriveners, they adopted the banking techniques of northern Italy, accepting deposits from a wealthy clientele. As with Clayton and Morris, both scriveners and goldsmiths allowed their customers to write 'drawn notes'

---

3. *Equivalent to over £80,000 in 21st century money.*

4. *Equivalent to over £360 million in 21st century money.*

5. *Edwin Green, in the* Illustrated History of Banking

authorising payments on their behalf, the origin of cheques. The goldsmiths also circulated 'running notes' drawn on the bank's own account, rather than on the account of a customer.

W ITHOUT MUCH ADO, a huge step forward in creditary expertise was about to emerge. Running notes could circulate, and so long as they did so no-one cashed the cheque. The inscription began to use a standardised terminology: '*I promise to pay*'. These new notes, which some scriveners also began to copy, slowly developed as a form of currency among merchants in the London market. The credit-manufacturing banks of early Renaissance Italy had now taken up residence in northern Europe's rapidly-emerging financial centre of London, and its bankers were improving their art continuously.

Like their Italian predecessors, London's goldsmiths grew rich and successful on the proceeds, and successive kings and governments turned to them increasingly for loans. Prominent among them was Edward Backwell, the '*great money man*' according to the indefatigable Samuel Pepys. During Cromwell's Commonwealth, Backwell built a tidy business taking money deposits from other goldsmiths and then lending them on to the Treasury. The ledgers of his business survive, which explains why he is sometimes hailed as the father of English banking.

With the restoration of Charles II in 1660, an era of financial exuberance dawned in London, matching that in Sweden under his near-contemporary, Charles X. The year after Charles returned to the throne in Britain was the same year Stockholm issued its first banknotes. Baltic merchants in London cannot have taken long to brandish their smart new creditary instruments among their competitors and customers around the financial district of London.

In England the economic rebound from Cromwell's austere Commonwealth was robust. Even such calamities as the Great Plague in 1665 and the Great Fire of London in 1666 failed to arrest progress. In the midst of it all, in 1665 King Charles's Treasury introduced 'Orders of Payment' which government departments used to make purchases. They were a financial hybrid : the logic of royal tally sticks combined with the latest Swedish idea of circulating official bits of paper.

King Charles's Treasury allowed its payment orders to be assigned, or transferable, thus making them all the more popular among potential purchasers. As ever, the ability to offload a debt to someone else before it matures serves as a powerful marketing tool. In effect 'the order of payment' of 1665 thus became the ancestor of Treasury Bills, still used on a large scale today to enable the government to borrow funds, not from one particular lender, but from the financial market at large.

The city's goldsmiths, who were by then accustomed to their own system of running notes, another form of transferable debt, bought the innovative Government chits in large volumes. The two did not seem all that different.

As so often happens in the evolution of debt and credit, early success ran away with the system. The goldsmiths would have done well to heed the London misfortunes of the Italian Medicis back in the reign of Edward IV. By 1671, six years after introducing its new paper, the government found itself unable to honour over £2 million of debt, and declared a 'Stop of the Exchequer' on any orders not repayable from specified future revenue. In short, the king welshed on his debts.

MAYHEM ENSUED IN the City of London. Many of its goldsmiths were ruined. Among them Backwell just about survived and struggled along in a small way for a further ten years. The goldsmiths who did survive, or re-invented themselves, began to emerge as private banks. Lending to a larger number of individuals was a much safer bet than lending to a single borrower such as an unreliable sovereign government. Then as now, a prudent banker will always spread his risks, he does not concentrate them.

The son of a successful horse dealer, Richard Hoare, had been apprenticed to a goldsmith in 1665. In 1672 and with the financial disruption of the previous year conveniently behind him, he was made a Freeman of the Goldsmith's Company. That accolade entitled him to keep his own ledgers. Timing is everything, and in 1673 Richard Hoare took over the established business of Robert Tempest, a beleaguered goldsmith in Cheapside and turned it into a bank.

By way of identification, Hoare hung a leather bottle over his door, and Hoare's sign of the Golden Bottle has survived ever since becoming one of the oldest corporate logos in the world. Hoare's earliest surviving daily Cash Book is that of 1677-78. Payments and receipts on behalf of customers totalled £78,000, loans and repayments were £16,000 and the purchase and sale of goldsmith's wares £11,000. The business cost just £499 [6] to run for the twelve months to 21 July. It was still some way behind the scrivener firm of Clayton and Morris just around the corner, but Hoare's was destined to survive and prosper.

6. *Again, around £100,000 in modern money*

Other private banks emerged in London from the debris of the 'Stop of the Exchequer' debacle. Child and Co began banking in 1673. Coutts was established by John Campbell in 1692. Somewhat later, others like Martins (founded in 1712) and Glyns (1753) chose the City of London money market as their base, where they could specialise in discounting Bills of Exchange and currency trading. A couple of miles to the West, banks such as Hoares, Childs and Coutts preferred the West End of London where their regular customers were aristocrats, politicians and prosperous office-holders.

During the century following London's financial disaster of 1671, a private banking sector evolved which was to provide Britain's wealthy citizens with the most sophisticated financial services available anywhere in the world. By 1770 there were fifty private banks in London. Between them, London's scriveners and goldsmiths had inadvertently spawned an innovative and powerful industry, partly aided by the dishonesty of King Charles II - yet another useful rogue of creditary history.

The new banking sector gave Britain's rich, and its aristocracy, far greater liquidity in managing their assets, by contrast with their counterparts in continental Europe; their wealth was still locked in country estates. That liquidity enabled Britain's social elite both to mastermind, and to deliver pump-priming finance for, the Industrial Revolution. They all invested at home. Much more recently that provides a model which today's Third World plutocrats would do well to observe.

Before the seventeenth century was out, England devised two more new weapons for its remarkable creditary armoury. Once again the stimulus was the expense of war. After the 'Glorious Revolution' of 1688, the protestant Prince William of

Orange was crowned king in 1689. He brought with him, or encouraged, some of the financial expertise of his native country. The Dutch influence around the rest of Europe was still pervasive, just as it had been in Sweden.

King William pursued the deposed King James to Ireland, defeating him at the Battle of the Boyne in 1690, and at much greater expense went to war with France. King Billy needed money quickly and in large quantities. Sadly for him the British Treasury was woefully depleted. It was a situation tailor-made for an ambitious Scots entrepreneur, William Paterson.

His main preoccupation was to create a Scottish colony somewhere, almost anywhere in fact. Eventually his dream took shape in Panama, in the disastrous Darien project of 1698. It became a nightmare which brought financial Scotland to its knees, impoverished its wealthy and was to lead directly to Scotland's begging bowl Act of Union with England of 1707. Fortunately for William Paterson, another of his financial wheezes bore fruit first, just a few years before his entrepreneurial reputation was reduced to tatters.

FAMOUSLY, IN 1694 HE WON the enthusiastic support for another of his bright ideas from the cash-strapped Charles Montagu, Chancellor of the Exchequer.

Together with a group of fellow 'projectors', he formed a corporation which he grandly called "The Governor and Company of the Bank of England".

Over four hundred years later the same statement of authority is emblazoned on every British banknote. From the outset the new bank was a joint-stock enterprise, quite the latest thing. Its novelty was that of selling shares to the public to finance a bank, something that had never been done before. That innovation promptly raised the issue of who felt directly responsible for the prudent management of the enterprise. It is far less disconcerting to take untoward risks with other people's money, a shortcoming of joint-stock banking still recognisable in the twenty-first century.

The initial capital for the new bank of £1.2 million[7] was fully subscribed by some 1,272 shareholders - although that modern term was not yet in use - in just twelve days. Paterson's public joint stock Bank of England met with clamorous opposition from London's private goldsmith-bankers. The whole idea of a government bank was objectionable to them, and an anonymous joint stock bank to boot. Prominent among the many objectors was Richard Hoare, who resorted to the growing fashion for pamphlets to publicise his opposing views.

It was all to no avail. The financial straits of the government were too great, and the embryo central bank was here to stay. It proved to be another vital step in the origin of economies. The bank's Royal Charter even required goldsmiths to discontinue issuing their 'drawn notes'. So the ancestors of cheques were promptly banned. That drove most goldsmiths to lodge their gold with the Bank of England instead. The Bank soon provided loans which funded war with France until the Treaty of Rijswijk in 1697.

Not surprisingly, Britain's new central bank quickly proved to be a very profitable enterprise and the idea was soon imitated elsewhere. Already by 1695, a Bank of Scotland had

7. *About £240 million in modern money. As with the all the other inflation adjustments shown in this chapter, they have been obtained using the Bank of England's very helpful on-line Inflation Calculator.*

been founded. Cautious to a degree, Scotland's politicians required all the joint stock proprietors of their Edinburgh establishment to be naturalised Scots, and it was specifically forbidden to lend to the state.

South of the border there was no such constraint. The Bank of England was not just a source of loans to support hefty government spending. It also arranged the flow of payments to the army in Europe, accepted and paid Bills of Exchange for commercial customers and permitted its 'sealed bills' to be used by the Treasury as payment for government spending. It opened bank accounts for private citizens - as it still does today, on a small scale - most notably the goldsmith-bankers of London.

THE BANK OF ENGLAND avoided the pitfalls which had befallen similar enterprises elsewhere, most prominently in Sweden. Maybe its pattern of business had a lot to do with that. The most important of its activities was not selling new debt, but dealing in existing commercial bills, the widely popular Bills of Exchange.

Until something as prestigious as a London Accepting House had confirmed that a businessman's IOU was good enough to be transferred to other creditors through the market, it was just another piece of paper with no third party value.

Yet once it had been 'accepted' it could be bought by the Bank - in other words exchanged for a different and more popular kind of IOU, the bank's own banknotes - and thereby it became as good as money. Buying in acceptable commercial debt paper to improve liquidity was one of the Bank of England's most important activities. It undertook to do so even *in extremis*, serving as the 'Lender of Last Resort'.

However there was a price to be paid. The Bank levied a deliberate premium, in effect a penalty rate of interest, which was above interest rates ruling elsewhere in the City of London. It became known as the 'Bank Rate'. Through various financial transmogrifications and its tragic misuse in the latter half of the twentieth century, the Bank Rate has retained the same name for most of the past three hundred years.

Where Sweden had failed with its banknotes some forty years earlier, the Bank of England succeeded. Modelling its system with care on the success formula of London's goldsmiths, the Bank was issuing its own 'running notes' from its inception in July 1694. The earliest to have survived is dated 1699, number twelve of the series. Its wording reflected that used by the goldsmiths and matches that appearing on every British banknote to this day. The Bank's Chief Cashier '*promises to pay on behalf of the Governor and Company of the Bank of England*'.

The surviving 1699 Bank of England note has two other distinctive features. Modern banknotes are denominated in small and round sums. This earliest of English banknotes is made out for the astonishing sum of £555 [8] - more than eleven times the face value of any British banknote in modern times.

Although the Bank did eventually issue £1 notes from 1797, it was again banned from doing so in 1825. Even after the Bank had been in business for over a century its banknotes were still far from being a currency for the common man. Like almost all creditary innovations down the ages, they began their existence as a system tailor-made to the specific requirements of prosperous merchants, whose commercial activities meant they had to uphold a creditworthy reputation.

------

8. *In excess of £100,000 today.*

There is also a significant clue to be found on this rare survivor from 1699. Its detail inscription reads: *' I promise to pay to Thomas Powell or bearer . . .'* Thus is revealed the true nature of a British banknote. In essence, it was a bank cheque made out to one Thomas Powell, or any of his chums. The 'payment' which the Bank of England promised was nothing more than recording an entry in a bank account. It is not, and never was, an entitlement to receive gold coins, bullion or indeed anything tangible.

LIKE THE PIONEERING CLAY tablets of Sumer, the Bank of England banknote was debt in the abstract. Small wonder that so many nineteenth century economists found the system difficult to comprehend, and even more difficult to accept. This was no ordinary cheque, however. Like the banker's draft (known as a cashier's check in the US) which enjoys such popularity in Britain's secondhand motor trade, it is not a cheque drawn on the personal account of a customer at the bank.

Rather it is drawn by the bank itself on its own account, a running note issued by a central bank. As is so often said by secondhand car salesmen, *'a Banker's Draft is just as good as money'*. To be more precise, most everyday money is in fact simply a mass-produced, durable Banker's Draft. There is no fooling a creditary economist.

The true banknote has one further peculiarity. The cheque is not made out to anyone in particular, but to 'bearer'. We are back to the game of 'pass the parcel' invented by Sumerian merchants almost 4,000 years earlier. It is an artifice which makes the Bank of England the clear winner. In principle the Bank is always willing to honour its Chief Cashier's cheque but in practice it hardly ever gets round to doing so. Instead each bearer, or creditor, simply offloads the bank's IOU onto someone else in payment of another and subsequent debt.

Most people would be quite delighted if one of their own cheques went uncashed just once in a while. The Bank of England does it all the time, and the permanent gain is called seigniorage; perhaps giving it a French name makes it sound less contentious. By agreement, the Bank then hands over its welcome windfall to the government to spend.

No-one familiar with the limitless spendthrift capabilities of governments will be remotely surprised by that. If anyone ever attempted to claim back the 'seigniorage' from the government and its tame bank, all they would ever receive would be another cheque. The purchasing power with which the public originally bought the freshly-issued banknotes has been spent, and is gone for ever.

Normally it is only commercial banks which return quantities of banknotes to the Bank of England to exercise that 'Promise to pay'. Even then, they typically do so only to swap notes that are worn out for newly-minted replacements. Sometimes a bank will pay large bundles of spare cash into the Bank of England, at which point the Bank does actually honour its 'promise to pay'. It marks a credit to the account of its customer in its ledgers. That is all the Bank's 'Promise' involves.

Such a transaction would not be open to anyone or any organisation without an account at the Bank of England. Just the same goes for any ordinary cheque; it depends on having an account at the bank on which it is drawn. So when Britons cheerfully circulate Bank of England banknotes, they are handling cheques which they would not be permitted to cash themselves.

The logic of banknotes was to be neatly demonstrated by the Irish in 1970. During a four month strike by its banks, much of Ireland's commerce survived by the simple expedient of circulating 'uncashed' cheques. The Irish, adroit innovators of creditary logic, were manufacturing and using homemade banknotes. By dint of circumstance the Irish also re-discovered a delightful bonus for any central bank. Like anyone else issuing them, uncashed cheques are always a bonus in the issuer's pocket.

THE BENEFIT TO THE Bank of England of issuing banknotes, indeed the benefit to any issuing bank, is substantial. Already by 1699 the total value of its 'running notes', its perpetually circulating uncashed cheques, had already passed £1.3 million and by 1720 was approaching £2.5 million. By 2013 it had topped £54 billion, in other words approaching £1,000 for every man, woman and child in the country.

That constitutes a whopping interest-free gift from the note-holding public to the British government. Originally, banknotes did pay a small rate of interest to acknowledge that 'loan'. It all sounds almost too good to be true but the irreversible bonus to bank and government is not entirely free. It is offset by the substantial cost of printing a billion or so new high security banknotes each year.

For all that, the principal business of the Bank of England in its early years was not in banknotes, but in Bills of Exchange. This remained true for well over a century and into the Victorian era. The Bank of England's much-vaunted Bank Rate is definitely not a price to strike a balance between supply and demand somewhere in the economy. Strictly speaking the 'interest rate' is just a rake-off the Bank demands for discounting, or buying in first class Bills of Exchange. So it began life as a calculation of business risk, and has remained so ever since.

The bank rate has never been a market-clearing price, despite the belief of many twentieth century economists that should be its function. As late as 1844, that perceptive observer Thomas Tooke was to point out that accepted Bills of Exchange accounted for 90 per cent of circulation, and Bank of England notes only for the remaining 10 per cent.

BILLS OF EXCHANGE begin as simple trade debt, a commercial agreement between two businesses. These private IOUs were then endorsed by an 'Acceptance House' to make them generally acceptable. Unlike a crude IOU, Bills of Exchange followed a formalised structure which then enabled them to circulate. It is almost certain the merchants of Sumer had a similar system 4000 years earlier, albeit recorded on clay rather than on paper. Like Sumer's clay tablet, London's Bills of Exchange passed from hand to hand among businessmen, and at each exchange they were endorsed anew. The lengthening list of such endorsements steadily increased their acceptability in and around the financial marketplace.

Sophisticated financial machinery of the City of London grew up around Bills of Exchange and the original function of the Bank Rate was to underpin the system. Yet in the 20th century, this simple yet effective financial instrument for all forms of commerce fell out of fashion, as did local stock exchanges. Instead the commercial banks took over the rôle of providing business finance with their overdrafts and loans, but that in turn is beginning to fade.

The cost of a paying a bank bureaucracy to run its nationwide, and even international, business places a heavy claim on any income generated by local accounts. Corporate banking which deals in very large numbers makes more commercial sense. Individual banking dealing in much smaller numbers - yet where the management task of assessing a borrower's creditworthiness is every bit as great - arguably does not.

So is the creditary principle turning a corner once again in the twenty-first century?   It would be logical for Bills of Exchange, in an updated, electronic form, along with a local stock exchange to make a comeback. The Acceptance House function, though electronic, would greatly benefit from being local. A revitalised system of Bills of Exchange could go a long way to meeting complaints about unenthusiastic banks reluctant to lend to small businesses, complaints[9] which became increasingly widespread as the twentieth century progressed. If all that such enterprises require is working capital - and that is usually the case - suitably endorsed, negotiable Bills of Exchange could well be just what they need.

Like the tally sticks which had preceded them, Bills of Exchange proved to be an essential part of the very ingenious creditary system which effectively launched the Industrial Revolution. They provided a simple way for traders and merchants to convert their cobweb of credits and debts back into working capital. Bills of Exchange ensured that credit generated in the financial marketplace was fed back into productive commerce of the economy, rather than disappearing into the

9. *As the first specialist Director for Smaller Firms of the Confederation of British Industry, the author frequently encountered this complaint. Large banks and small firms with a strictly local credit reputation, do not mix.*

unproductive maw of asset price inflation. It was an effective system which provided its users with short-term finance, but a long-term equivalent was also required.

The solution to that also arrived with William of Orange. His entourage introduced a distinctly Dutch influence to the commercial practices of London. The change was one for the better, for Holland had much to offer. In the view of Adam Smith, writing over eighty years later, '*Holland, in proportion to the extent of land and the number of its inhabitants, is by far the richest country in Europe.*' One of the ways the Dutch had built their business enterprise was through trading in shares. It is paradoxical that Smith admired the result but vehemently opposed the means.

It had been essential to spread the daunting risk of running the massive Dutch East India Company. Now they were to teach the English how to do it. Encouraged by the government of Queen Elizabeth a century earlier, Sir Thomas Gresham had imported the low countries invention of a bourse into London. It had not been an unqualified success.

Until the arrival of the Dutch, trading in issued shares in England was dominated by those of just three companies: the Hudson's Bay Company, the Africa Company and the British East India Company. The shares were difficult to obtain. A petition to King Charles II in 1681 complained that the profits of the last were kept in very few hands. Its modest issue of just 550 shares was held away from the market by only about forty people.

The arrival of Dutch entrepreneurs quickly changed all that. Their familiarity with broking techniques stimulated London's joint stock enterprises. By the time the (joint stock) Bank of England was founded five years later in 1694, shares in at least fifty-three companies, in all kinds of businesses, were already being traded vigorously. Harsh financial lessons were soon learnt and three years later legislation was introduced to restrain any malpractice by brokers.

Under King William, London soon discovered how an anglicised bourse could breed a commercial, and much later an industrial, economy of entirely new enterprises, yet already another cloud was on a not so distant horizon. Creditary advances only rarely make smooth progress.

THE SUCCESS OF THE Bank of England had naturally invited imitation elsewhere in Europe, and not just in Scotland. Where the Scots adapted the powerful new banking machinery with great caution, across the Channel the French were inveigled into doing quite the reverse. And the man who did it as another Scot.

As Europe's nation states jostled for power and influence, France's Louis XIV ran up huge debts in his wars with the Spanish, the Dutch, the Germans and eventually the British. More money went on his grandiose projects. Louis's palaces at Versailles and the Louvre, testimony to his extravagance, were dauntingly expensive.

By the time the sun king died in 1715, the French state was in debt to the tune of almost three billion livres, a sum dwarfing its annual revenues of just 80 million livres. It was a treasury problem closely matching that of Sweden half a century earlier. France's indebtedness created a golden opportunity for an ingenious Scots entrepreneur; another creditary rogue.

The man who sprang to France's rescue was John Law, a habitual advocate of institutional answers to awkward financial problems. Under his guidance, the Ferme General was given the task of collecting direct taxes, while the French Compagnie des Indes was reorganised as a state monopoly for overseas trade.

So far so good, but John Law's third innovation for the French was much less successful. Just twenty-two years after his compatriot William Paterson peddled his proposal for a Bank of England to the government in London, Law did the same with the government in Paris.

John Law's Banque General was founded as a private company in 1716. While Paterson's creation in London had to wait a whole 250 years before it was nationalised, Law's new bank in Paris achieved as much in two. In 1718 it became a state monopoly with the new title of Banque Royale.

In an attempt to revive the French economy, the Banque began to issue banknotes on a prodigious scale. It had observed London's success, and its motto was evidently "whatever the British can do, we can do better." In 1719 nearly a billion livres were issued in banknotes, and by October 1720 the total had risen to 2.7 billion, when the Bank of England across the Channel restricted itself to a total of just £2.5 million.

At such short notice there was nowhere constructive to place finance on such a scale; the regular economy had no use for it. Instead the credit was pumped by investors into the shares of existing enterprises such as Compagnie des Indes. A flood of credit instruments from the Banque Royale fuelled a Europe-wide stampede for joint stock shares as their prices escalated.

Funds from as far afield as Amsterdam and Switzerland streamed into the shares of London's South Sea Company. Shares in France's Compagnie des Indes, in which John Law had a large personal stake, rose to stratospheric values. On paper at least he briefly became the richest man on earth.

THE BUBBLE BURST, INEVITABLY, in August 1720. Share prices slumped in both England and France. Holdings in the Compagnie des Indes became practically worthless, and by November the banknotes of the Banque Royale ceased to be legal tender. Palmstruch's Swedish flirtation with such potent pieces of paper had lasted three years. John Law's flirtation in Paris had lasted just two.

The South Sea Bubble was only the first such stampede driven by a credit expansion, and certainly not the last. The easier it is to create credit, the more difficult it is to control. The lessons are still being learnt two centuries later.

Not all the originators of economic practice made a constructive contribution. Sometimes their development was disastrous. John Law was forced out of France and died in poverty in 1729. For an adventurer in the very deceptive business of banking, it was ironic that he should expire in Venice where it had all begun. It was to be another 80 years before his dreams of a unified French financial system were fulfilled. The much more respectable Banque de France was eventually formed in 1800, several years after the Revolution.

Despite the catastrophe of its South Sea Bubble, London's business in joint stock companies recovered and continued to expand. Traders on its venerable Royal Exchange, however, were a boisterous lot and eventually chucked out. They had to find new meeting places and the coffee houses of the City of London were all to keen to win the business. In 1760 a club was formed by 150 stock brokers at Jonathan's Coffee House in the City of London. The trading of joint stock companies begun in the reign of King Billy had now come of age. Within thirteen years, the coffee house club of traders in shares was renamed the London Stock Exchange, in 1773.

CENTRAL BANKING AND paper banknotes had been the twin creditary innovations of the seventeenth century. Their eighteenth century sequel was orderly trading in the equity of joint stock companies, an achievement which in Britain took two hundred years. Together they created a sophisticated creditary infrastructure which was about to give birth to the Industrial Revolution.

The eighteenth century was a period of proliferation in finance. In 1765 Frederick the Great of Prussia authorised a note-issuing bank, the Königliche Giro und Lehnbanco. Its success was limited because Frederick declined to deposit his own treasury funds with it.   Fifteen years later the Anspach-Bayreuth bank was established and served as the royal Treasury as well as a credit institution. It did survive, eventually to become the forerunner of the modern Bayrische Vereinsbank.

Britain's financial services industry fostered by the private banks of London was coming of age. Beyond the charmed circle of the City, financial expertise was expanding in another direction, to parts of the country well distant from the financial hothouse of the City. The development can be traced back to the drovers, those entrepreneurial herdsmen who moved live cattle from the countryside to big markets like London. Long before refrigeration, droving was the only way to transport fresh meat. To this day, there are many traditional tracks across moorland and open country still known as 'drover's roads.'

The finances of a successful drover business were, of necessity, quite complicated. He bought animals from farmers, drove them to market, sold them for their meat value and only then made any money. From such mercantile activity in the provinces emerged the 'country banks'. One such, popularly known as the Black Ox bank, was founded in Llandovery by David Jones, a former drover, in 1799. It began life in the town's King's Head pub which still displays fascinating records of the enterprise.

As David Jones and Co it remained in the family over four generations and when its goodwill was eventually sold to Lloyds in 1909 it was to be the last surviving private bank in Wales. As its modern corporate logo shows, Lloyds was to become the Black Horse, rather than the black ox, bank.

The private provincial banks were a key component of Britain's creditary structure in the Victorian era. Provided they were at least 65 miles from London they were permitted to issue their own banknotes. They met the needs of wealthy and financially literate people living 'in the provinces.' Banking was no longer an esoteric expertise restricted to London's Square Mile and the Strand.

In 1765 the ironmaster Samuel Lloyd teamed up with button manufacturer John Taylor to found a banking firm in Birmingham. It grew to become the principal ancestor of Lloyds Bank. Ten years later the Gurney family began banking in Norwich, opened branches throughout East Anglia. No doubt some of their early customers were Norfolk's turkey drovers, whose annual drive of 'bootiful birds' to London was a regular tourist sight in East Anglia; the birds were fitted with bootees to protect their feet on hard roads. In due course the Gurney family bank became a principal component of Barclays.

The eighteenth century's financial progress reached far beyond the shores of Europe. Across the Atlantic, another economic thoroughbred entered the creditary stakes for the first time. America had been the destination of sixteenth century colonists, notably into Virginia and into the extensive French territory of Louisiana in its South. They introduced a more backward-looking, class-driven vision of society, its economic structure too reliant on the barbarous slave trade from West Africa.

Conflict between Europe's catholics and protestants in the sixteenth century then generated a very different prospect for America. It eventually came to a head in 1620 when just one hundred Puritan dissidents sailed to America in the Mayflower. In retrospect perhaps no other ship in history has increased its complement of passengers quite so astonishingly down the years that followed. If modern American family history is to be believed, there must have thousands of them clinging aboard.

THE PILGRIM FATHERS may certainly have '*yearned to breathe free*'. But they were anything but '*the tired, the poor, the huddled masses, the wretched refuse of your teeming shore*' celebrated by Emma Lazarus in her sonnet at the Statue of Liberty. The Pilgrim Fathers were well-educated folk, versed in the value and the pitfalls of financial affairs, just as they were conversant with many other structures of Jacobean England.

In the early years, the New England settlers adopted the money and the methods they had known in the old country. There was little resource available in the new towns of New England, however, to replicate the London trade of goldsmith - certainly not enough to satisfy the needs of a rapidly-expanding agricultural economy. The colonists had to develop a different creditary method to finance their commercial enterprise.

Even before the Bank of England was founded or issued its first banknotes, the Commonwealth of Massachusetts had already circulated its own paper currency. The state decided that money should be issued exclusively by a central authority to represent the interests of the whole people. Knowingly or not, the structure adopted much the same philosophy proposed for Athens by Xenophon just about two millennia previously.

His vision, however, would have been based on using gold and silver coins. Theirs used a much cheaper material. The paper money of Massachusetts became full legal tender on 2 July 1692, two years before the first Bank of England banknote. It could be used to pay all debts, public and private. It was used to finance public spending and public works. It was lent by the state Treasury to private citizens at a low rate of interest.

Unlike the banknotes which were shortly to appear in London, or the banknotes which had already appeared - albeit briefly - in Sweden, New England's money was strictly a paper proxy for gold or silver. If anything, the monetary system devised by the New England colonists had more in common with the paper money of the Ming dynasty in China, and their predecessors, than anything seen in London. It was not a beefed-up cheque, some abstract token of indebtedness created within the banking system.

These prototype American bills of currency were circulated, and were also loaned out, exactly as if they had been chunks of gold or silver. The government revenue they generated, seigniorage, enabled taxes to be much reduced. Better yet, the state as a whole paid no external interest for the creditary medium which was fuelling its economy. Other American territories were quickly to copy the example set by Massachusetts, and the practice ushered in a period of unrivalled prosperity for colonial America. London noted, it seems with some concern, the financial and economic autonomy which America's novel creditary system was creating. The Bank of England in particular was perturbed by the way its recently-won dominant monopoly was being usurped.

From about 1720 onwards, the Bank persuaded the British Parliament to suppress all colonial money. That led to years of defiance in America, which came to a head in 1749 when the London Parliament passed the Resumption Act. It required all contracts and taxes to London to be paid in gold or silver. Bullion was so scarce in North America that the results were economically disastrous. A deep depression ensued. Prices fell and trade stagnated.

THE POLICY WAS ECONOMIC oppression, and became a fuse to America's revolutionary wars. Britain compounded its folly by backing yet another Bank of England brainwave, this time demanding that the colonies borrow 'bank notes' from it, at a price. The Chancellor of the Exchequer in Pitt the Elder's government, Charles Townshend, followed with his ill-considered series of American import levies known as the Townshend Acts. The aim was to obtain revenue from the colonies through tariffs on their imports of glass, lead, paints, paper and tea.

The merchants of Boston boycotted English goods in protest. Their maxim of "no taxation without representation" has echoed down the centuries ever since. There followed the legendary economic and then military conflict between London and America, with British troops sent to enforce its extortionate laws. That led to the Boston Massacre, more boycotts, and the forced repeal in 1770 of all the Townsend Acts save that on tea, which was retained to bolster the precarious finances of Britain's East India Company.

America's economic problems were not solved immediately by victory in its wars with the British, nor by its Declaration of Independence. The new Congress began issuing paper money without any particular limitation on quantity, least of all any link to quantities of precious metal. These 'continental' dollars soon inflated into oblivion. It was financial recklessness which almost destroyed the infant United States of America.

The New England states grew so antagonistic towards the conduct of financial affairs that they threatened to secede from the Union. The American Constitution was drafted in 1788 in a bid to rescue the situation.   There was to be no more hyperinflation. Jefferson made sure the great document embodied a gold and silver standard in explicit terms, set out in Article One, Section 10. There it languishes to this day.

In the midst of all this, Adam Smith wrote his *Wealth of Nations*. It took him thirteen years, on and off. Famously, it was published in the same year as the American Declaration of Independence. Historically, it was surrounded by extraordinary economic change.

When the book eventually appeared in 1776, London's Stock Exchange was still only three years old. It is hardly surprising that Smith had few words to say about joint stock companies, and those that he did were disparaging. Smith's grasp of the industrial system was sound but circumscribed, inevitably so given the times in which he was writing. He had a sensible grasp of the division of labour in a factory system, even though his first-hand experience of it must have been limited.

The Industrial Revolution, which Smith's twentieth century disciples sometimes appear to believe he invented, was barely into its stride. Even now we are probably only half way through it. Small wonder his primitive economics, though inspired, provided a less than adequate explanation of what was to unfold in the twentieth century. Richard Arkwright's innovations in the textile industry were just seven years old, the spinning jenny of James Hargreaves was just two.

Only the year before *Wealth of Nations* appeared, Boulton and Watt had opened their Soho Mint in Birmingham. The cheap mass-produced British coinage which it was to make possible, so important to the financial needs of ordinary folk, was still 40 years into the future. During the second half of the 18th century, very little silver or copper coinage at all was minted in Britain. Smith wrote his book in a world which still regularly used tally sticks and traded them in secondary markets.

DURING THE 18TH CENTURY the Industrial Revolution built its early momentum by producing high quality consumer durables. Their market was among the wealthy. There was no master plan, nor any significant preconception of what was eventually to happen. The key was a trickle-down permeation through the class, and wealth, structure of British society. The evolution of pottery and porcelain, one of the easiest to track, well illustrates the principle.

Within a period of fifty years pottery manufacture moved from being a localised folk craft to re-invent itself as an international, branded quality product.

Following their independence from Spain, the Dutch had been quick off the mark with their Delft pottery. Dutch potters came to London in the wake of William of Orange after 1688. London Delft dates from 1705, Lambeth Delft and Bristol Delft from not much later. Staffordshire pottery, an early portent of what was shortly to happen on the upper River Trent, and still does, dates from around 1697.

The next stage was to import far eastern technology. The porcelain expertise of China and Japan found its way into Europe, most notably to Meissen, which became Europe's greatest porcelain factory. It started manufacturing in 1709. Then the know-how reached Britain in the wake of another notable German export, the royal House of Hanover

Britain's leading eighteenth century porcelain producer was Chelsea, opened in 1745. Porcelain became the preference of royalty, so Royal Worcester in England and Sevres in France were established to meet the inevitable demand that generated among the aristocracy. Then in 1759 Josiah Wedgwood in Stoke-on-Trent transformed the potteries of Britain and beyond, developing his mass-produced yet stylish pottery for the middle classes. Other traditional trades followed a similar pattern.

Before the Restoration, the best domestic furniture in England had been made from solid oak. All that changed with the invention of veneers, the use of decorative wood especially walnut, and the influence of 17th century designers such as Grinling Gibbons. Wars in Europe cut off the supply of walnut. A substitute, mahogany from Cuba and the West Indies, changed

fashion for the next two centuries. Thomas Chippendale's
furniture designs were published from 1754, to be followed by
those of Sheraton and Hepplewhite. They gave birth to an
important new industry, that of the cabinet-maker.

In Sheffield, the invention of a bimetal substitute for solid
silver was brought about by the desire of the middle classes to
imitate the solid silver coat buttons of the rich, which they could
not afford. Such splendid fashions had supplanted the dowdy
puritanism of Cromwell's Commonwealth.

Thomas Boulsover made his 'invention' in 1743 when
repairing the handle of a decorative knife. He overheated it and
found its silver and copper had fused firmly together. So by
fusing a thin layer of silver onto a thick piece of copper then
rolling it out, Boulsover devised Old Sheffield Plate for his
button manufacture. His apprentice Joseph Hancock saw the
greater market potential, making articles such as silver tableware.

As early as 1762 Joseph Hancock established a water-
powered factory[10] solely to mass-produce Old Sheffield Plate as
a raw material for the town's silverware trades. It was one of the
first factories to specialise in an industrial semi-manufacture for
other businesses to use; another origin of economies.

Smith's division of labour was already dividing ever more
finely even ten years before his famous book was published. That
it could do so was testament to the financial flexibility of the
provincial banks. The family wealth generated from Sheffield's
renowned silverware trades helped pump-prime the city's steel
industry in the following century. Little or any of that was

10. See Mary Walton's Sheffield, Its Story and Achievements, published
in 1948. Hancock's Old Park Silver Mills, of which his father was the
managing director from 1949 onwards, was the company with which the author
grew up. Processing modern materials, it continued until the 1960s.

anticipated by Adam Smith in 1776. He had nothing to say about large-scale industrial enterprise. The labour-saving technology of mass production, that great invention of the middle industrial revolution was only beginning to take hold a century after his book was published. It never really occurred to him.

Nor did mass market consumerism with its advertising and marketing men in which the vast majority, not just the privileged few, would bathe in prosperity. The unprecedented advances beginning with steam power, then applying science, eventually using electricity to create the consumer society were beyond his wildest imagination.

A S WITH ANY OTHER MAN of his times, Smith found it nigh impossible to break free from a vision of society dominated by, and dedicated to serving, the ruling classes. He imagined that once the factory system had eventually *"accumulated its full complement of riches"* - all the pin factories, as it were, whose output could be absorbed by the needs of the rich - then *"economic decline would begin, ending in an impoverished stagnation."* [11]

Among Smith's circle of Scottish acquaintances was the inventor James Watt, just thirteen years his junior. Watt's first-hand experience of industry could have enlightened Smith on the realities and prospects of new industries. To exploit his prophetic understanding of steam technology, Watt wanted to establish a factory to build steam locomotives.

It would have been a far more costly enterprise than Smith's paradigm pin factory, and the emerging inventor was unable to raise the necessary funds from the banks. But for his

12. Encyclopaedia Britannica

severe misgivings about the newer methods of finance, Adam Smith might in turn have advised Watt how to raise money. Unlike his earlier compatriot William Paterson in 1694, Watt appears to have lacked the expertise, or the vital contacts and patronage, to form a joint stock company. In any case Adam Smith was deeply opposed to the stock exchange then emerging from the simple beginnings of Jonathan's coffee house.

Thwarted in his ambition to manufacture steam locomotives, Watt formed a partnership with the wealthy Matthew Boulton, to create the less costly Birmingham Mint. The steam age would have to wait a further fifty years.

WEALTH OF NATIONS was conceived amid the first green shoots of the Industrial Revolution, and it was written when much of the financial infrastructure was still too novel to be easily comprehended. The book is oddly ambivalent about paper currency, that notably success of the Massachusetts authorities. On the one hand, Smith had a slightly better grasp of its fundamentals than many of his academic successors, as he explained that *'the paper currencies of North America consisted, not in bank notes payable to the bearer on demand, but in a government paper, of which the payment was not eligible till several years after it was issued.'*

Having apparently understood it, however, Adam Smith took a bizarre dislike to America's sensible currency system. *"To oblige a creditor to accept of this as full payment for a debt of a hundred pounds actually paid down in ready money was an act of such violent injustice as has scarce, perhaps, been attempted by the government of any other country which pretended to be free. It bears the evident marks of having originally been a scheme of fraudulent debtors to cheat their creditors".* So much for one of the foundations of creditary economics. It was strong stuff indeed from the man hailed as the father of economics, and his hostility warrants closer investigation, particularly since it echoes so closely the bellicose policies of the emerging Bank of England.

Back in 1763 at the age of forty, Adam Smith had been persuaded to resign from the Chair of Moral Philosophy at Glasgow University, where he had taught for the previous thirteen years. His university post paid just £200 a year. The prominent politician, and future Chancellor of the Exchequer, Charles Townshend arranged for Smith to receive instead an income of £300 a year from the wealthy Buccleuch estate.

Townshend had married the recently-widowed Duchess of Buccleuch, and recruited Adam Smith to serve as tutor to the youthful new Duke and his younger brother. The Buccleuchs were among the greatest Scottish landowners, and Townshend had bought himself a bargain.

Smith promptly abandoned his vilification of Scotland's landed aristocracy. Instead he busied himself in his new rôle of tutor and accompanied his aristocratic protégés on the Grand Tour. Adam Smith found much of the travel tedious, although in Geneva he met and was much impressed by Voltaire. In Paris he met the Scottish philosopher David Hume, then a diplomat at the British embassy, who introduced Smith to the literary salons of the French Enlightenment.

There in turn he met the social reformers calling themselves Les Économistes led by Quesnay and Mirabeau, better known since as the Physiocrats. François Quesnay's groundbreaking *Tableau Economique* had recently been published, in 1758.   Its influence on *Wealth of Nations,* although not unbounded, is readily evident. Had Quesnay not died in the meantime, Smith would have dedicated his own book to him. The Physiocrats believed in the existence of a natural order, regarding the state's rôle as simply that of preserving property, and advocated free trade rather than the interventionist ideas recommended by their adversaries, the mercantilists. This much Smith largely accepted.

He was less impressed by the Physiocratic notion that agriculture was the only source of true wealth.   As the 18th century progressed another and greater source of wealth, manufacturing industry, was becoming ever more evident in Britain, rather more so than in France. Adam Smith's views on that prospect were semi-prophetic.

ONE MAY WELL CONTEMPLATE what ideas passed between Smith and his patron Charles Townshend. It is hard to believe a Chancellor of the Exchequer would not seek some insight from the philosopher and emerging economist he had just recruited to tutor his stepsons. Just four years after employing Adam Smith, Townshend embarked on his disastrous clutch of Parliamentary Acts in 1767 which did so much to precipitate the secession of the American colonies.

It would have been patently churlish, and probably damaging to his own livelihood, for Smith to disparage Townshend's disastrous policies in public. Whatever he thought privately, it was later the view of Benjamin Franklin, ambassador to London, that banning the colonial paper currency had been a prime cause of the American Wars of Independence. Yet

Franklin also had something of an axe to grind. Together with his brother he owned a printing company producing the paper currency, and in 1729 published a pamphlet to recommend it.

So there may yet be grounds for postponing the canonisation of Adam Smith. He was surrounded by pre-steam age technology and that inevitably restricted his vision. In his day, horse-powered canals were quite the latest thing; windmills for grinding corn were the norm. The 'dark satanic mills' were almost all driven by water wheels.

It was in the sphere of creditary economics that Smith was at his weakest; he believed economics should be entirely mechanical, an amoral calculus. He could not grasp the emerging devices of sophisticated finance. In part that is illustrated by his ill-willed and seemingly absolute rejection of the sensible paper currency devised in the American colonies.

In an era when moral philosophy was all the rage - he himself wrote a Theory Of The Moral Sentiments published in 1759 - he failed to spot the quintessential morality which is to be found at the very heart of any creditary system. Adam Smith missed the simple truth that the financial techniques emerging all around him each ultimately served the same purpose. They were all just different creditary methods for absorbing risk and simultaneously recording and then trading debts between one man - or business enterprise - and another.

If only he had told his friend James Watt that joint stock businesses financed through the stock exchange might be a good idea. Watt could well have built his steam locomotive works half a century before George and Robert Stephenson marched into the global limelight. What then?

Chapter Six

1800 AD to 1900 AD

The Errors of a Wise Man make your Rule,
Rather than the Perfections of a Fool.
WILLIAM BLAKE, 1810

WHEN THE SAGA of economics reaches the nineteenth century it divides in two. In the material world the industrial revolution began to unfold at an unprecedented speed, most visibly in Great Britain. In the intellectual world, by contrast, developments were rather less convincing. English-speaking sages devised an anthology of inklings which is frequently referred to as 'classical economics'.

To help matters along, perhaps we should refine the conventional vocabulary. This book takes a purist approach: here "Classical' does not mean 'timeless' or 'perfected'. As an adjective to describe writings about economics from Adam Smith to approximately 1850, it is so used for the last time in the present book. Here the word 'Classical' is reserved for that remarkable civilisation which the Greeks - in a sweeping geographical sense - devised. The Romans then raised it to unprecedented levels of success but could not maintain the rate of positive progress. As always, economies like most other things must move one way or another, they rarely stay in the same place for very long.

By accident rather than design the Romans allowed 'Classical' civilisation to rot, especially in the West. Too many elementary financial mistakes were made, not that they were understood as such at the time; Chapter Four of this book examines the prolonged decline in more detail. Not for the last time, purely monetary phenomena were tragically confused with the products of the physical economy. It has been a recurring misconception ever since "money" was invented. Or to re-quote John Hume writing in 1742, "Money is none of the wheels of trade: it is the oil which renders the motion of the wheels more smooth and easy".

ALTHOUGH IT BECAME a model for many societies much later, Classical civilisation and its inspired ideas about philosophy, mathematics, democracy and governance gradually fizzled out in the half millennium after Christ. It was long gone by the time Mohammed made his appearance in the seventh century. In every realistic sense the Classical era was history.

The word itself deserves, in pursuit of clarity, to be reserved exclusively for that quite remarkable epoch. The tattered remnants of the Roman empire in the East survived in Constantinople where it stagnated, or worse. Eventually the city fell to the Ottomans in 1453. Some still see the Roman Catholic church as the empire's continuation in the West; the Pope, the vicar of Rome, is perhaps regarded as the spiritual successor to the western Emperor. More realistically, perhaps, the eastern half of the Roman empire became the Orthodox Christian church, rooted in Emperor Constantine's city of Constantinople, the earlier name of Istanbul [1].

However that was all a very different Roman civilisation from the one known to that founder of its Christian tradition, Constantine the Great. Acclaimed emperor by his troops in England, more precisely in York, the Rome of which he took charge as its first Christian leader traced its pagan, mythological origins back to Romulus and Remus of almost a thousand years previously.

So "Classical civilisation" as understood in today's western intellectual tradition had survived for about a thousand years, very roughly 500BC to 500AD. The study of economics was not grafted onto the intellectual tradition for a further 1300 years. Applying the adjective "Classical" to the early exponents of economics was an unwarranted step by intellectual romantics who concocted a seriously misleading label. They really were pushing their luck.

As already noted in the preceding four chapters, economic activity had been under weigh for at least 10,000 years before people deemed it worthy of academic study. Economic activity in the guise of farming, merchanting, manufacturing, international trade and even derivatives, then later the invention of money and later still the invention of banking just happened, rather like the weather. It was all too commonplace, so that few paid much attention to the

1. *The original luxury railway train the "Orient Express" still ran by a variety of routes from Paris to Constantinople, not to "Istanbul." That came later.*

underlying mechanics of what was gradually taking place. [2]   Sadly, economists seeking to improve on the commonsense of Adam Smith made matters worse by their chosen line of argument.

They formulated their inklings, not from observing objectively what was happening around them on a daily basis, but rather from their myopic blend of *ex cathedra* presumption and distorted retrospection. They wrote about the past, while ignoring the present as being uninteresting.   If they speculated about the future, they uniformly displayed a profound lack of imagination.

Much of it was piffle. As noted at the start of this book, economics has consistently been the science that never was. In fairness, the opportunities for early economists to examine the real-life foundations of their chosen discipline were strictly limited. They had very little relevant academic material at their disposal, and such academic enquiry was quintessentially imitative or pedagogic. By and large they were just shooting in the dark.

The fascinating strands of diligent scholarship in so many specialised fields,   knowledge which has been raided ruthlessly in the preceding chapters, were not available to them. Nor were they quasi-Biblical prophets, endowed with visionary insight into the industry and consumerism which unfolded over the next century or more. That was all far beyond their imagination.

---

2. *One may observe much the same phenomenon with family photograph albums in our own era. They do not show any interest in the commonplace. If future generations were to take the available evidence at face value, twenty-first century humanity spent most of its time wearing scant clothing, standing on beaches and waving joyously at cameras. People rarely bother to take photographs of their everyday activities - activities just too familiar to bother about. Exactly the same goes for the origin of economies.*

The early economists spent much of their time brooding over a minuscule factual base, not helped by the way they were locked in vitriolic personal rivalries.   Based on historical principles, this book applies to that academic pastime the name it merits.   It was primitive economics, too often an exercise trying to work out just how many axioms could be balanced on the head of a manufactured pin.

NOT ALL THE EARLY economists ignored the fundamental components of the creditary principle. Some showed a passing interest in what should have been the twin of Adam Smith's division of labour.   It figures in the writings of Jeremy Bentham as it did in those of the man who so intensely disliked him, Karl Marx. Famously he labelled Bentham *"the insipid, pedantic, leather-lipped oracle of the commonplace bourgeois intelligence of the nineteenth century"*. Vitriol indeed.

   In more analytical passages of Marx, debt and credit were regarded as an instrument of economic exploitation and/or repression between the classes, rather than as the basic building block of political economy. Marx had no concept of the creditary principle as explained so far. In his idiosyncratic view, credit and thus debt, could not have emerged until after money existed. It was principally an antisocial mechanism to impoverish the working class.

   As has been shown in previous chapters, his assertion that money emerged before formal credit was back-to-front.   Marx missed the historical reality by at least three thousand years. The primitive economists were simply guessing. This is scarcely the first book to take the line of least admiration for the over-revered fathers of economics. Reviewing their correspondence a century later, John Maynard Keynes acidly observed that "*the almost total obliteration of Malthus's line of approach and the complete domination of Ricardo has been a disaster to the progress of economics. Time after time in these letters Malthus is talking plain sense, the force of which Ricardo with his head in the clouds wholly fails to comprehend.*"

At their rare best, the primitive economists sought to explain a few of the more self-evident economic mechanisms around them. Yet in so doing, they were not the originators of the price mechanism, nor the notion of factories. Nor did they devise the principles of employment, nor the payment of rent, nor the fascination with gold, nor the mechanics of overseas trade. Such practices were understood and being acted upon by merchants and tradesmen from ancient Sumer onwards. For the primitives, other economic phenomena were just too commonplace, a range of over-familiar activities unworthy of their attention.

The conspicuous contrast between the uninspired economic observation of early economists and the active work of political philosophers - who can often claim fair copyright for mechanisms they describe - is overlooked too often. Economists were at best the audience of contemporary events, never the performers. Professional doctors cure people of illness, professional engineers build machines and bridges, professional lawyers legislate and fight cases in court. Professional economists just passively observe the commercial and financial ingenuity - and mistakes - of others.

There was also a matter of timing. By the time the Industrial Revolution was getting into its stride, many of the primitive

economists were already dead.   David Ricardo died in 1823, Jeremy
Bentham and France's Jean Baptiste Say in 1832.   The Rev Thomas
Malthus died in 1834, and James Mill in 1836.   The grim reaper was
having a field day among the early pioneers of economics.   Their
intellect is not in dispute; men such as Jeremy Bentham pursued a
breadth of interests, despite the envious calumnies of Karl Marx.

        Not without fair reason is Bentham's mummified body
preserved to mystify future generations of economists in the London
School of Economics, in the city centre.   Karl Marx must make do
with a cumbersome granite approximation four   miles to the
north-west in the suburban wilderness of Highgate cemetery. It is
an occasional place of pilgrimage for his scattered admirers.

T HE PRIMITIVE ECONOMISTS had scant opportunity
        to apply their undoubted intellect to the wondrous
        economic activity of the Industrial Revolution as it was
        about to unfold all around them. So we should leave them
in their reverie and move on, from those early nineteenth century
intellectual inklings of economics, to the very different sphere of
practical advances remarked at the start of this chapter.

        It is an unfortunate coincidence of history that the 1820s and
1830s which witnessed the demise of the early economists were the
same two decades in which economic activity began to undergo
transformation beyond their wildest imagining. The economic order
familiar to the primitive economists was disappearing rapidly. In
1832, the same year that Say and Bentham died, the antiquated Palace
of Westminster, dating back to the sixteenth century and even earlier,

was catastrophically burnt down. As if symbolically the fire was caused by over-enthusiastic stoking of Westminster's boilers with large quantities of redundant Exchequer tally sticks which had been stored there, disused relics of a bygone creditary age. Tallies now just kept the legislators warm, their economic function already forgotten and not respected. None of the primitives spotted the irony.

For those who did look for portents of the economic future, there was much to observe. When he highlighted the importance to the classical economy of navigating the Mediterranean, Adam Smith was unquestionably mining a much richer seam. Less than a century after he wrote it, transport was to become the remarkable force driving the most conspicuous economic advances since 9,000 BC.

The great English painter J M W Turner observed something exceptional was happening when he painted "Rain, Steam and Speed" in 1844; or six years earlier in "The Last of the Fighting Temeraire". He portrayed a sailing warship being hauled to its demise by a steam-powered tug. The remarkable changes in propelling ships did not escape his eagle-eyed attention, and they probably would not have escaped Adam Smith's attention either, had he encouraged James Watt to build steam engines.

Even if the primitive economists hadn't a clue what was unfolding around them, contemporary painters and writers were far more alert. One can but wonder exactly what was in the mind of the romantic poet William Blake when, writing his epic about Milton, he composed the short poem Jerusalem in which he included the interesting line: '*bring me my chariot of fire*' . It was a timely request. In the same year that Jerusalem was first printed, and just about twenty minutes' stroll from William Blake's home near today's Leicester Square, one of the earliest steam locomotives spluttered around a circular demonstration track behind a fence. It was ambitiously nicknamed *'Catch Me If You Can'* by its Cornish inventor Richard Trevithick. At a modest twelve miles an hour that 'chariot of fire challenge' would not have over-exerted the more sprightly nineteenth century Londoners.[3]   Surely a man as naturally curious as William Blake would have strolled across town to take a look. And then he wrote Jerusalem.

TREVITHICK'S WHEEZY RAILWAY was presented as a circus curiosity; but that did not last long. As he suspected his entertainment was also a significant pointer to the economic future, as others well noted, but it did not interest the primitive economists. Adam Smith, however, might well have seen the point.

Richard Trevithick's adventurous technology demonstrated in Bloomsbury was soon to be taken very seriously in the north of England. The pioneers of steam power, like Richard Trevithick, or William Hedley of Newcastle were experimenters, using coal energy to mine coal. All around them, horses were still the normal source of power for land transport and in warfare, but that was changed by the Napoleonic wars. Wartime military demand inflated the price of horse fodder, while the price of industrial coal came down. The cost advantage tilted in favour of coal to generate steam.

---

3. *The site of Trevithick's circular demonstration railway was more or less where the Senate House of London University now stands.*

Just ten years after the Battle of Waterloo the era of railways properly began, at a level far beyond the efforts of early experimenters with their colliery locomotives or gestures of civic entertainment. Boosted by a nationwide sense of salvation, the confidence that followed Britain's victory over Napoleon in June 1815, one unanticipated effect was to push enterprise and innovation ahead much faster than before. The shackles of horse power were about to be broken. Transport was a principal beneficiary of the post-Waterloo zeitgeist, and it moved ahead rapidly.

Until the Stockton and Darlington Railway opened in 1825, steam power had been used mainly by slow Newcomen engines driving pumps to prevent mines from flooding. Now a revolution in transport was to revolutionise the depth and breadth of economic activity for the future generations.

While this book has been formulated we have been in the throes of that revolution as, for the first time, transport and communications have been separated into different technologies. Until the 1840s they were effectively the same thing.[4] Thanks to the triumphal mood following Waterloo, Great Britain became the global centre of science and innovation. Amid great scientists like Humphrey Davy and Michael Faraday, one man led a different revolution. He was not an academic nor theoretician at all. He was the practical-minded engineer of the Stockton and Darlington

---

4. *The hilltop-to-hilltop mechanical semaphore signalling stations of the Royal Navy in the early nineteenth century, (and arguably carrier pigeons) were early portents of the separation; their legacy survives only in local names such as "Telegraph Hill". However they were almost insignificant compared with the invention of, first, the electric telegraph and then of the telephone.*

Railway. Its evident success was widely noted in the north of England. The impressive railway led to its engineer being invited by the merchants and businessmen of Liverpool and Manchester to build an even better, an even more advanced railway for them.

THE TOWERING PRESENCE behind the greatest revolution of the nineteenth century was George Stephenson (1781-1848) son of an illiterate colliery fireman. There was no money for his schooling; Stephenson did not learn to read and write until he was 18. From low colliery wages he paid for himself to be taught reading, writing and arithmetic. He was a determined young man and that never left him, fortunately blessed with the practical intelligence, and contrarian stubbornness, which the north of England can frequently generate.

George Stephenson was struck cruelly in his thirties by an angry public controversy over the true inventor of a coalminer's safety lamp. Was it Stephenson's idea, or was it Sir Humphey Davy's? Fashionable opinion in the South of England sided with the erudite Sir Humphrey; surely such ingenuity was far beyond the abilities of some uncouth North countryman. The latter, they concluded, must therefore have plagiarised Davy's work.

Even though Stephenson had demonstrated his safety lamp a month before Davy presented his version to the Royal Society, it took almost twenty years before his true inventiveness was fairly acknowledged. The intelligentsia of the south of England was too introspective and conceited to be aware of what was afoot. The miner's lamp episode left George Stephenson with a lifelong distrust of the theorising scientific experts of fashionable London. Ten years later he had his revenge. His Stockton & Darlington Railway of 1825 had moved both transport technology and the business methods of his time into a new dimension.

Stephenson's railway in County Durham was much more than just some obscure colliery tramway. It was a publicly-subscribed enterprise, authorised by its own Act of Parliament. The railway was intended from its outset to carry passengers as well as freight, the first to do so, between the northern coalfields and coal docks on the River Tees.

Although it was regarded as the world's first main line railway, the S&DR was still no racing track. Its first passenger train took two hours to complete the first twelve miles, no faster than a stage coach. The speed of horses still ruled unchallenged, as it had done for several thousand years. Eventually speeds on the Stockton and Darlington did reach as high as Trevithick's 10-12 miles an hour, but that paled into insignificance compared with Stephenson's achievements of just five years later.

W ITH HIS VISIONARY Liverpool & Manchester Railway of 1830, George Stephenson probably did as much as any clearly identifiable figure in history to transform the material lot of mankind. Its opening has been appropriately hailed since as *The Day The World Took Off* [5]. The railway's innovation was however very specific; much of it had been seen before, albeit in a different setting. Steam power had been

5. *In a BBC Television series of that name.*

around since the days of Thomas Newcomen's pumping engines. Purely as a curiosity, steam energy had fascinated Hero of Alexandria in Classical times, around 60AD.

The L&M was not the first tracked railway, nor was Stephenson's the first steam locomotive, nor was his enterprise the first recognised railway company. The quintessential difference from anything seen before was speed, driven by a remarkable leap in locomotive technology. On October 1829, his suitably-named "Rocket" was the easy winner of a locomotive competition for the railway staged on level track at Rainhill near Liverpool.

In George Stephenson's brilliance we can see one of the historic turning points of economies. Doggedly determined to build the railway the businessmen wanted between Liverpool and Manchester, he overcame every kind of obstruction. His experiences with the miner's lamp had been most educative; he well understood whom his opponents were. Influential canal owners and stage coach operators objected to his proposals; they were doing very nicely out of their existing business arrangements. Wealthy landowners sought strenuously to protect their landscaped acres and the farms of tenants who provided much of their income.

Expert engineers declared the treacherous bogs of Chat Moss to be impassable. When he wanted an overbridge built at an angle, a skew bridge, and civil engineers could not fathom it, George Stephenson took a turnip and carved one for them. Meanwhile intellectual snobs believed nothing important could emerge from anyone like him, while London's financiers reckoned they knew a good deal when they saw one and his wasn't.

Yet despite all the discouraging obstruction, George Stephenson saw every one of them off. It all seems rather workaday almost two hundred years later, but in its day the Liverpool & Manchester Railway was brilliant because it was so simple. Never has Occam's Razor been put to better use.

Around Stephenson there were all kinds of fanciful ideas in embryo, many of them revealed as crackpot, not the least those to be seen at Rainhill. His Rocket was different from everything else. It incorporated a water-filled boiler with multiple flues of hot gases flowing through it from a firebox. Exhaust steam from its cylinders was blown into the chimney to draw the fire. Unlike some of the weird and wonderful techniques for transferring power from steam cylinder to driving wheel, Stephenson used a simple crank. The other engineers displaying their over-ingenious ideas at Rainhill must have been kicking themselves.

STEAM LOCOMOTIVES exploiting his no-frills approach to the technical design survived longer than many other more exotic contraptions seen down the decades. Britain's last "Stephenson technology" steam locomotive was suitably named *Evening Star* (the choice of the works staff) and emerged from Swindon locomotive works in March 1960. So Stephenson's revolutionary locomotive technology survived in front-rank service in Great Britain for over 130 years. The Chinese were building them for another thirty years after that.

In contrast to the relatively unassertive George Stephenson, his competitors such as Isembard Kingdom Brunel surrounded themselves with self-publicity. Brunel's bridge across the Tamar at Saltash bears one of the largest signatures ever seen. His broad gauge railway track was doomed by a Royal Commission in 1845, although it was not until 1892 that the last broad gauge train chuffed its way out of his superb Paddington station. Brunel's steam locomotives were sluggish; and not for nothing was his GWR derided as the "Great Way Round". He was afraid of gradients and his level, roundabout routes later had to be bypassed with 'cut-offs'.

About a century after Stephenson's Rocket took to the rails, a locomotive using the same technology touched 126 miles per hour, four times the top speed of its ancestor at Rainhill [6]. Almost a century on again, electric trains running as fast as that record-breaking LNER steam locomotive are still considered remarkable.

Until the advent of the Liverpool and Manchester Railway with its rocket science of high technology locomotives, the maximum speed of transport on land had been dictated by animals. Inland canals, quite the latest technology in the days of Adam Smith, were simply horse-powered, as were all road wagons.

Stage coaches occasionally went at the gallop if the roads were good enough, which they rarely were, but that was the upper limit. The handful of steam locomotives built before the Rocket had been designed as substitute horses - the objective had been to haul more, and do so more cheaply, not to haul faster. Throughout the previous four millennia the speed, cost and inconvenience of land

─────────────────

6 : The Gresley pacific "Mallard" achieved that speed when racing down Stoke Bank in a braking trial on the East Coast Main Line between Grantham and Peterborough in July 1938. It is a world record which still stands after 79 years.

transport had made little progress, until George Stephenson changed everything. His revolutionary changes were in cost and speed. His vision of the future must surely rank alongside any in the world before or since. Stephenson's intercity railway enabled the businessmen of Liverpool and Manchester, the cotton kings, the merchants, the shipping men, their bankers and their insurers, to move comfortably between their two cities, conduct their necessary business together and return to their own homes that same evening.

Liverpool grew from its slave trading origins to become one of the most important shipping and insurance cities in the world. That prominence lives on the Royal Liver Building which still dominates the Mersey waterfront. Manchester became the world centre of the cotton trade, a status it held for a hundred years.

For the first time since around 1500BC inland cities, just as they had done in Sumer, became a great economic driving force, the centres of industry, commerce and wealth generation. They no longer needed to be ports taking advantage of cheap sea transport. In Britain towns such as Leeds and Sheffield, lacking any shipping access to the sea, grew quickly to exploit the opportunity.

AS RAILWAY NETWORKS expanded the same pattern of inland economic development spread around the world, nowhere more remarkably so than in the United States of America. Without railways the open ranges of America would have remained a wilderness of savanna. Such mobility was unprecedented; as shown by the Liverpool and Manchester Railway, the era of business travel had dawned. It was to transform the world economy over the next two hundred years and continues to do so. The economic and business advantages of speedy railways, first as Stephenson's vision, then as everyone's experience, became increasingly obvious throughout the civilised world.

The doubters were soon overcome and Great Britain built an entire network of main line railways within twenty years of opening the Liverpool & Manchester. Over those two decades steam trains transformed how people lived, where they worked and when and how they sought their recreation.

Before 1830, hardly anyone lived more than a couple of miles from their place of work. Thanks to Stephenson, by the middle of the nineteenth century ordinary citizens would regularly travel not just two, but sixty miles to work and back in a day. The steam railway made commuting possible, while the ambitious new railway companies actively encouraged that repetitive daily routine with extensive urban development on previously rural land.

They invented the suburbs, perhaps the most noteworthy of which was "Metroland" designed by the Metropolitan Railway, building leafy dormitories north west of London into the Chiltern hills. The objective was to provide regular paying passengers for its network of commuter railways. Before then and since Roman times, only the well-to-had been able to contemplate living anywhere well removed from the town centre on their country estates.

Within a century the tables were turned. By the late twentieth century, only rich people could afford to live in great city centres; the ordinary people moved to their fringes. London's economy in particular was transformed. Commuter railways meant it could bring together an array of talents from a broad catchment area stretched right across southern England.   Such labour variety and expertise had never been seen in one place before.

London grew rapidly to become the largest city in the world and was to remain so for over a hundred years. Skilled workers and professionals - reasonably well-off people with no desire to live in squalid conditions in an insanitary city - now became available to London's employers on a daily basis and in their millions.

The   daily   gathering   of   people   created   the   modern metropolis. It was manifest in a multitude of finely-divided talents, innumerable service industries and a myriad customers now with substantial discretionary income at their disposal. There had never before been a division of labour to compare with it. Cities were once again in the vanguard of economic progress - but they were a new kind of city using a new kind of transport. Where Sumer, or Greece, or Rome, or Cordoba, or Venice, or Antwerp or Amsterdam had gone before, London and its railways was to eclipse them all.

TRANSPORT INNOVATION, like creditary innovation before it, was a primary cause of a new kind of civilisation. If steam-hauled passenger trains changed completely the way people lived and worked, steam-hauled goods trains were equally revolutionary. They alone could assemble the huge quantities of food, fuel, building materials and other supplies which such a concentration of population demanded.

Railway companies moved with great enterprise to meet the burgeoning demand.   For the transport of perishable foodstuffs such as meat, fruit and vegetables, fast trains to Smithfield or Covent Garden were essential. London could now afford to import beer in bulk from the admired breweries along the River Trent. Rail transport was now cheap enough to transport such bulk products inland at prices which were realistic to the ordinary man.[7]

Speeding overnight fish trains from Cornwall and Scotland to London were a triumph of nineteenth century railway management, devised long before refrigeration was invented. Time was of the essence. Distant ports such as Aberdeen, Padstow, Fleetwood and Grimsby now shared in London's prosperity. They could now send their highly perishable produce to Billingsgate's huge market.

As many inland people tasted fresh fish and more varied vegetables for the first time, diet improved. So did communication. The overnight mail trains and later the overnight newspaper trains, a peculiarity of Great Britain, were massive steps forward in the progress of communication which continues still. Few countries could match Britain's rail-borne ability to deliver the news. So the United States never spawned national newspapers, a distinction which had significant impact on its regionalised political attitudes.

The low costs of freight railways transformed the economic geography of Britain's industry. It was now an economic proposition to move bulk products such as coal, minerals and bricks

---

7. *The supporting pillars of the freight-only undercroft at the Midland Railway's St Pancras station were originally spaced to match the size of standard beer barrels stored there after their journey from breweries along the River Trent. With the station's more recent rebirth as the terminus for international Eurostar trains to Paris, Brussels and beyond, its beer barrel-inspired pillars have now been revealed for all to admire in its splendid pedestrian precinct.*

long distances inland without over-inflating their delivered price. For the previous five thousand years, bricks had of necessity been made very made close to where they were needed. Building materials had never moved very far other than for cathedrals and aristocratic houses - and Stonehenge.[8]

Profitable mining of inland coalfields, such as those of the Welsh valleys, was only made possible by the railways. A number of railway companies emerged, all engaged in strenuous competition to shift Welsh coal down the valleys to the coal ports, especially Cardiff. The Welsh capital enjoyed an economic boom, creating numerous millionaires along the way.

One of them even built Cardiff Castle, a nineteenth century nod of acknowledgement to King Edward III, or even the Romans of almost two millennia previously. Working conditions along the narrow coal seams - the product often sought-after anthracite - were harsh and the coalminers were often poorly treated. Not surprisingly the Welsh mining valleys became a nursery of trades unionism.

Slate quarries around Snowdonia in North Wales enjoyed a comparable benefit. The pioneering narrow gauge Ffestiniog Railway opened in 1836 to transport roofing slate to a new harbour at Portmadoc (nowadays Porthmadog) from where it was shipped

---

8. *The railways themselves also exploited cheap brick manufacture. Especially in London, their railway cuttings yielded hard London clay as they climbed out of the low-lying valley of the River Thames. As they did so railway contractors built portable kilns to turn the cuttings clay into bricks on the spot, and sold them to local builders. The resultant "London commons", bricks with a distinctive grey-yellowy colour, became the standard building material for housing in the railway-inspired suburbs as London spread rapidly outwards.*

around the world. Portmadoc itself became a shipbuilding centre. From then on, roofs made of slate, rather than clay tiles, became commonplace, even as far afield as Australia. The Ffestiniog Railway was the pioneer of economical narrow gauge railways all over the world, claiming a number of historic firsts as it emerged once steam power arrived in the 1860s. Before the Ffestiniog Railway was built, roofing slate went down the mountain on pack ponies and was prohibitively expensive.[9] By 1900, two more standard gauge railway companies had reached Blaenau Ffestiniog, all three vying with one another for its highly profitable slate traffic.

THE ECONOMIC REVOLUTION was fundamental. Everywhere it went rail transport dictated how and where factories might be built and how the entire economy might develop. All was determined by the routes, speed, price and reliability of freight transport.

Beyond that, economical freight even for semi-manufactures now determined how cheaply and so how frequently they could be moved from one factory to the next. In turn that promoted the degree of specialisation in each factory, and so strengthened the depth of entrepreneurial and technical skill brought to every stage of industrial production. It was the same principle as Adam Smith's specialising pin factories once again, but now transferred from adjacent benches to distant counties. The expertise of the

---

9. *An international mining engineer once told the author that "the man who invented the hundred-ton dumper truck doubled the world's reserves of copper." [Quoted by the author in a letter published in* The Economist, *July 1973.]*

66industrial system advanced a long way in just seventy or so years. It was now a nationwide activity, well beyond the way in which some of the earliest industrial semi-manufactures had been transported. In eighteenth century central Sheffield the closely-packed 'Little Mester' small cutlery and silverware firms had relied on the old-fashioned horse and cart. Everything stayed in Sheffield.

In a sense it was the end of a first phase of the Industrial Revolution, a phase dating back to Josiah Wedgwood's factories mass-producing pottery for the middle classes in Stoke-on-Trent from the 1760s. His products could only move by horse and cart, or maybe canal. The railways ushered in its next, and most dramatic, phase. Craft factories gave way to national, even global, industries.

As George Stephenson built the Liverpool & Manchester, his son Robert was principal engineer for the London & Birmingham. Two generations of Stephensons realised where all this could lead. They even left future historians of industry, and inquisitive economists, a valuable trail of clues in their Prospectus for the London & Birmingham Railway of the 1830s. It offered the following inducements to potential investors: *"First, the opening of new and distant sources of supply of provisions to the metropolis; Second, easy, cheap and expeditious travelling; Third, the rapid and economical interchange of the great articles of consumption and of commerce, both internal and external; and lastly, the connexion by railways, of London with Liverpool, the rich pastures of the centre of England, and the greatest manufacturing districts; and, through the port of Liverpool, to afford a most expeditious communication with Ireland."* Stephenson was not just a down-to-earth engineer; he also had a prophetic vision for the future, an exceptional combination. When his son Robert was designing the London & Birmingham Railway, they discussed which track gauge to use. George told his son to build it to the same gauge as his Liverpool & Manchester, in turn the same as the Stockton & Darlington. *"Make them all the same. They might be a long way apart now, but they will all join up together one day"*.

AND JOIN UP THEY DID. Since his day, Stephenson's original Stockton & Darlington gauge prescription has become the standard throughout Great Britain and all of Europe except Ireland, Finland and Iberia, across the whole North American continent, throughout China as far as its Russian frontier and for Japan's Shinkansen bullet trains. It was used for Australia's transcontinental east-west route to Perth, opened in 1917. Almost ninety years later Australia completed a north-south route to Darwin, the Ghan, again using the Stephenson gauge.

New railways in Spain are now being built to Stephenson's standard gauge in the twenty-first century, replacing the awkward anomaly recommended by Isembard Kingdom Brunel. The gauge is now the norm for new-build railways anywhere in the world, from Europe to Japan. The Chinese are currently rebuilding at least one African railway to bring it up to Stephenson's standard.

Almost two hundred years old, Stephenson's railway gauge will prove to have been the most enduring global standard of the Industrial Revolution. It has survived unscathed where so many other would-be standards - notably in colour television, or videotapes, or electric plugs, or even the sockets for charging mobile phones - conspicuously failed to materialise.

THE RAILWAYS OF GREAT BRITAIN totally transformed what was already a long-established economic landscape. More dramatically, the railroads of the United States created a new one from scratch. Work began early, not long after the opening of the Stockton & Darlington. From the outset there were far-sighted Americans who could clearly see the huge implications for their own country.

The foundation stone for the very first, the Baltimore and Ohio Railway, was laid on the deliberately chosen date of 4 July 1828. The guest of honour was the 91 year-old Charles Carroll, sole-surviving signatory to American Declaration of Independence of exactly 52 years before. At the inauguration ceremony, Carroll declared: *"I consider this among the most important acts of my life, second only to my signing of the Declaration of Independence, if second even to that."*

Using British-made locomotives and track, railway services on the B & O began in 1830. Over the next two decades, a remarkable 9,000 miles of American railroad were constructed, threading through hills, linking towns and farmlands as they encroached on the Mississippi. The economic benefits became obvious, and in 1855 the Federal government in Washington decided to step in.

For the next decade and more it operated a land grant system to open up the West. Together with various state governments, Washington gave the burgeoning railroad companies 180 million acres of virtually uninhabited land (almost five times the area of England) beyond the Mississippi.

The development of America's railroads was supported with subsidies. Companies such as the Union Pacific set about spanning the entire country; the first transcontinental railroad was opened in 1869. The American West was opened up, not by central planners nor by teams of bureaucrats, but by buccaneering railroad promoters and owners of often precarious banks. With a network of railroads a world-ranking economy was thereby created out of a wilderness.

Railways not only defined the extent of economies in the 19th century. They redefined entire countries too. The railways of continental Europe were at the heart of the unification process which herded the previous disparate provinces and princedoms of Germany and Italy into single nation states.

It was the promise of a trans-continental railway to Vancouver which alone persuaded the distant Pacific territory of British Columbia to join a confederation to form Canada. It was only the promise of the trans-continental railway line from Brisbane to Perth which persuaded Western Australia to join a Commonwealth and so create modern Australia. It involved building a dead straight railway across the Nullarbor Plain.

When Czar Alexander III gave his blessing to building a trans-Siberian railway in 1891, he did so knowing full well that huge enterprise would help bind his far-flung territories in the East to the Russian homeland in Europe. Just twenty-four years previously, Russia had sold its far eastern territory of Alaska to the United States for a low price. The Czar was determined to hold on to the rest of his vast possessions in the Eurasian continent, and a connecting railway was his answer.

E VEN BEFORE THAT in April 1852, a diminutive locomotive worked its laborious way out of Victoria terminus in Bombay for just 20 miles to Thana. Its pioneering train conveyed four hundred members of the privileged Anglo-Indian gentry. *'They little knew that the invention they had introduced to India would later prove, more than any ruler or dynasty, the single factor that unified the vast sub-continent, shaped its consciousness, hastened its freedom from colonialism and was to be seen as the most valuable and enduring legacy left behind by its British rulers.'* [10]

By the time Indian railways were nationalised a century later, they had become the fourth-largest network in the world with almost a million and a half employees. Every day the 14,500 train services in India cover a distance equivalent to almost two return trips to the moon. They have been the driving force behind India's burgeoning economy for over 150 years. Just as in Europe and North America, they brought inland centres, as well as ports such as Bombay and Calcutta, into the collective prosperity. Landlocked Bangalore, equidistant from the Arabian Sea and the Bay of Bengal, was to become a global centre of the IT business.

Alone of the major continents, Africa still lacks a significant railway network. Only South Africa can boast a developed railway system using its own manufacture of track and rolling stock and its own capital for construction. Former colonial territories to the north depend on outside help for all of these. The Belgians built a

10. Leading article, The Times, London, Wednesday 18 April 2002.

railway from the Atlantic coast to the copper mines of the Congo. It has since been largely destroyed by civil war.

The British built a railway from the Indian Ocean to the fertile high altitude farmlands of Uganda. The resultant Kenya-Uganda railway has been more successful. Its watering stop built in the middle of nowhere was Nairobi, a name simply meaning 'sweet water'. The location was then chosen as the engineering centre for the line, a direct African equivalent of Crewe or Swindon. Nairobi grew to become the largest African city anywhere between Johannesburg and Cairo. The main towns of inland Kenya trace their growth and importance to the arrival of the railway.

Embryo states of Africa originally looked to European colonial powers to build their railways and trigger the economic expansion they alone could generate. That came to an abrupt end with European 'decolonisation' in the 1960s. A Second Colonial Era, now under the control of the Chinese, is currently building or rebuilding African railways. Once the Europeans had been sent away, China moved in and was quick to build the Tan-Zam (now Tazara) Railway from Dar-es-Salaam to the Zambian copper belt.

Then in 2013 it was announced China would build a new standard-gauge railway line across Kenya. It would replace the old East African Railway (as the Kenya-Uganda railway had been renamed). Ambitions run high, eventually aiming to reach north of Kenya to Sudan and ultimately the Mediterranean.

If completed, that could create the Cape-to-Cairo railway of which Cecil Rhodes had dreamt, over a century previously. Africa still needs many thousand miles of railways to be constructed before it can even begin to unlock its full economic potential. By the end of the nineteenth century the railway revolution had, in seventy years, transformed economies out of all recognition in most other parts of the world. In so doing the process revealed a third foundation of the economic mechanism.

THE TRANSPORT PRINCIPLE determines the extent or breadth of economic activity. It works with the Specialist and Creditary Principles; together those two determine its expertise or depth. As noted in Chapter Two they are a kind of double helix, spiraling upwards through time to determine the complexity of an economy. To complete the picture we now add the third prime dimension of economic activity.

Transport governs the diameter, the geographical extent of that helix. The three functioning together embrace the true origins of economies. They can encompass a Neolithic village 'state' of farmers, or a city state from Sumer onwards. Sea transport then gave ports an obvious economic advantage from Classical times. The coming of the nineteenth century railway spread that transport advantage much more widely, most obviously in North America.

The twentieth century dream of a United States of Europe was thwarted because, though necessary, the three are not sufficient. They need to be backed by compatibility, not just not of the creditary system and its offshoots such as taxation, but by political homogeneity and a standard regulatory infrastructure as well. Cultural and language uniformity help too. Given all that - a tough call beyond Europe's deep-rooted and very diverse political traditions - the continent could have moved far further in the direction of its pioneering dreamers. They got it back to front trying to impose a single currency on diverse economies. Hard experience has shown a unified Europe to be less and less plausible as each year passes, though the doctrinaire diehards will be the last to surrender.

There was nothing fundamentally new in any of it. The essential rôle of transport in any economy traces back well before the Mediterranean seafarers of classical times. Yet it took George Stephenson's sudden change in speed and reliability, and everything they in turn made possible, to reveal just how potent is the transport principle. Until something changes, it is more difficult to spot the evolving pattern concealed by relative inertia. If further proof of the transport principle's importance were needed, a similar process of rapid change was to be seen all over again from 1960 onwards with the advent of jet aircraft.

The transport principle in the origins of economies was obvious enough by 1850, but none of it seems to have made any impact on the nineteenth century economists. Instead they were engrossed in their own glass bead games. Far too much intellectual effort was wasted by them on how to calculate the 'value' of something. Any perceptive auctioneer could have resolved their monotonous controversy in a sentence. [11]

It might be possible, for admirers trawling their voluminous writings in meticulous detail, to claim some primitive economist included a passing reference to almost any economic phenomenon,

---

11. *Economic value is something that only emerges in a marketplace. Many people confuse it with sentimental value, which arises in the human psyche.*

even transport. That is scarcely the point. The sum total of their efforts was not to explain how economies may be made to grow (see Chapter 1). That was what was happening all around but their attention was elsewhere. It is not as if they needed to look far. As noted, as early as 1832 the Stephensons had left them a helpful clue in the Prospectus for the London & Birmingham Railway.

Karl Marx was then still sixteen years away from writing his *Communist Manifesto*. Then in a forlorn attempt to develop a mathematical basis for his political prejudices he wrote *Das Kapital*, persevering doggedly in the British Museum. The Museum is just over half a mile from Euston Station, main terminus of the London & Birmingham Railway. It would have taken just a ten minute stroll for Marx to discover what was happening in the real economy. In thirty years of wasted effort, writing a pretentious tome he eventually abandoned, there is no significant evidence he bothered to do so.

NINETEENTH CENTURY ECONOMISTS were being blinded by the obvious. The fundamental dimensions of economic development - the troika of the creditary, the specialist and the transport principles - never even occurred to them. Yet all three were becoming apparent by 1840, it seems at least to J M W Turner and arguably William Blake. In the following decade a forward-looking investment community thought of little else. It was seeking profit, not rarified intellectual enlightenment. Always follow the money. Collectively the transport and communications, specialist and creditary principles are a path which any developing economy must explore and adopt. The pattern was all around them yet the primitive economic theoreticians still could not see it. John Maynard Keynes pointedly remarked: *'practical men, who believe themselves to be quite exempt from any intellectual influences, are usually the slaves of some defunct economist.'*

Never is that more true than each time such practical men chirrup 'land, labour and capital'. There are many businesses which can and do prosper without any one of them. An inspired computer software company can, and typically will, thrive without any of them. But it still needs technical expertise, creditworthiness and a reliable means of communication.

If the primitive economists could not bring themselves to recognise the importance of railways, there were other remarkable developments around them which also deserved their attention. One such was the rapid advance in banking, to which we may return in a moment. Another was to transform the stock market, fundamentally just another way of agreeing debt and credit.

The changes had been triggered by the success of the Liverpool & Manchester Railway. In the 1830s the early railways were promoted and financed by solid men of commerce. Their commercial success transformed the function of the London stock market. Previously a gentlemen's gambling club, it now became a source of industrial finance. That creditable progress was then turned to pecuniary advantage by a new breed of City slickers.

The Railway Mania of the 1840s was in full swing. Railway projects were much more than three-friends-in-an-alehouse, back of an envelope musings. Each railway proposal needed all the paraphernalia and expense of a Private Bill in Parliament. They involved costing and negotiating with sub-contractors and their thousands of navvies, designing unprecedented works of civil engineering, including great tunnels and bridges.

Then all the mechanical needs of rolling stock, track and signalling had to be included. Beyond that, negotiating often tricky changes in land use and building substantial stations along the route were all part of the project. The suggestions that the 1990s dot com boom was like the railway mania were well wide of the mark.

ONCE THE RAILWAY CONCEPT took hold, its economic and industrial consequences proved to be phenomenal. Yet if its effects were felt primarily in the industrial, commercial and transport economy, its origins were firmly rooted in Britain's House of Commons. The flood of new railway projects was not regulated by the demands of the marketplace, but by the law. The sanction of Parliament for any new railway was essential. *"In the Parliamentary session of 1840 not a single railway Bill was passed, while 1841 saw no more than a short branch line. But then there gradually developed a startling and indeed terrifying change, due to two principal factors. First, the grand trunk lines had already been completed and were earning excellent dividends. Second, from 1843 the money market in London was in a very easy state, Bank of England reserves were exceptionally high, interest rates were low and money was generally abundant. Investment in foreign securities had become very unpopular, while London stockbrokers who until then had avoided railway shares noted that the London and Birmingham, the Grand Junction and the York and North Midland were paying 10 per cent."* [12]

Building new railways had in effect become a political lottery. By 1845 optimistic schemes were being hatched for new railways to be built into every corner of the country, on the off-chance the body politic might just agree to them. The railway mania reached its zenith that year. Railway projects were being approved in Acts of Parliament at the rate of five a week.

Newspapers which circulated widely among the investor classes, publications themselves made feasible because the railways could now deliver them on time, fanned the flames and in the process created a new advertising medium. Hare-brained railway projects were constantly being presented in the financial gossip mills as copper-bottomed investment opportunities

The stock market was in a frenzy, energised by the way investors could buy parcels of shares in new railway ventures with merely a ten per cent deposit. In the event a third or more of them were never built. When the crash came in 1846 and promoters called in the remaining ninety per cent, many families lost everything.

Over just a few years the origins of popular financial capitalism had descended into mayhem. Then into the limelight stepped another of the useful scoundrels of economic progress, an ambitious linen draper from York called George Hudson. The newly-galvanized London stock market was rapidly falling in love with railway company prospectuses. George Hudson was the man

---

12.   *'150 Years of Mainline Railways' O S Nock, p.20*

who worked out how to convert that stock exchange romance into a personal fortune. He was the originator of practices, sometimes dubious, which were to dominate the City of London into the twentieth century.

H
UDSON WAS AMONG THE first in the City of London to recognise exactly what the engineer George Stephenson and his successors were creating, and exactly what could be done to exploit it. Hudson was about to invent financial engineering. Within the space of a just few years he became Britain's wheeler-dealing 'Railway King'.

George Hudson became the master of mergers and takeover bids, almost certainly the first the world had known. It would have quite been impossible before then without an active, and liquid, stock market. His ingenuity was another origin of economies, if not exactly one of its most reputable. It was highly effective nevertheless. Hudson devised a set tricks in creative finance which, in various guises, were to permeate the London stock market for the next century and more.

Already by 1844 Hudson had engineered a merger of the North Midland, the Midland Counties and the Derby and Birmingham Railways. That created the Midland Railway. But there was a positive side too. The finances might have been questionable but Hudson's new baby mushroomed to become the largest business enterprise on earth. The Midland Railway thrived moving fuel from the Midlands coalfields to London. With its extensive route network, large fleet of locomotives and rolling stock, an advanced engineering centre in Derby and grand stations like London's St Pancras, the Midland Railway company grew to become the largest enterprise on the planet. It was quite the Shell Oil, General Motors, IBM, Microsoft or Google of its day. Meanwhile gyrating through the boardrooms of the fashionable railway companies, Hudson turned himself into a previously unknown breed, an industrialist.

Eighty years previously Josiah Wedgwood had transformed the three thousand year old notion of a craft workshop into a large factory. However the primitive transport of his time meant Wedgwood's activities - and himself - were of necessity confined to a single location. Thanks to the railways, George Hudson, that prototype twentieth century entrepreneur, travelled the length and breadth of the country with ease, inserting his fingers in a wide variety of commercial, and potentially profitable, pies.

Over the next century the new breed of industrialists would evolve to become some of the most powerful people on earth. But exactly like the notorious pioneers John Law or Johan Palmstruch before him, George Hudson overdid it. In his case it was not just a matter commercial excess. He indulged in fraud as well, later revealed in his dealings with the Eastern Railway. It emerged he had been bribing Members of Parliament and milking large sums from his companies for his personal use.

Hudson was found to be paying dividends to some people out of capital subscribed by others, one of the earliest exponents of the so-called Ponzi scheme. Although it was clearly not known as such at the time, the principles of his fiddle rapidly became apparent.

Versions of it made their appearance in Charles Dickens' novel *Martin Chuzzlewit* of 1844, and again in his *Little Dorrit* in 1857. However it was not until 1920 that the American Charles Ponzi pursued the fraud to such excess that he gave his name to the grossly dishonest practice.

THOMAS CARLYLE in one of his pamphlets called Hudson the "big swollen gambler'. The Railway King ruined many of those who too innocently believed his grossly optimistic promises, and eventually he even beggared himself. Yet his contributions to economic progress were at once both financially destructive and at the same time beneficial.

By the time he died in 1871, George Hudson had almost single-handedly created some of the principal transport arteries of Britain's twentieth century commerce. From Hudson's time onwards, shareholders were no longer just the genteel, remote proprietors of an enterprise. They were often its ordinary customers and employees as well. Widespread popular trading in industrial shares became commonplace; for decades in Great Britain they were dominated by 'Home Rails'.

Shares in businesses which are themselves simply financial go-betweens and in the banking industry itself, which so animated London's stock market in the later twentieth century, were still far in the future. Consigned to the past, however, was a primitive stock market which had been the private domain of hooray henries trying to make a fast buck from shares in the East India Company. London's much-enlarged investor community needed its own mass-circulation source of information.   Gossiping coffee shop society around the City of London was no longer adequate. When the *Financial Times* was first published in February 1888, such was the dominance of railway shares on the stock exchange that its front page featured railway company news and little else.

The inaugural FT's headline stories examined the Southern Railways, the Midland Railway's annual report, the Great Northern Railway and included a long letter about the Metropolitan District Railway. There was just space on the first front page for a report headlined *'Russia and Finance'*. Effectively the same riddle, wrapped in a comparable mystery inside a broadly unchanging enigma was regularly to be found in editions of the same newspaper for the following century and longer than that.

The time has come for all serious students of economics to grasp the essential contribution of transport and communication to their enquiries. It was as true of the nineteenth century railway as it had been of the Spanish galleon, or of the primitive sailing vessels of the Classical Mediterranean wisely observed by Adam Smith. Or of the donkey caravans of Anatolia which conveyed the earliest recorded international trade. Or of high speed container trains racing all over modern Europe through the night. The next chapter shows how the essential contribution of air travel is another part of the same broad picture.

It is as true of the much-maligned container juggernaut as they obstruct traffic and block motorists on motorways. In our own world it is true of camel caravans traversing Asia, as they probably did on the ancient Silk Road. It is seen in the huge road trains with multiple trailers racing through the Australian bush, or massive container ships to be seen loading and unloading against the clock at container ports like Southampton, Rotterdam, Singapore or Yokohama every day of the year. That is how economies work. Sooner or later, mainstream economics is bound to come to terms with the relevance of transport to the subject.

Two millennia ago the Roman Empire could do little about speed, but at least its soldiers could minimise journey times by building straight roads. They moved armies and conveyed diplomatic and military intelligence. Speed was vital. The later Ottoman Empire also understood that essential principle and built its communications network on good roads as well.

While rail transport was making most of the economic headlines, behind the scenes another of the unseen hands was busily at work. As noted in Chapter Four, merchant banking in its earliest form had now existed for seven hundred years since its invention in Italy. That industry, too, was about to make vital if reluctant steps forward; the creditary system also had to move with the times.

FOR ALL ITS LONGEVITY, and still more of a profession than an industry, banking was not prepared for the economic upheaval of the Industrial Revolution. As always, necessity rather than ability was to be the mother of invention. Until the middle of the 18th century banking customers in the English provinces were mainly landowners and cattle merchants. Even so they depended heavily on London banks for deposits and loans. Only in exceptional cases, such as Smith & Co of Birmingham and the Gurneys of Norwich did bankers in 'the provinces' handle Bills of Exchange and other payments, and provide financial services.

Then from the 1750s country banks, far from the patrician Bank of England, began to increase in number. The Bank itself, at the heart of the constantly-evolving financial City, was as yet only half a century old and was still developing its own expertise. There was no prototype elsewhere to follow, not even the Bank of Venice. Progress could only depend on financial prudence, trial and error.

Good commercial ethics, first seen in the earliest farmers of 9000BC, were still as vital as ever. Of the new country banks, one well-known example should suffice as illustration. As mentioned previously, in 1765 the ironmaster Samuel Lloyd and button manufacturer John Taylor established a banking firm in Birmingham. It was the ancestor of today's Lloyd's Bank. Along the way Lloyds duly acquired the Black Ox bank of the cattle drovers founded in Llandovery, central Wales in 1799.

At the beginning of the eighteenth century there were no more than a dozen country banks. A hundred years later there were over 600. Their development exactly matched economic expansion in the early stages of the Industrial Revolution. As ever the specialist principle and the creditary principle must march hand in hand. Banking then needed to advance much further following the railway revolution. A far more ambitious industrial system, with its geography broadening from just one locality to an entire country, placed unprecedented demands on Britain's financiers.

The industry soon fell foul of a bureaucratic mentality. Its unimaginative supervisors spent much of their time trying to catch up with the past, rather than looking to future economic potential. Meanwhile unimaginative politicians meddled without much forethought, still seeking perfection for familiar financial phenomena that had already passed into memory. In those apposite words of William Blake, '*The Errors of a Wise Man make your Rule, Rather than the Perfections of a Fool.*'

BACKWARD-THINKING POLITICAL economists were far more concerned with any theoretical damage banks might do. That took priority over any positive progress they might generate, especially so in the Anglo-Saxon world. Inability to grasp economics was the one consistent element in the interference of politicians for the next two hundred years. Of course there were some steps in a positive direction. The Banking Co-partnerships Act of 1826 ended the exclusive privileges of the Bank of England, and permitted the formation of commercial joint stock banks with any number of shareholders. The Bank of England was no longer the only joint stock financial enterprise in town.

Provided they were not based closer than 65 miles to London, the new limited liability banks were permitted to continue issuing their own banknotes. Until the nineteenth century, such notes issued by provincial bankers were commonly in circulation. However any joint stock banks based closer to London were forbidden to do so. Even the Bank of England had its *amour propre*.

The largely arbitrary limit of 65 miles had a distinctive effect on the geographical shape of Britain's industrial economy, an effect still visible even in the 21st century. The implacable Law of Unintended Consequences was busily at work. The rule kept capital-hungry heavy industries away from London and the Home Counties.

More than that. Serving on the management boards of the country banks, especially, were the new breed of experienced industrialists. They understood the financial needs of commerce and industry at first hand unlike the Bank of England or the genteel private banks of Fleet Street and the Strand. That hasn't changed much since, either. Britain's major concentrations of heavy industry in the nineteenth century inevitably gravitated to regions well away from London, to South Wales, the Midlands and the North.[13]   Far removed from the refined metropolis their financial requirements were properly understood by their local bankers.

Potential local investors could reach well-informed judgement through direct observation. Location of raw materials had a bit to do with it, as they had since the gold and silver mines of King Gyges over two and a half millennia previously. With the advent of cheap rail transport, however, even that factor of location began to wane in importance.

Matters changed once more when the geographical restrictions on banking were lifted. Newer mass-production industries, such as motor manufacture, entirely creations of the twentieth century, took root conspicuously closer to London, in

---

13. *"Where there's muck, there's brass".*

centres such as Luton, Dagenham or Slough. Then industrial food manufacture began to supplant simple supplies of raw foodstuffs sold in bulk in markets. That industry also found a twentieth century base in the Home Counties, much closer than 65 miles from London. A simple geographical banking rule had a profound effect on the shape of England's commercial development.

Political attention was directed elsewhere, with adverse results. The Banking Charter Act of 1844 decreed that no bank other than the Bank of England was henceforth allowed to issue new banknotes. The era of bureaucratic restrictions on banking was now closing in, even though the process was gradual. In a sense it could trace its origins to Venice half a millennium previously. Those renaissance banking ventures were firmly regulated by the Senate.

In Britain much the same political imperative decreed four hundred years later that issuing banks would have to withdraw their existing notes from circulation in the event of their being involved in a takeover. Even if no-one acknowledged the creditary principle existed, no-one was left in any doubt of its potency.

It was recognised that larger banks could become too powerful. Meantime the Bank of England was restricted to issuing new banknotes only if they were 100% backed by gold or up to £14 million in state debt. Flawed logic which had been fading for six hundred years was suddenly back in fashion.

The 1844 Act blindly exempted demand deposits from the legal requirement of the 100 per cent reserve demanded for the issue of paper money. It is hard to fathom the logic. For the commercial community using cheques, demand deposits were every bit as effective as money [14].   So even if banknotes were not allowed to play their full part in a fast-growing economy, the banks themselves were still allowed to support it with their credit ledgers. One scarcely needs to be a paid-up creditary economist to comprehend the illogicality of that.

THE BANKING ACT OF 1844 was a Pyrrhic victory for the uncomprehending "Currency School", which even argued that the issue of new banknotes was in itself major cause of price inflation. John Hume's notion of 'financial oil' just two centuries previously had evidently been forgotten completely. Economic insight had gone into reverse. Although the railway mania both in Parliament and on the Stock Market was approaching its zenith in 1844, it evaded the attention of the perpetrators of the Banking Charter Act. They were not interested in what the real economy was doing.

The Act required new notes to be backed fully by gold or government debt. The government however retained the power to suspend the provision when the going got tough. This happened several times: in 1847 and 1857, and during the 1866 Overend Gurney crisis. Currency School orthodoxy was evidently a system designed for debt management when it was not needed. It was quasi-economics for a sunny day only. When events took a downward turn, the Currency School rule book was pushed aside.

---

14.   *The author's own experiences with the Bank of England when a Travel Allowance was introduced in ignorance of credit cards in 1966 (page 12 onwards) again showed how the traditions of high-level financial incomprehension die hard.*

Worse, the restrictive 1844 Act only applied to banks in England and Wales. So three commercial banks in Scotland and four in Northern Ireland still issue their own sterling banknotes, under Bank of England regulation.   To put it at its kindest, nineteenth century political imposts on the Britain's banks were not characterised by anything so edifying as logical consistency.

Many emerging banks outside London could trace their origins to the cattle drovers, canny entrepreneurs who needed to sort out tricky finances with much care. Their banks were small to begin with, so amiable mergers were really rather sensible. Banking generally needs to spread its risks, and that is difficult for a very small bank. Yet as another ruling of the Banking Charter Act, when such provincial banking businesses did merge to form larger banks, they immediately forfeited their right to issue notes.

Once again, logical consistency had taken a holiday. Understanding the creditary principle should help guard against such misconceptions. Britain's venerable Midland Bank started trading in England as the Birmingham and Midland Bank, in 1836. Then in 1891 it merged with the Bank of London, to become the London and Midland Bank. After a period of expansion throughout the British Isles it was to become Midland Bank in 1923. It had established itself as the largest deposit bank by 1934. Almost sixty years later it was itself acquired by HSBC [15].

15. Formerly the Hongkong and Shanghai Banking Corporation. The author was its principal media spokesman and worldwide head of PR, marketing and publications 1984-86 when the bank's global headquarters was still in Hong Kong but it was already concerned by '1997'. By then the bank had subsidiaries in five continents.

That merger created one of the largest banks in the world, as a rapidly-changing and increasingly criticised industry headed into the twenty-first century. Hongkongbank had started life as an overseas merchant bank for the Far East trade in the nineteenth century. From that it spread across much of the world.

Times change. With the scheduled handover of Hong Kong to China in 1997 on expiry of the "unequal treaties" which had added the New Territories to Victoria island, the basic law would probably change as well. So HSBC sought a base well clear of its home territory in the Far East, and preferably in London. Through buying Midland Bank, it succeeded.

BANKERS CONSTANTLY SEEK to operate under regulatory regimes which can be trusted. They move with the times, just as the bankers of Antwerp moved to Amsterdam amid the turmoil of the sixteenth century. HSBC's principal business until 1949 had been with pre-Communist China through Shanghai. Even so, it always retained its headquarters in Hong Kong. That ensured it could function under English commercial law. Banks choose their regulatory regimes.

The relocation, even of a very large bank like HSBC, illustrated a more general principle. It is not difficult to move a bank. It has no factory. Such mobility is too easily ignored by countries which flatter themselves as future global financial centres. One badly-handled banking problem brings a swift end to any such political or commercial ambition. Many are watching what happens to Deutsche Bank and Commerzbank over the next couple of years.

Barclays Bank was formed in 1896 through the merger of the concerns Barclay, Bevan, Tritton, Ransom, Bouverie and Co with Gurney and Co. Aware of the excessive length of such names, the Bank's originators chose plain Barclays as its brand. The word 'Ransom' offered less than helpful connotations around the financial community anyway. The English private banknote eventually disappeared completely; the Bank of England won its remunerative monopoly over note issue south of the border. The last English private bank to issue its own banknotes was Fox, Fowler and Company in 1921. The government and the Bank of England were jealous of the money made from seignorage by a note-issuing bank.

Across the Atlantic and in the wake of the Declaration of Independence, the USA experimented with a "Bank of the United States" twice. However president Andrew Jackson doubted whether the government had such powers and withdrew the bank's privileges in 1836. Five years later it went bankrupt. Central banking was proving nothing like so simple as it appeared just by observing the activities of the Bank of England from a comfortable distance.

One key difference was that the Bank of England been functioning with increasing success since 1694. Its century and a half of financial expertise was in turn built on hard-won creditary expertise dating back to Sir Thomas Gresham. That was crucial. As had been demonstrated in both Sweden and France, early attempts at central banking, largely out of the blue, could all too easily end in disaster. Despite the evident attractions of a government running its own central bank to sell its own debt, it is something very difficult to get right and extremely easy to get wrong.

THE EARLY UNITED STATES OF AMERICA concluded that for the sake of financial prudence, its commercial banks would be authorised, not nationally at Federal level, but individually by the constituent states of the Union. That led to a multiplicity of banks across the nation when the trend in, for example, the UK was the opposite.

It was essentially a defeatist decision by the American government and was to become an increasing impediment in the country's financial system until the 1980s. For about half a century until then, the principle of anti-Federalism was enshrined in the MacPherson Act. That meant, for example, that a cheque drawn on a bank in New York was an unrewarding piece of paper to banks in New Jersey immediately across the River Hudson. It was hardly the most convenient arrangement for the many who commuted across the river each day to earn their living.

The geographical impediment in turn became the driving force behind American Express, which devised an ingenious way round the inevitable problem of interstate money transfers. The company, founded originally in Buffalo, New York in 1850, started out with a vital toehold in the key state for finance. Two years later it took another step toward national status by acquiring the Wild West's famous brand Wells Fargo. Its broad geographical reach meant selling travellers's cheques to people going far away from home was a natural progression. Years later, American Express pioneered credit cards with a similar purpose in mind.

Amid the chaos of the nineteenth century, and surrounded by ham-fisted regulations, the American government was still unable to regulate its own debts. Providing intelligent nationwide banking services to a sophisticated and increasingly prosperous people was even more difficult. The National Banking Act of 1861 at last clarified the situation. The new rules permitted 'national banks' to be chartered and regulated by the Federal government, while individual states were allowed to authorise state banks within their own territory. The various states had their own ideas about how to regulate their banks.

At one extreme stood the important state of Illinois (there were others) which did not even permit banks to operate from more than one branch. Thus the major international bank Continental Illinois had to run its entire operations, everything from its retail 'high street' banking to complex international banking deals to accommodating its senior management, from a single large building in Chicago. That imposed eccentricity, dating back as far as the early nineteenth century, survived until the 1980s. Old traditions die hard.

AMERICA'S NATIONAL BANK concept flourished. In less than twenty years over 2,000 national banks were issuing their own notes - state banks were not permitted to do so. By 1900 there were about 4,500 note-issuing banks, which became a fresh cause of confusion. So in 1913 it was decided to establish a centralised note-issuing bank for America as a whole. That institution was the Federal Reserve, and each national bank was required to place deposits with the new federal system. The Fed's

Board of Governors was appointed directly by the President; any notion of 'free market' capitalism was firmly excluded.

Earlier qualms of President Andrew Jackson were long forgotten, and the USA at last had something broadly equivalent to the state-run Banque de France or the Deutsche Bundesbank. It was simple nationalisation, elsewhere the avowed objective of a rising tide of socialism. It was also inevitable : a lesson from thirteenth century Venice onwards was that banking, exceptionally, is one industry which must be regulated to survive.

Hard-won experience on either side of the Atlantic demonstrated how the evolution of banking was a treacherous path in the evolution of economies. That was even more true of central banking. No kind of banking was anywhere as straightforward as most people might chose to think. Only when something goes wrong, as it did in Iceland in the early twenty-first century, do ordinary people suddenly discover the real fragility of banks.

Knowledge of what has gone before, of the pitfalls as well as the potential, is vital for anyone who would set up a central bank even today. Far too many people, including many economists, take it all for granted. They wrongly assume that because some clever and wary people did get it right in the past, anyone could get it right. Nothing could be further from the truth.

It is still possible to find examples of recently-founded central banks, even in the 21st century, which are teetering on the brink of disaster. The European Central Bank in Frankfurt, which sits at the heart of the much-critised Euro, is probably one of them. It has become embroiled in a gigantic cat's cradle of interbank debts around Europe which threaten to bring the entire edifice crashing down within twenty years of its creation. It is 'administered' by a European Commission which is itself so haphazard in its own financial management that its auditors have refused to sign off its Annual Accounts for years on end. At the time of writing, once again serious questions are being raised about the realistic survival prospects of the Euro.

There is little which is new in any of that. The intrinsic weaknesses date back as far as thirteenth century Venice. As noted previously, the House of Bardi had already collapsed by 1295. The ECB has lent money around Europe with profligate abandon. It is clearly unaware of the fate of John Law who did much the same in France just three hundred and fifty years earlier. Those who ignore the lessons of history are condemned to relive them.

WITHOUT ANY ACCEPTED orthodoxy on what will actually work, different countries had all kinds of different ideas on the best way to manage their banks. The one thing they could never do was leave banks entirely to their own devices. Scottish banking was organised quite differently from that of England, for example, and remains so still. The Scots took note of the formula adopted for the early Bank of England and promptly chose to do something different.

As ever the natural temptation is to put powerful economic - and especially creditary - institutions in the hands of a government-owned monopoly. The philosophy has a long pedigree, tracing back at least as far as the disastrous coinage mismanagement of the

Roman empire. The Sumerian Temple was a monopoly too, if rather more benign. With little evidence to support their conclusion, politicians trust themselves far more than they trust others.

Following the Tudor reformation which opened the doors to organised commerce, many early, large English enterprises had begun life as state-licensed monopolies. Before their dissolution the monasteries[16] had also imposed a unilateral and remunerative control on what could be done. The names, at least, live on. How many old English towns still have an Abbot's Mill? Or a Monk's Fields, or in the case of London the possessions of the Black Friars?

With the Reformation around Europe, and especially in England, economic prerogative was simply secularised, after which it continued much as before. Monopolies were sold in Britain for the benefit of the Privy Purse. Doing so was a principal activity of the exceptionally dishonest House of Stuart. In the broader scheme of things, remunerative monopoly imposed by assorted governments in many countries is almost the norm.

Politicians want the money, and use their draconian powers of legislation to grab it. Greed, rather than any alleged lack of confidence in 'free market' management, is usually at the root of it. However in Scotland the monopoly powers of the Bank of Scotland were allowed to lapse in the early 18th century, a foretaste of the Scottish Enlightenment.

---

16. *The principle lives on in the Catholic church, notably the insistence that priests must remain unmarried - rather than celibate, which is different. When a married priest dies, his estate goes to his widow. When an unmarried priest dies, his estate reverts to the church.*

In 1727 the Royal Bank of Scotland was founded, also in Edinburgh. The two banks were rooted in different political camps, and for many years were bitter rivals. Elsewhere in Scotland some banking services, such as discounting and exchange, were still provided by commercially-driven merchants. As the pace of economic change gathered speed, so did the demand for banking services. It was not long before new businesses emerged to fill the void.

The problem with the two Edinburgh banks was that they granted most of their credit to familiar figures and enterprises - in Edinburgh. Before a Glasgow merchant could borrow from one of them, he would have to make himself well-known in the capital. Only the more substantial Glasgow tobacco magnates found themselves to be sufficiently creditworthy.

Initially, the problem was partially solved by a growing number of small private banks which simply borrowed large sums from the Edinburgh banks and then lent them on in lesser amounts to merchants from Glasgow and elsewhere; an early example of a financial intermediary. A more satisfactory solution was found when merchants themselves in Scottish cities and major towns outside Edinburgh began to set up their own banks.

WHEREAS ENGLISH MERCHANTS were not given the same freedom to set up in business as bankers, there was no legal restriction in Scotland to prevent Scotland's entrepreneurs from doing it for themselves. The Edinburgh banks were horrified at the proliferation of provincial banking companies and joined forces to try and drive them out of business. Some provincials were small and vulnerable but others, such as the Dundee Banking Company, were made of sterner stuff and survived attacks from Edinburgh.

Another banking survivor of the era was the British Linen Company which emerged as a potent force in the banking business. Originally formed in 1746 to promote the Scottish linen industry, the company soon developed banking services which it offered to customers through its offices in many parts of Scotland.

The British Linen Bank was effectively the pioneer of branch banking in Scotland, but not the first to attempt it. Bank of Scotland had tried, unsuccessfully, to establish a branch network in the 1690s and again in the 1730s. It was more successful at its third attempt in the 1770s. The Royal Bank, by contrast, maintained just one branch for many years. This was located in Glasgow but it soon became one of the busiest bank offices anywhere in the United Kingdom.

Nearly all the Scottish banks which opened in those early years issued their own bank notes and there was a clear danger, in the 1760s, it would lead to monetary instability. Some modest regulation were imposed by a Scottish Statute in 1765, and the opening of the Note Exchange a few years later soon regularised the matter. Note issue became one of the most popular and profitable activities of the Scottish banks. The existence of the Note Exchange also nurtured more mutual respect in inter-bank relations.

Early Scottish banking still went astray. In 1769 the Ayr Bank was set up, a joint stock bank which vigorously extended a network of branches around the principal cities of Scotland. Within three years however its lending was out of control and it failed in June

1772, taking thirteen private banks in Edinburgh with it. Despite such setbacks Scotland's provincial banks survived and flourished; by 1810 there were 25 such banks in Scotland in addition to the three public banks of Edinburgh. Scottish finance took on a distinctive character of its own.

For all the vicissitudes of credit management, by the end of the eighteenth century, England, Scotland and Wales were still the only places where deposit banking was a familiar part of the community in rural centres as well as in the major towns and cities. That geographical diversity was essential. As events of the following century were to show, technical inventiveness in finance, the essential way forward to facilitate the division of labour, was not a peculiar privilege of major towns and cities in Britain by any means.

It was the widespread availability of the latest creditary techniques which made possible the development of Britain's Industrial Revolution. For much the nineteenth century, the banks of continental Europe were playing catch-up. Yet the basic creditary principle was hard at work behind the scenes. It is a perennial necessity : the more credit agreements an economy can sustain, then the greater the division of labour it may attain.

Another major development of commercial banking in the eighteenth century was lending by cash credit rather than by cash itself. Although the bulk of business finance was achieved by discounting Bills of Exchange, the cash credit (forerunner of an overdraft) was an increasingly popular lending device. It was developed by the Royal Bank early in the century but, eventually, all banks offered advances to their customers by this means. In a sense the banks had rediscovered the technique developed by the earliest banks of the Italian Renaissance.

The fourth major element of this emerging banking system was the acceptance of deposits and paying interest on them. This was by no means a new idea but the Scots were the first to develop it as a significant and continuing activity on a large scale. Significantly it first developed in Glasgow where the pace of industrial and economic progress was at its most rapid and the resultant demand for funds was at its greatest.

THROUGHOUT THE INDUSTRIAL Revolution the banking system on both sides of the Atlantic grew in a markedly dynamic and, on the whole, relatively stable basis, although politicised supervision and profligate lending ensured there were many setbacks.

For all that, branch systems were enlarged and new provincial banking companies continued to be formed. The rapid growth of industry and commerce was such that many of the smaller provincial banking companies and private banks were too small. They ceased to be able to provide the scale of financial services required by their customers.

From time to time, Scotland's banking system came under scrutiny, in whole or in part, from the English government at Westminster. In 1826, concerned that the note issues of an otherwise under-developed English banking system had contributed to the commercial crisis of that year, the government determined to curb note issues throughout the United Kingdom.

The outcry from all quarters in Scotland was such that Parliamentary Committees of enquiry were set up and the Scottish banking system, in general and the note issue, in particular, were held up as being worthy of imitation. Foremost amongst defenders of the system was that arch-patriot Sir Walter Scott.

A further series of commercial crises in the 1830s and early 1840s forced the government to return to the vexed subject of monetary controls. Despite protests from Scotland, English legislation was passed which restricted issuing of banknotes to those banks already in existence. Since that time, few major banks have been formed.

It has sometimes been claimed that this marked an end of Scotland's most dynamic period of banking development. That was not the case. The number of branches continued to grow quickly; volume of lending and deposit-taking pursued a healthy rate of growth. London was fast developing as an international financial centre, not least in part due to transformation of its Stock Exchange, and in the 1860s the Scottish banks began to open offices there as well. This provoked a storm of protest from English banks but their protests were overcome.

In 1874, Clydesdale Bank opened three offices in the north of England. Once again this caused outrage from English bankers and the government appointed yet another Committee of Enquiry. Evidence was taken but no report was produced. Nevertheless Clydesdale, and other Scottish banks which were about to follow its example, abandoned their plans to open English branch networks and there the matter stood for a century. The Scots confined themselves to Scotland, apart from their London offices, and in return the English banks agreed not to set up operations anywhere north of the border.

Their decision was an important one because, at the time, banking was under-developed in England. The Scots would have had the strength to stage takeovers for many English banks. However over the next thirty years English banks, by processes of merger, acquisition and takeover, and also by extensive branch openings, consolidated their position and created the 'Big Five", the principal London clearing banks.

MAKING SUFFICIENT CREDIT available to the most inventive borrowers in commerce had put one set of strains on the financial system. Another was demand for, and shortage of, coins. By the late eighteenth century there were in chronic shortage. Britain's Royal Mint was using essentially hand-crafted production, showing little technical advance on the moneyers of classical Rome.

Provincial mints spotted an opportunity. The first issue came from the Anglesey Copper Mining Company in North Wales. From 1787 they churned them out in a wide variety of designs - depicting persons, buildings, coats of arms, local legends, and political events. Their trick was to copy the wording of Bank of England paper money : the obverse of the tokens read "we promise to pay the bearer one penny" - probably as a bank credit, in the unlikely possibility the 'bearer' had a bank account.

Denied the funds to develop a factory for steam locomotives, the ever-resourceful James Watt instead turned his attention to the coinage problem. He established a steam-driven coin factory in Birmingham, the Soho Mint - a less expensive enterprise than manufacturing entire locomotives.

Its creditary logic, however, was lacking. In 1797 the Soho Mint produced an ill-fated coinage whose metallic content sought to match its nominal value. These cumbersome objects were rudely known as cartwheels. Their ostensible purpose was to render any local token coinages illegal.

The prohibition failed and within just a few years cartwheels from the Soho mint were replaced by smaller coins. King George III's advisers had been led down that defective route by circular economic logic which had regressed about 2,500 years. Even King Gyges of Lydia had been ahead of them - not that they were likely to have much inkling of his involvement. The original realisation of Lydia had been that a coinage which was considered more valuable than its intrinsic metal content would work.

Municipal tokens re-appeared in 1811 when a wave of prosperity caused by the Napoleonic wars caused another dearth of silver coinage. Then in 1816 the Treasury adopted the Boulton and Watt steam-driven machinery and built a new and much larger government mint on Tower Hill, where man-powered mints had operated for centuries. The result was the world's first mass-produced coinage. At long last an industrial solution was found to relieve a centuries-old shortage of acceptable coins. It was another origin of economies.

By the time machine-made coins began to tumble off the Tower Hill production line, Adam Smith's *Wealth of Nations* was already forty years old. He had witnessed a different world in which the ancient tally stick had still been commonplace. Once a reliable coinage became plentiful, wooden debt devices were abandoned by the Exchequer. Many were stored in the Palace of Westminster and eventually, their financial purpose now forgotten, they were used as fuel. As noted previously, over-enthusiastic stoking in 1832 caused a spectacular fire which consumed most of the Palace.

WELL AWAY FROM commerce and finance in the English-speaking world, things were different. Not every country followed economic doctrines concocted by the primitive economists, especially in continental Europe. They had their own ideas, and different sets of experts. In France and Germany the financial needs of farmers were a high priority. Germany built its network of landesbanken, France's largest bank was the Crédit Agricole. Although it could not have been seen as such, France tacitly acknowledged the same creditary needs as those of the first ever-farmers ten millennia previously.

In Japan, emerging banking industries were deliberately steered toward the development of industry, rather than financing stock market transactions or furnishing the desires of wealthy individuals. The Industrial Bank of Japan set a fine example, one which stood the country in very good stead as it embarked on twentieth century economic expansion.

With their different starting points, Germany and France took a distinctive approach to economic development. As they looked across the English Channel, they realised they were lagging behind. They also had different political dynamics.

Neither country had experienced the tough but modernising Enclosures Acts which had transformed the structure and efficiency of British agriculture. Instead they had to accommodate a large voting bloc of a politically-minded peasant farmers. That never arose in the United Kingdom which had already reformed its agriculture well before it extended its voting franchise, starting with the Great Reform Act of 1832 and continuing over the next century.

France took a collectivist approach. Companies were obliged to join a Chamber of Commerce, a legal requirement unknown in Britain. The local chambers wielded great power in a community as a result. The Chambers also ran the ports and airports for the community, a better route than central government diktat. As noted later in this Chapter, it is a principle worthy of further attention.

Germany was more corporatist. Institutions requiring the involvement of industrial enterprises came on the scene early. Companies were required to set up management boards which included representatives of workers, and eventually worker directors appeared on the boards of major corporations.

It was an enduring concept. Part of the rules setting up the European Common Market were still advocating compulsory worker directors in the 1970s. Such dirigisme found little support amid the much more free market philosophy of industrial Britain, where its Civil Service promptly labelled the notion "prole control".

Several decades before that, Keynes was well aware of the different economic architecture of other countries, which fascinated him, but did not merit much investigation on his part. There are others, but perhaps one economist worthy of more detailed consideration than most is Silvio Gesell.

G ESELL'S INFLUENCE was far greater than his perceived reputation, probably because he did not write in English. Nevertheless his thinking held sway over economic policy in Switzerland for over a century. Given the success of the Swiss economy against the odds, he is worth more attention than has been paid so far.

He was born in 1862 in what is today Belgium, then part of the Prussian empire. Rather than go to university, he became an apprentice merchant in Berlin with his brother. Then at the age of 25 he moved to Buenos Aires where he opened a branch of the merchant business. The depression in Argentina was damaging the economy, and merchanting businesses are always very vulnerable to that. Drawing on his first-hand experiences on the nature of economic depression, Gesell wrote *Die Reformation des Münzwesens als Brücke zum sozialen Staat* ('The reformation of the monetary system as a bridge to a just state'). He then handed the Argentine business back to his brother and returned to Europe in 1892.

For much of the time between 1900 and his death in 1930, Gesell owned a farm at Les Hautes-Geneveys in the Swiss canton of Neuchatel. That too was instructive. Someone with practical experience both as a merchant and as a farmer does enjoy a helpful advantage in understanding economics over a cabal of academic economists who had neither.

They strongly resented his interference. His fellow German-speaking economist, Joachim Starbatty of the University of Tübingen in Germany wrote that *"economic science owes Silvio Gesell profound insights into the nature of money and interest, but Silvio Gesell has always been considered a queer fellow by economic circles. To be sure, he was no professor, which already raises suspicion."* Only a 'professional' academic could be quite so patronising as that.

The suggestion that economic wisdom might somehow be rooted in the real world, rather than in a closed mutual admiration society of scholastics, was anathema. Such were the academic conventions of the nineteenth century. Others were less patronising: *"I am a humble servant of the merchant Gesell"* wrote Irving Fisher of Yale University, apparently in surprise. It was still the view that to understand economics properly one had to be a full-time professor, rather than move in the inferior sphere of a commercial economy.

Silvio Gesell founded two magazines about economics, although their intellectual influence, even within the non Anglo-Saxon sphere was greater than their commercial success. That said, his second magazine, *Der Physiokrat*, was forced into liquidation by censorship laws when World War One broke out. In 1915 Gesell left war-torn Germany and returned to his Swiss farm in Les Hauts-Geneveys, where he stayed until he died. Probably because he wrote in German and Spanish, and never had any direct contact his with the contemporary English economists, Gesell's influence in the Anglo-Saxon sphere was limited.

However he did have at least one British admirer in John Maynard Keynes. On page 355 of his General Theory of Employment, Interest and Money' Keynes wrote that *"Gesell's standpoint is both anti-classical and anti-Marxist. The uniqueness of Gesell's theory lies in his attitude to social reform. His theory can only be understood considering his general point of view as a reformer ... his analysis is not completely developed in several important points, but all in all his model shows no fault. "*

K EYNES'S MORE GENEROUS assessment of Gesell is honourable; it says nothing about Gesell being required to join a professors' trade union before being permitted to write about economics. Nor had Keynes; he first made his name publishing *"The Economic Consequences of Mr Churchill"* when he was a journalist on *The Times*.

The great man's analysis, however is not completely developed either. He omits to point out, or never knew in the first place, the nature of how genuine advances in economies emerge. Almost every step forward had been the work, not of lofty-minded professors, but of practical merchants like Silvio Gesell, a path virtually without deviation reaching back to 3000BC if not earlier.

Proof of the pudding is in the eating. The authorities in Switzerland have consistently taken a Gesellian line in their economic policies. From unpromising beginnings and with few natural resources, Switzerland has emerged as, per capita, the most prosperous country in the world. Today's economists would do well to follow Keynes and investigate the roots of that success.

The essence, however, is to discern what works for an honest and progressive merchant and commercial community in any culture. It is, and has to be, the antithesis of ingrained, corrosive corruption.

That has been the origin of successful economies for the past five thousand years; it is scarcely rocket science. When Silvio Gesell first put his thoughts in writing, he was following a tradition of economic morality stretching back to the merchant community of ancient Sumer - the practical application of the creditary principle.

It was not just Gesell who helped create the distinctive political economy of Switzerland. The country's cantonal structure and constitution, mainly determined by its mountainous topography, inevitably mean its regional attitudes are very independent.   Is anyone really surprised that led it to stand aside from trendy concepts of European union encompassing so many disparate and deeply-rooted cultures? The Swiss could see it would not work.

That said, it is a nation which manages to combine the best of both worlds. It has wide cultural diversity for a country of eight million people; yet its land area of 42,000 square miles is only about a third that of Pennsylvania. Switzerland contrives to accommodate, in fairly congenial harmony, no fewer than four different languages and indeed cultural groups: French, German, Italian and Romansch. One need look no further than the various combinations of 'SBB, FFS, CFF' on its railway carriages to see this multilingualism put into daily practice.[17] To avoid any hint of linguistic favouritism, its stamps are identified as 'Helvetia', the Latin name for the region.

---

17. *Respectively Schweizerische Bundesbahnen; Ferrovie Federali Svizzere; Chemin de Fer Fédéraux Suisses.*

Switzerland's ingrained culture of independence has proved a major economic benefit. By steering clear of what later expanded into the much-criticised European Union, it gained a lot of ground. The idle-minded "globalisation" entreaties which countries on all its frontiers obeyed were studiously avoided. So it is now more prosperous than any of them and its national finances are in much better shape. Gesellian enterprise, clarity aforethought and financial prudence do clearly work.

WHEN IT WISHES TO CO-OPERATE Switzerland does so willingly. The world's largest hadron collider, CERN, straddles the Swiss-French border. Nuclear particles jump in and out of the European Union ten thousand times a second. It is the world centre of impartial treaties. Conditions of war are driven by the Geneva Convention. Prudent banking is driven by the Basel Accords. Berne is home to the Universal Postal Union. The Red Cross is based in Switzerland, which adopts the symbol for its national flag. Geneva is the base for United Nations agencies and there are more besides.

All that for a small country bereft of most natural resources barring hydro-electricity, mountain scenery and hilly pasture. In principle it started with a huge economic disadvantage compared with countries enjoying open access to the sea, large populations and ample natural resources. In World War Two, its railway routes through the Alps were vital to the Axis powers of German and Italy to the north and south respectively. It was starved of food imports and in dire economic straits.[18]   Yet its economic recovery has left the rest of Western Europe for standing. Switzerland is surely a rôle model to which the culturally diverse nations of Africa might yet pay attention. Sooner or later they must look beyond their predilection for civil war, genocide and murderous internal strife.

One might fairly regard the Swiss approach to accommodating cultural distinctions as more elevating than most, compared with countries where inter-regional strife is the norm and has been for centuries. Meanwhile its ultra-reliable banking industry attracts the constant attention of third world kleptomaniacs as a safe place to keep their typically ill-gotten gains.

Yet the greatest influence of Switzerland's unique political outlook is its geographical location at the crossroads of Europe. As explained in Chapter Four, the arduous journey across the Alps through Switzerland played a significant part in the origins of merchant and private banking. The opening of the Gotthard rail tunnel in 1888, followed by the Simplon tunnel in 1906 and the Lötschberg tunnel in 1911 changed all that.

Switzerland could afford to pay for all of them, and continues to dig much longer Alpine tunnels in the twenty-first[t] century. Such was the strategic significance of its transalpine railways to the combatants in the First World War, three years after the Lötschberg tunnel opened, it was in everyone's best interests to leave the Swiss alone. Let them continue to be the logistics manager of Europe, adamantly protecting their own neutral status as they did so.

18. When the author first visited Switzerland as a child in 1951, there were still twelve Swiss francs to the pound. Such has been its superior economic performance since, the Swiss franc is now well on its way to parity.

Nineteenth century railways were the bedrock of the nation state, and in the process revealed the Transport Principle as a fundamental force in political economy. Railway systems were built geographically, nation by nation.

International frontier stations became the great crossroads of European culture and commerce in particular. That rôle is far more apparent where countries share land frontiers : a classic example is Basle station even today, on the three-way frontier of France, Germany and Switzerland. It is as romantic as ever; one almost expects to bump into Agatha Christie in its waiting room.

As this book now tracks the advance of economic activity into the twenty-first century, the transport principle based on newer technology is changing things once more. The achievements of George Stephenson cast a long shadow, but the independent nation state created by his railways has probably passed its prime.

A S NOTED AT THE START of this chapter, in the material world the Industrial Revolution unfolded with unprecedented rapidity and ingenuity. Stephenson's contributions were higher speed and lower cost, but the consequences of those two changes were far greater than it sounds. His Prospectus for the London & Birmingham Railway (page 280) although written for tough-minded investors, was as close as any document before or since to providing a completely accurate prophesy of a new kind of civilisation.

In the intellectual world, by contrast, developments had been rather less convincing. The infant wisdom of economics lived in a cocoon of its own, disdainfully ignoring the reality of economic advances all around. Meanwhile advances in manufacturing collectively pushed prices in the same direction : downwards.

No entrepreneur will build a factory whose products are more expensive than those of existing competitors. Either his output is better, or it is cheaper - most often it is both. Across the economy, the direct and inevitable effect of market capitalism is gradual deflation. Possibly a surprise to those more familiar with what happened in the the twentieth century, it is the converse, inflation, which is the historical aberration.

One inflation index which avoids being over-clouded by shifts in consumer taste is postage. Perhaps its takes a specialist in the stamps of Great Britain (such as the present writer) to demonstrate just how much postal rates came down after Rowland Hill's pioneering 'Penny Black' in 1840. In July 1860 sending a letter from Great Britain to New York cost a shilling. By November 1902 the same thing cost fivepence, a fall of almost sixty per cent.

Between the end of the Napoleonic wars and the beginning of World War One, a matter of ninety-nine years, the purchasing power of the British pound just about doubled.[19] Inevitably so, given the march of expertise in an entrepreneurial economy. It was to be a very different story in the century to come.

19. *As shown by the Bank of England's long term chart of inflation, published in 1994 to mark its own 300th anniversary.*

Chapter Seven

After 1900 AD

The evil that men do lives after them.
The good is oft interred with their bones.
WILLIAM SHAKESPEARE
JULIUS CAESAR

B EFORE IT RECEDES into some airbrushed archive
of selective amnesia, the twentieth century deserves
thoughtful examination. Neither a disaster nor a triumph,
it turned into an eclectic cocktail of economic opposites.
At its best, the twentieth century witnessed the heights of industrial
progress in the West. At its least impressive, for a hundred years
after the First World War it was corrupted by a succession of
misguided experiments in political economy.

The economies of advanced countries enjoyed a whirlwind
of progress in scientific and technological achievement. Led by
unprecedented innovation, augmented by a new culture of research
undertaken by commercial enterprises, its fruits were manifest in a
profusion of new materials, new products, revolutionary changes in

technology and in manufacturing methods. Prior to the twentieth century, innovative research had been the work of inspired individuals, rather than the offspring of commercial investigation.

Progressively after the First World War such collective research became the norm, backed by organisations like CERN, or NASA or the National Physical Laboratory. Crowning all this, the ingenuity and volume of industrial production moved to previously inconceivable heights, at least in the leading countries. The twentieth century became the first-ever era of near-universal abundance.

NOT FOR THE FIRST time in history many of the most original advances emerged from military conflict. It seems to focus inventive minds even more powerfully than the profit motive. In the space of just over thirty years there were two appalling wars of an almost global involvement, those of 1914-8 and then of 1939-45. Only the Armageddon-like prospect of nuclear annihilation prevented any more.

Remarkably continents which were not extensively caught up in the conflict, specifically much of Africa, notably Latin America and swathes of Asia ended up as the least prosperous regions of the twentieth century. It is a paradox, or maybe it was simply a matter that there was nothing about them worth fighting for, and so they were overlooked.

A transformed level of industrial output in the West meant that a broadly-based consumer society first glimpsed in the nineteenth century reached unprecedented levels. Never before had quite so many enjoyed such generous slices of quite so much. By

1959 a British prime minister was truthfully able to declare in his election-winning slogan *"You've never had it so good."* [1] Free market capitalism, led by the north Atlantic democracies, and despite its grossly-criticised flaws, generated a phenomenal level of material prosperity. By the end of the century, producers were looking for customers, rather than consumers looking for goods.

Another distinctive ingredient in the economic cocktail was the division of the world into the haves and have-nots. If the First World of the West bathed in relative abundance, and the Second World of the Communist bloc collapsed, the Third World stagnated. In the second half of the century it expelled so-called 'colonial' regimes which at their best sought to extend to those countries the prosperity of the West. The result, too often, was more poverty.

Meantime the morose expectations of Adam Smith and Karl Marx were consigned, in the latter's own phrase, to the dustbins of history. Both philosophers had anticipated that industrial prosperity would be an exclusive perquisite of the few, the masses held in poverty simply to furnish a sumptuous lifestyle for the rich. Marx even tried to devise a mathematical formula to show he was right.

It was a forlorn quest he eventually abandoned. Having reached his intellectual impasse, however, he unfortunately failed to put anything more perceptive or constructive in its place. Many of his admirers would consider he had sufficient ability. Both men were subsumed by the pointed observation of J K Galbraith *"The experience of being disastrously wrong is salutary. No economist should be denied it, and not many are"*.

1. *Harold Macmillan, British prime minister 1957-62*

It took just one man to show how far-fetched the miserable prognostications of the primitive economists really were. Henry Ford did so by the most direct route of all, creating a twentieth century form of capitalism which entirely confounded those previous prophets of doom. However his was not some lofty intellectual construct as was theirs. On the contrary it was a down-to-earth arrangement for making himself extremely rich. And to do that, he chose to make his workers and customers rich too.

ENRY FORD DID TO THE world economy of his own era much what George Stephenson had done almost a century before. Both men both revealed what it took to become an economic pioneer. Neither had a lengthy education, quite the contrary. They were never bound by any conventional wisdom taught in a classroom or seminary, but left totally free to think for themselves.

Both acquired their outlook as trade apprentices. Working as a brakeman controlling the winding gear of a coal pit, George Stephenson made shoes and mended clocks to supplement his income. He was illiterate until he was eighteen. Henry Ford famously dismantled a watch.

Far more than any 'professional' economists, George Stephenson and Henry Ford are two founding fathers of economies. We should judge talent by what it achieves, not by its vain hopes or conceited proclamations. Yet such innovators are often seen as irascible and intolerant by those around them. They typically are those who 'cannot suffer fools gladly'. As perfectionists, such men are usually unable to make that desirable concession. Anyone incompetent working close to them is soon found out, dismissed and typically nurses a grudge thereafter. True pioneers normally collect a full share of enemies and the 'evil' that men do lives after them.

The industrial production of the motor car set a pattern which was then imitated many times elsewhere. The twentieth century became the era of mass production. Yet just like Stephenson's Rocket, Henry Ford's business enterprise could trace its technological roots deep into the previous century.

The world's first working four-stroke internal combustion engine had been demonstrated by the German inventor Nikolaus Otto back in 1862, before even the high summer of the steam railway. Otto was born in 1832, two years after Stephenson's Liverpool & Manchester Railway opened, and five years before the first German long-distance steam railway between Leipzig and Dresden. After Otto's first demonstration it then took a further twenty-four years before another German, Karl Benz, began to produce road vehicles using such engines.

Next, in 1891 the Englishman Herbert Ackroyd Stuart built an oil engine which was licensed to the engineering company Hornsby. The progressive invention of the internal combustion engine was proving to be an Anglo-German affair. Two years later in 1893, a third German, Dr Rudolf Diesel, obtained a patent for his compression-ignition oil engine which dispensed with the need for spark plugs. By 1900 he was even using peanut oil as a fuel - a century before the fashion for renewable energy. In total, almost forty years was spent developing internal combustion until came the man who was to draw it all together. Born just fifteen years after George Stephenson died, the genius of America's Henry Ford was in manufacturing rather than discovering new science or technology.

Just as Stephenson had built his great enterprise on preceding decades of clever technology which created the external combustion engine, so Ford built his great enterprise on preceding decades of clever technology which created the internal combustion engine.

H ENRY FORD DREW SOME of his inspiration from the mass production techniques already devised for sewing machines. The first such were manufactured in the USA in 1839. The man who worked out the potential of production line logic was Isaac Singer (1811–65) who improved on the design concept for the machines, drew up patents and formed the Singer Sewing Machine Corporation in 1851. It was destined to grow into a worldwide company.

To speed up sales, Singer also pioneered part-payment, more popularly known as hire purchase. One of his sewing machines could be acquired for a down payment of a modest five dollars. Another step forward in creditary technique was marching hand in hand with the improving specialisation principle, the normal pattern. Success only took Singer twelve years. In 1863 he retired to England.

Henry Ford was well aware of Singer's success when he set about making motor cars half a century later. His simple philosophy for mass-production was to shape most of twentieth century manufacturing, for everything from fizzy drinks to Liberty ships. In many ways it became the century of Ford. As with George Stephenson he was rapidly surrounded by imitators eager to copy his success formula for large-scale commerce.

Henry Ford believed in standardised designs, manufacturing in very large numbers, using ultra-efficient methods and paying his workers high wages. He made his money out of high volume, not out of extravagant profit margins. So did his employees. The more they were paid, he reckoned, then the more they would spend. Exactly sixty years after Marx's *Communist Manifesto* had dolefully predicted that workers would always be the downtrodden and impoverished slaves of capitalists, Henry Ford demonstrated reality to be the opposite.

Customers benefited too. When the Model T Ford was launched in October 1908, it cost $825. A success from the start, its price fell every year until it cost just $360 in 1916. So capitalists did not, after all, merely seek to increase their profits at the expense of everyone else. Rather, Henry Ford saw himself as the catalyst of a general economic prosperity in which everyone else could share.

In the process the price of the Model T became a textbook example of the deflationary effect of natural capitalism. It blazed a trail to be followed even more dramatically eighty years later with the emergence of electronic information technology.   By the time the last Model T car came off the production lines of Detroit in 1927, over fifteen million had been built. By then Henry Ford had built his huge River Rouge complex near Detroit. It was the largest factory in the world. Ford did not want to rely on other suppliers, so he opted to manufacture everything from steel to the smallest components.

For his Model T and its pick-up truck variant, the target customer was the American farmer. Ford's commercial logic was inescapable. A farmer would have every incentive to expand his output once he had effective transport to run his farm, while his means of transport had to be cheap enough to buy and rugged enough to maintain.

Henry Ford judged it right and America's farmers did just what he predicted. His proved a far more effective way to expand agricultural production than collective farms devised by twentieth century intellectual communists, which served only to wreck levels of output in some of the most fertile stretches of eastern Europe. One cannot make the poor rich by making the rich poor.

S TEPHENSON AND FORD stand head and shoulders above their contemporaries as two originators of the Industrial Revolution. Both built on the past; almost all the economic achievements in the first half of the twentieth century traced back to inventions of the nineteenth.

By 1875 much of the future groundwork, from railways to the possibilities of the motor car to the new chemistry and electricity, was there for those with eyes to see. It is therefore both surprising and tragic that Karl Marx (1818-1883) proved to be so stubbornly unobservant, particularly so when he proclaimed that *"the philosophers have only interpreted the world in various ways; the point is to change it."*

One might argue that the originator of industrial plenty in factories had been the eighteenth century's Josiah Wedgwood (1730-1795). Much of it was already apparent even half a century before

Marx was born. The creditary structure of the British economy was also in place by the mid-nineteenth century. Numerous banks serving a variety of financial purposes were all to be found within easy walking distance of the reading room of the British Museum.

Marx was surrounded by a rapidly changing economic order. He should have been in his element. Instead he ignored it. Between his birth and publication of *Das Kapital,* the British parliament passed ten Factories Acts to improve workers' conditions. Practices thus outlawed such as child labour, until then normal on farms, are still prevalent in parts of the Third World.

Great Britain set up its Factories Inspectorate in 1833. Marx seemed oblivious to that as well. As an exponent of political economy, he was far more of a politician than an economist. As an example of his political insight, his *Critique of the Gotha Programme* of the early 1870s was remarkable. It contrasts markedly with his ham-fisted economics. Yet his grossly-political economic simplifications seen to have nurtured his popularity - certainly not his insight.

George Stephenson's world-changing Liverpool & Manchester Railway opened for business when Karl Marx was still only twelve years old. Robert Stephenson's London & Birmingham Railway opened before he was twenty. Its southern terminus at Euston station was only about half a mile from where the philosopher wrote *Das Kapital* in the British Museum.

Did he ever bother to stroll up the road and indulge in some old-fashioned curiosity? It seems unlikely. No quoted element of Marx's volumes acknowledges the importance of transport to economic progress. Surprisingly so. He was preoccupied with economic progress for many years: it was the very essence of *Das Kapital*. One might reasonably think he would have shown some inquisitive interest in what was actually happening.

Marx did not observe so much as surmise. His economic rationale was far more pseudo-mathematical than empirical. His political visions were apocalyptic rather than realistic. At least that made for good box office. Well over a century after his death there are still many who see him as their intellectual inspiration. Yet how many of his admirers ever do anything more than recite his catchiest slogan, engraved on his semi-monumental tombstone in Highgate cemetery? The evil that men do lives after them.

A T WHICH POINT WE should move on. The rôle of world's leading country in economic progress since the beginning of the Industrial Revolution has been shared between Great Britain and the United States. The switch from one to the other about coincided with the First World War. But before the nineteenth century emergence of economically dominant industry, it had been agriculture that counted for more. In Europe, both France and Spain covered a much greater area than Great Britain and until the early nineteenth century their agricultural economy gave them greater power.

The narrow defeat of Napoleon at Waterloo in 1815 was not just a momentous military victory. It was a historic reversal in the rôle of economic leadership. In the century which followed, and partly as a result, Great Britain successfully turned itself into 'The Workshop Of The World'.

Eventually the vast agricultural potential of the United States was unlocked by its railroads and America's economy overtook that of Great Britain. Since then, the USA has continued to lead the world economic order, now for more than a hundred years, and to the envious resentment of many. Beyond any sensible dispute, the twentieth century was to be America's century.

Men like Henry Ford led the way, and in the process he became one of the richest Americans ever. But not the richest. The four richest Americans have each pioneered one of its four leading industries: oil, steel, railways and much more recently information technology. It does seem that history has space for only one such ultra-rich entrepreneur to emerge from the early days of any major innovation. Then his imitators spread the financial success among many. The fifth richest American, John Jacob Astor, made his money from property development.

The most successful American ever was John D Rockefeller, who made his money by creating Standard Oil. The second was Andrew Carnegie born in Scotland to poor parents and moved to the United States in 1844. His timing was good. The industrial revolution triggered by the railways was rapidly unfolding. His first job was as a railway telegrapher and from that he moved into business in US Steel at just the right juncture. The railways and civil engineering generated a huge market for his products.

The next richest was Cornelius Vanderbilt, founder of many American railroads. The fourth richest has been Bill Gates, founder of Microsoft. Slightly further down the list, of the next thirty-five richest Americans, seven more also made their money out of railroads. Seven made their money out of banking. Six made their money out of retailing of whom five are members of the Walton family alone, founders of the huge Walmart enterprise.

Much more recently three more joined the list. They made their fortunes out of the IT revolution and their number is likely to grow.[2] No matter what the industry, however, it always seems to be the original pioneers who make the real money rather than those who succeed them. Much the same pattern is now to be observed in post-communist Russia. After the collapse of Communism it quickly spawned a single generation of ultra-rich oligarchs which seems unlikely to be repeated.

It is a wealth pattern which can be traced back over two and half millennia to the plutocratic success of King Croesus of Lydia. No-one seems to have made quite so much money out of money since. That said, many lesser fortunes must have been made by innovative entrepreneurs in developing Mediterranean mints and coinage over the next four hundred years.

We can only surmise there would have been comparable financial success among the pioneer merchants of ancient Sumer two millennia before that. If their individual identities have perhaps been preserved in early cuneiform records, no-one so far seems to have unearthed them. Doing so would be an interesting challenge to today's archaeologists.

In our own time the development of industry after Henry Ford's pioneering efforts has been amply chronicled in many places, and needs no detailed repetition here. Countless businesses are

---

2. *Larry Ellison of Oracle; Jeff Bezos of Amazon; Mark Zuckerberg of Facebook.*

contemplated, many established. Only a few were destined to survive and prosper, their commercial origins often happenstance. What became Britain's Imperial Chemical Industries emerged from a chance discussion on a transatlantic liner in the 1920s.

THE GOLDEN RULE is that many acorns are ambitiously planted, but only a few ever grew into oak trees. That has been the rationale for encouraging the small firms sector, but its essential serendipity has never fitted comfortably with the bureaucratic mindset which seeks predictability above all else.[3] Burdens heaped on small firms by regulators and tax authorities are typically draconian. Yet a myriad small firms, rather than a few large firms, are the prime generators of fresh employment. And somewhere among them is the next Henry Ford.

Another unsurprising rule is that almost no industry, or technology, lasts for ever. They unfold, often explosively, then settle down and gradually fade into the background again. The technology of the steam locomotives had already reached maturity around 1900 with the work of George Jackson Churchward at Swindon for the Great Western Railway. He would have seen nothing unusual (apart from its size) in the last steam engine built for British Railways as it emerged from the same Swindon works in 1960.

If Henry Ford's Model T was the first modern motor car, its technical innovation had about run its course by 1980. Attempts to revolutionise the technology - such as replacing reciprocating

3. *The same pattern repeated itself time and again in the author's direct experience as the CBI's first Director for Smaller Firms in the late 1970s.*

engines with a rotary Wankel engine - came to nothing. Car manufacturers now routinely swap engines, power trains and expensive major components such as the floor pan. There are no trade secrets left.

T HE PRIVATE CAR is nowadays just a commodity. Competition has been reduced to body-styling, advertising gimmicks and more importantly, price. Maybe the advent of the electric car, a remarkably long time in the making [4], will shake things up a bit. As this is being written Sweden's Volvo has announced it will cease manufacturing conventionally-powered cars around 2020, and others are following suit.

Governments are enthusiastically hopping aboard the bandwagon. The global trade consequences of abandoning petroleum should not be overlooked; it is a political minefield. Should electric cars become the norm, then the Henry Ford internal combustion automobile will have lasted for about a century.

Another such mature industry which will be instantly familiar to most people in the United Kingdom is the double-deck bus. The basic design concept - one-man operation with a front entrance, a six-cylinder diesel engine in the rear - was established by 1960 and has barely changed since. Cosmetic styling apart, brand new buses

---

4. *The author wrote an extended news article on the subject, entitled* 'Field Day For Electric Cars' *and published in the* Financial Times *way back in 1967. The main difference since has been in battery technology. That said, electric propulsion had already been used for fork lift trucks, and milk floats quietly doing early morning house to house deliveries, for many years before that.*

being introduced in 2017 are virtually indistinguishable from their predecessors of fifty years earlier. They have become the routine mainstay of passenger transport in Britain's towns and cities.

Road transport flourished in the twentieth century much as rail transport had done in the nineteenth. In Britain it was given a boost at the end of the First World War; the military effect again. Army surplus lorries and demobilised army drivers became the foundation of a road haulage industry. They had the advantage of selecting the most profitable business. Railways, by law being common carriers, had to accept any freight offered to them.

So Britain's railway industry, already struggling to recover from gross dilapidation after being requisitioned for the war effort, was left to pick up the commercial dregs. The high point of the railway industry was around the First World War. The time from inception to maturity was about a century The railway's relative decline was then exacerbated by massive improvement in the road network. Not since the Roman Empire had so many new roads been built anew with such definite purpose.

A comparable post war surplus pattern was evident after World War Two. America had manufactured large numbers of Liberty ships and T2 tankers. They were bought up by enterprising Greek and Hong Kong shipping magnates, who turned them into global fleets and thus became extremely wealthy. In turn that development was to be over-shadowed by what happened next

Among the most potent improvements in the 'transport principle' in the latter half of the twentieth century was the advent of the container ship Once again, there was nothing particularly revolutionary about the technology. They use a conventional marine diesel driving a single propeller from an engine room which requires less and less manpower. Attempts to copy the nuclear reactors used in America's aircraft carriers came to nothing. Only one nuclear-powered cargo ship was ever built, and the Russians built one nuclear icebreaker. It was another technological dead-end.

Although navigation techniques made great advances with the advent of GPS, and manning levels were reduced to an absolute minimum, the major change in the cargo ships of the twentieth century was in their speed and size. The economic impact of that was substantial. Deep sea container ships were already becoming the worldwide norm by 1970.[5]

When Britain abandoned Commonwealth preference on joining the EEC, container shipping was still in its infancy. Trade patterns half a century later are very different. Britain's European trade is still transported in articulated container trucks, to be seen in their thousands crossing the English Channel on ferries and passing through the Channel Tunnel beneath it. The driver of an articulated truck can move just one international standard container. A crew of fewer than thirty on the latest container ships can move 20,000.

It is probably cheaper for Britain to transport a bottle of wine from Australia or New Zealand than to transport one from France

---

5. *The author wrote the first substantive article on the 'container revolution' to be published in the* Financial Times, *appearing on 8 July 1966. Unusually it took the form of a lengthy item on the publisher page, when the regular slot for such industrial feature articles was on the O.P. Even then the paper rated the subject as important. Within fifteen years containers had gone from being a novelty to being the norm.*

or Spain. By the turn of the century the cost of container shipping fell to the point at which it was economic to despatch garbage in containers for disposal in India. It was now a cheaper option than using landfill sites around England.

Containerised shipping began in the United States, to supply its war in Vietnam, another innovation with a background in war. Its large-scale operation needs a freight catchment area generating thousands of boxes a week. So Britain's trade is concentrated on Tilbury, Felixstowe, Southampton and Liverpool. Gone are the days when smaller ports and wharves shared Britain's overseas trade more equally; it is another shift in the location of industry.

CONTAINER SHIPS ARE proving to be another origin of economies. In the process an economic pattern is half-repeating itself. It was the efficiency of shipping around the Mediterranean which gave birth to the international economy of the Classical world. Now the pattern is global, and the main difference between the two is political. Navigation and trade around the classical Mediterranean came under the umbrella of the Roman empire, a *Pax Romanus* and its uniform currency. Today it depends on international co-operation through trade pacts; but that does not have to be the product of a Treaty of Rome.

Where container ships now shape the global spread of industry, a parallel change in air transport determines how it is managed. The gentle revolution began in about 1960 with the introduction of jet aircraft. Jet engines emerged from the 1930s followed by a race to develop the fastest fighter aircraft in World

War Two. The new 1960s passenger jets typically flew at 550-600mph, almost four times the speed of piston-engined aircraft of only ten years previously. The effect on the North Atlantic business community in particular was fundamental.

The acceleration meant it was now possible to travel between Europe and America in about six hours, a twentieth of the time it took a transatlantic liner. Previous aircraft such as the "whispering giant" Bristol Britannia using turbo-prop engines had still taken twelve hours to make the trip.

Before that, piston-engined aircraft such as the Boeing Stratocruiser had taken a whole day, including for Britain refuelling stops at Prestwick in Scotland and Gander in Newfoundland. As a mode of travel, the popularity of flying such long distances in slow piston-engined aircraft had been limited. Until the 1960s the regular way to cross the Atlantic was on grand ocean liners such as the Queen Elizabeth, competing for the 'Blue Riband' fastest crossing; it was all very heroic, but about to become obsolete.

As a mode of transport, although stylish and luxurious, the time spent in crossing the Atlantic by sea meant that managing a business spanning both continents required a high level of decentralisation. It was almost impossible for one man to run both ends day to day. All that was now about to change.

From 1960 onwards, an intercontinental business could be run by a single management team based in, for example, either New York or London. Crossing the Atlantic was no longer a prolonged relaxation or a star-studded spectacle. Management could be there and back again in just a few days. To demonstrate the new travel potential at least one prominent show business personality contrived to present concurrent weekly television programmes on both sides of the Atlantic. That was David Frost, who bathed in the publicity.

In and around Europe, a similarly radical change emerged. Speedy jet aircraft such as the BAC 1-11, and its European variants, meant that from a single location - typically London - a business's subsidiaries and its factories anywhere west of Russia could now be visited 'there and back again' in the day [6].

The previous trend toward business decentralisation was reversed. Over the next couple of decades there emerged a new kind of corporate structure, one which located top management well away from the rest of the enterprise. Back in the nineteenth century, Mr Arkwright had typically lived in a house next door to his mill. A hundred or so years later his great-grandson could live a thousand miles from the mill and yet be just as effective in managing it.

NOWHERE WAS THIS NEW structure of business management more evident than in London, which developed rapidly as the specialist centre for managing an international business. Only top management were involved. In that pursuit Britain's capital enjoyed the double benefit of being English-speaking, and of a longitude position just half-way between the geographical extremes of the Far East and California,

---

6. *In the 1980s as international director of Marketing and Public Affairs for what was then Chemical Bank of New York (now J P Morgan) the author was responsible for its branches in Edinburgh, Frankfurt, Zurich, Geneva, Paris, Milan, Madrid and Barcelona, working from just a single base in London.*

being eight time zone hours apart from each. That meant London-based directors could talk with their offices in Japan or Hong Kong at the beginning of their normal working day and with their offices in San Francisco or Los Angeles at the end of it. It is no coincidence that from then onwards, the principal language of international commerce became English rather than French. In the European Union, the divide is between participants born before or after 1960.

Much faster air transport in the latter half of the twentieth century reshaped the way intercontinental businesses were managed. They became more feasible and more profitable. Although "globalisation" in the sense of standardisation has generated some political displeasure, the global shift in business management has been entirely logical. As an example, one British chemical company reduced its management team to just six, based in a small suite of offices in London's St James's Square.

With a single PA-receptionist to man the fort, six keyboard-savvy top executives could comfortably supervise its corporate issues and company operations throughout Europe. Such slimmed-down top management meant that lines of communication became informal and efficient: The CEO or the CFO was readily on call just next door. The other side of the same coin was that 'the provinces' were denuded of such top management - in British many towns and cities the most senior representative was a regional manager, earning a fraction of his - or her - superiors in London.

Managerial impoverishment of Britain's provinces was in full swing. That had knock-on social effects as the higher discretionary incomes of such Londoners set them apart. It became a source of some resentment elsewhere in the country, which in turn had long-term political repercussions.

One might again draw a comparison with classical Rome two millennia previously. Everything from live theatre to stylish restaurants to museums and "culture" with their supporting professions was concentrated in what was transformed into a metropolis for the wealthy at the expense of the rest of the country. The stratospheric level of London's domestic property prices was in major part a consequence of the same wealth transfer process.

N O LONGER WAS THE geography of business management being driven by proximity to raw materials or sources of energy such as coal. The determining factor was now proximity to an intercontinental airport. For London the magnet was Heathrow: a similar pattern could be discerned around Frankfurt airport in Germany, or Schipol airport in the Netherlands, in Paris and Milan, or further afield in New York, Chicago, Atlanta and as far afield as Singapore and Sydney.

A key difference however is that of distances: the industrially-advanced region of western Europe is relatively compact, so its internal flying times are comparably brief. The entire region would about fit into the expanse of the United States between the Mississippi and the Atlantic Ocean.

For its internal flights western Europe business does not have to contemplate distances as great, or as time-consuming, as New York to San Francisco. Beyond the continental scale of business travel, a different set of criteria now applied to the intercontinental routes. Globe-trotting businessmen now demanded regular daily flights to all the world's major destinations. Their new routine of running businesses meant they could no longer afford to wait a whole week for the next scheduled flight. Meantime global airlines were facing a different challenge.

Their cost structure meant they needed to run the most economical aircraft and to operate them as fully as possible. With the advent of much larger jet aircraft, there was a further shift in commercial geography. As the twenty-first century dawned progressive airlines have switched to concentrating their scheduled services on fewer business routes, and in practice that means operating out of a radiating hub. The cost advantage they gain in a ruthlessly competitive industry is substantial.

The 1960s notion of a network with scheduled flights linking everywhere with everywhere else became obsolete. Once again it is a matter of simple arithmetic. An airline providing a full schedule of flights linking a hundred different destinations with a traditional network would require, in principle, five thousand routes to do so. An airline concentrating all its services through a single hub can serve that same hundred destinations with just a hundred routes.

However such operations then need hub airports with four runways unless they have no national or regional traffic as, for example, Dubai. The logic is inescapable. Despite that a number of governments - including the United Kingdom - still cannot fathom the concept of hub operation, and persist in extending undersized, obsolete airports. They are wasting time and money. Four runway hub airports are an origin of economies still in the making.

WHILE FASTER JET AIRCRAFT transformed the physical means to manage a company which spanned the globe, an even greater revolution was in train, that of global communication. It has been separated from transport, progressively, ever since the 19th century. Until then, communication was no faster than transport : at its fastest a man carrying a letter on a horse or a sailing ship.

The separation began with invention of the electric telegraph in 1837 by English physicists William Cooke and Sir Charles Wheatstone. Morse Code was devised a year later. That was even before Sir Rowland Hill set up Britain's uniform penny postage on 6 May 1840, a much cheaper standardised mail service using prepaid stamps and made famous by the 'Penny Black'. Postal services of course relied on conventional road and rail transport to reach their destination. They have never been separated from physical transport, even into the era of air mail.

The first public telegraph line was installed in 1843 between Washington DC and Baltimore. Samuel Morse sent the first message *"What hath God wrought?"* on 24 May 1844. Just six year later the first undersea telegraph cable was laid between England and France, although it was to survive only a few days until severed by the anchor of a French fishing boat. By 1858 a transatlantic telegraph cable had been laid between Newfoundland and Ireland. Queen Victoria sent President Buchanan a congratulatory message on 16 August. Already by the 1840s the electric telegraph was the normal way of controlling signalling and train movement on railways.

T HE NEXT STEP WAS the telephone, invented by Scotsman Alexander Graham Bell (1847-1922) at the age of 29. He beat a competing inventor, Elisha Gray, to the patent office by a matter of hours. Over the next hundred years telephone technology in developed countries advanced to the point at which manpower was no longer needed to connect and switch standard calls. Using a minuscule quantity of electricity the marginal cost of providing telephone services effectively shrank to almost zero, once the infrastructure had been provided.

The first mobile phone (more precisely called a cellular or cell phone as in the USA) was invented by Dr Martin Cooper of Motorola and the first demonstration call was made in 1973. Forty years previously a two-way mobile radio telephone had been used by the Chicago police to stay ahead of the city's gangsters. Perhaps that was a kind of war as well. It certainly led to an important innovation.

In the twentieth century radio came into its own. Michael Faraday and then James Clerk Maxwell had laid the theoretical groundwork in the nineteenth, but radio had to wait until Guglielmo Marconi (1874-1937) perfected the system and successfully transmitted a radio message across the Atlantic in 1901.

It then transpired he had in the process infringed a number of patents registered eight years earlier by the Serbian-born Nikola Tesla (1856-1943) working in the USA. An America citizen from 1891, Tesla was a fertile inventor, at times working with Thomas Edison and George Westinghouse. No matter who devised which bit, radio was very much a product of the United States around the turn of the century. The next step was television. A bit like steam railways, the basic technology began as entertainment but steadily migrated into communication.

Although the German Paul Gottlieb Nipkow registered a patent for transmitting pictures by wire in 1884, it was John Logie Baird (1888-1946) who demonstrated a system at Selfridges, the department store in central London, in 1926. His system was then adopted by the British Broadcasting Corporation, but its mechanical technology of rotating discs was replaced by a wholly electronic system invented by Philip Farnsworth (1906-1971) of the USA just a decade after Baird's pioneering demonstration.

That was all in monochrome : the first colour television was designed by the Radio Corporation of America and broadcasts began in 1953. Like the telephone before it, radio and television depended on detailed research, many thousands of hours in laboratories and some highly sophisticated equipment.

The neatest invention of the telecommunications era was set out in just a short letter published in *Wireless World* in February 1945. In the space of four hundred words, the English radio enthusiast, later cinema celebrity and space commentator Arthur C Clarke (born 1917) just followed the implications of basic Newtonian physics.

It became a classic example of "it's so simple, it's amazing no-one thought of it before". His outline proposal laid the foundations for global communications which will last to the end of the Industrial Revolution and probably well beyond. Clarke started from the observation that the further an object is from the earth, the longer it takes to complete an orbit. The moon takes 28 days.

RGUABLY A TWENTIETH CENTURY successor to Galileo, Clarke then realised there had to be some distance from the earth at which a complete orbit needed precisely 24 hours. If any object could be sent into space at that height and positioned directly over the equator it would then appear, as seen from the earth below, to be quite stationary.

The satellite would be synchronised with the earth's rotation, or as it is now expressed "synchronous".   In his letter Arthur Clarke also pointed out that such a satellite *"would be in brilliant sunshine half the time. Its operating [duration] might be indefinitely prolonged by use of photo-electric elements."* Prophetic words indeed. The necessary orbit was about 22,000 miles above the earth's surface and, as Clarke acknowledged, the technology to launch such a satellite into space already existed. His letter remarked that the German V2 weapon, a ballistic rocket designed and used to bomb London, could handle a payload of 2000lbs.

All Clarke needed for the payload of his communication system was "a few hundred pounds". So his idea *"required nothing new in the way of technical resources. It should be possible within 5-10 years."* Arthur Clarke's 1945 letter ended with *"I'm afraid this isn't going to be of the slightest use to our postwar planners but I think it is the ultimate solution to the problem."* He was being overly pessimistic.

With the defeat of Germany just a few months later, its V2 rocket programme was acquired by the United States in its entirety. It became the basis of the US space programme, which included launching satellites for communications. The first such, Telstar, went into orbit in 1962. Seven years later, and more as an act of political propaganda, the same programme put a man on the moon. Within a decade or so of that event, Arthur Clarke's original concept of synchronous satellites had become the norm . Today his simple astronautical formula is known as the Clarke Orbit.

There are now several hundred communication satellites scattered along its path. They have become the foundation, not only of global telecommunications, but also of position-finding. The mapping technology of GPS exploits an ever earlier principle, Euclidean trigonometry, to define an exact point anywhere on the earth's surface. John Harrison's chronometer had been superseded.

In a remarkable wartime decade which saw the invention of electronic television and Arthur Clarke's historic brainwave, the modern electronic computer was also born. Once again the main motivation was the challenge of war. It was another Briton with a remarkable mind, Alan Turing (1912-54) who developed a machine at Bletchley Park in total secrecy. Its purpose was to decipher traffic from Germany's very sophisticated Enigma coding machine used to encrypt its military communications. Not unreasonably, German scientists believed they had developed a coding technology which was almost certainly unbreakable.

Alan Turing's first contribution was a paper published in 1936 in which he devised the algorithm. It remains the basis by which all computers work; a set of instructions for accomplishing a task which can be fed into and followed by an electronic calculator. Mechanical calculators may be traced to 87 BC, when an unknown Greek craftsman built a device, the Antikythera mechanism, to calculate new moons. Devising computers took centuries. In Italy Leonardo da Vinci, mathematics pupil of Luca Pacioli, had conceived a mechanical calculating machine in 1500, while a machine to calculate logarithms was developed in England by Edmund Gunter in 1620 and is widely regarded as the first successful analogue device. The slide rule was invented the following year by the clergyman and mathematician William Oughtred, and then in 1642 Blaise Pascal of France built a mechanical digital calculator.

THE NEXT ADVANCE was that of the mathematician Charles Babbage. In 1822 he built a large device to improve the accuracy of calculating arithmetical tables. His futuristic machine is considered to be the most beautiful computer ever. Much more recently the British Museum has constructed a working reproduction which is on display. However by the time Charles Babbage designed his mechanical difference engine a newer technology understanding using electricity, thanks to the pioneering genius of Michael Faraday, was beginning to loom over the horizon. It took a long time to develop it to drive computers.

Another step forward was the inspired realisation that all calculations could be simplified to a system using just two numbers, the binary system based on one and zero. In terms of technology that simply meant switching from 'on' to 'off' in an electrical circuit. Such an elementary concept would have been beyond the mathematicians of classical Greece, who even debated whether one, the "monad", was really a number. The Romans never quite came to terms with it either.

Yet as Chapter Four sought to show, zero was also the basis of the new arithmetic which had made efficient banking feasible in the thirteenth century. Not until 1939 did the electronic computer see the light of day. It was the work of the American physicist John Vincent Atanasoff (1903-95) whose father had emigrated from Bulgaria in 1889. That helped lay the groundwork for Alan Turing's greater achievements at Bletchley Park.

His machine became known as the Turing-Welshman Bombe and could undertake millions of programmable calculations with astonishing rapidity. Next came the semi-conductor transistor, which dispensed with the need for bulky, expensive thermionic valves. The technology of computers was on the march.

Another key advance was the integrated circuit in which transistors, resistors, capacitators and all their connecting pathways could be combined in a miniature piece of electronics. The device was invented almost simultaneously by two Americans, Robert Noyce and Jack Kilby who patented it in 1958.

Kilby won the Nobel Prize for physics in 2000, while Noyce went on to found Intel, the company which now supplies four-fifths of the world's microchips. *"What we did not realise was that the integrated circuit would reduce the cost of electronic functions by a factor of a million to one. Nothing had ever been done like that before."* commented a contemplative Jack Kilby years afterwards.

Then in 1968 the American engineer Ted Hoff invented a way to print all the 'thinking' parts of a computer onto a single chip of silicon. The electronic manufacturing task was now as simple as printing the pages of this book. Hoff had joined Intel as its twelfth employee, and his invention was marketed in 1971 as the Intel 4004. Over the next decade fortunes were made in America by the men and their companies who devised all the software to operate on the new, cheap, computers.

Matters had come a long way since Ken Olsen, president of Digital Equipment, had declared that *"There is no reason why anyone would want a computer in their home."* For some time that also remained the view of the establishment computer manufacturer IBM, until Apple proved them wrong.

THE ONE MAN WHO pulled it all together was (now Sir) Tim Berners-Lee. In1989 he established the principles of the Internet. Together with colleagues working at CERN in Switzerland, they devised the format that tells a computer how to display a webpage (HTML) the system that allows clients and servers to communicate (HTTP) and the system (URL) that enables applications such as email addresses, documents, pictures and services to be uniquely located. Thus emerged the World Wide Web.

By using synchronous satellites for global communication with the Web, the basis of the twenty-first century economy had been laid. All in all it took about fifty years and will undoubtedly go down in history as the greatest achievement of the second half of the twentieth century. It is proving to be another origin of economies.

As a result the fundamental Transport Principle had now divided into two. Transport and communication were no longer the same thing, as they had always been until the 1840s. The distinction gave birth to brilliant science and technology, some of it like Arthur

Clarke's the fruit of individual inspiration, much of the rest the creation of gifted scientists and inspired technicians like Noyce and Kilby working in company research laboratories.

Computers were not only used for communication. From the 1960s ways were found for them to drive machines and manufacturing processes. They could now do complex repeat tasks unaided. Henry Ford would have loved it. Clearly computers do not require wages, salaries or pension schemes. An era without any discernible labour costs was starting to dawn.

That will probably become a further phase of the Industrial Revolution. After its early stages when those who had the scarce knowledge to manufacture could charge more or less what they liked, the era of cheap labour then dawned. So the second half of the twentieth century was very different. It was the turn of poorer countries with ample reserves of labour to reap the reward.

From the Second World War onwards former trade secrets increasingly became public property, so that difficult manufacturing processes could easily be copied. 'Technology transfer' now meant that countries with large, cheap workforces could take over the activities, pay low wages and move into global markets. Then by the turn of the century that all began to change again.

Cheap labour cost businesses are now being displaced by enterprises in advanced countries which effectively have no labour costs at all. Computers can do almost everything. The era of 'cheap labour' is drawing to an end, and a further phase of the Industrial Revolution is now dawning. More about that, and its likely evolution in the foreseeable future, toward the end of the chapter.

Where the twentieth century saw remarkable advances both in the specialist principle and in the transport and communication principle, positive progress in the creditary principle was much more spasmodic. Political economy took a battering too.

As noted at the start of this chapter, for a hundred years after the First World War the world economy was marred by catastrophic experiments in political economy. The era of Communism (1917-1990) in the Second World was only one of them, if undeniably the worst. The First World endured its due share of illogicality as well.

The creditary disasters included Great Britain's decision to return to the Gold Standard in the 1920s. The man who took the fateful decision was Winston Churchill, as Chancellor of the Exchequer. The concept was a political hocus-pocus obliging countries, by law, to tie their currencies to gold by maintaining a fixed price. How this 'optimum' price was to be arrived at in the first place was never properly explained. Nor was the precise economic significance of how much gold there happened to be in the world explained either.

The intended effect of the Gold Standard was to trigger exports of gold if a country traded badly enough, or imports if it traded well enough, to influence the costs structure of its economy. Or so the theory went. In principle reduced gold reserves should then reduce money supply, and cause deflation to the point at which its exports would become internationally attractive again.

The gold standard conspicuously failed to work as anticipated. Its most apparent effect was unemployment, and was duly abandoned in 1931. Winston Churchill went before the House of Commons and apologised. At the ensuing Macmillan Committee enquiry into what had happened, the harshest critics were Keynes and the rising trade union leader Ernest Bevin.

To his great credit, the governor of the Bank of England Montagu Norman thereupon appointed Keynes to the Bank's court. In effect that made him a non-executive director. Keynes, originally a financial journalist on *The Times*, held this position until his premature death fifteen years later. His influence, implicit rather than publicised, was vital in what happened to the Bank Rate over the next two decades. It barely shifted from two per cent.

PROGRESS IN THE TEACHING of economics in Britain between the two wars was punctuated by two publications which merit particular attention. The first was little remarked, except by Keynes. It was an Article in *The Banker* magazine in 1923 written by A H Gibson. He pointed out that in traceable history, high interest rates had steadfastly accompanied high inflation. Keynes himself remarked in 1930 it was *"the most thoroughly-researched phenomenon in quantitative economics, but most professional economists prefer to ignore it"*. Professional economists continued to ignore it for the next eighty years.

The misconception can be traced to the views of a Governor of the Bank of England, J Horsley Palmer, called before the Secrecy Committee in 1832. One of Palmer's answers could be taken as suggesting that raising interest rates would shrink the money supply, force commerce to use it more carefully and so combat inflation.

This off-the-cuff comment was seized by the Austrian economist Joseph Schumpeter (1883-1950) about a hundred years later as evidence that would be the beneficial effect of higher interest rates; so they could become the Philosopher's Stone for tackling inflation.

The notion was thus embedded in the canon of economics, and thereafter copied by one academic economist after another until it acquired the unmerited status of established truth   Had Schumpeter bothered to note of some of Horsley Palmer's other answers he could equally have reached the opposite conclusion.

A later economist, Thomas Tooke FRS (1774-1858) writing a decade or so after Horsley Palmer gave his evidence, pointed out that a rise in interest rates would probably attract foreign capital seeking a higher return and thus increase, not reduce, the money supply. This eminently sensible observation failed, however, to attract the attention of Joseph Schumpeter.[7]

Some eighty years later A H Gibson demonstrated in *The Banker* magazine the diametrically opposite effect. Raising interest rates causes inflation; it does not cure it. Keynes lugubriously labelled it the "Gibson Paradox". In reality of course it should have been labelled the Gibson Principle.

All to no avail. Confusion over the true effect of raising interest rates haunted received thinking on economics for the rest of the twentieth century. Even into the twenty-first century some

7. *Together with fellow Gang Eight economists, in December 1998 the author specifically re-examined J Horsley Palmer's original answers to the Secrecy Committee, still to be found in the archives of the Bank of England. That original source material, rather than the hearsay of what imitative academics subsequently assumed, makes it quite clear that his numerous answers on interest rates could be taken either way.*

economic journalists still seem to believe that if inflation rises, the Bank of England should raise interest rates to combat the process. Out of mental idleness it is still their knee-jerk response. Doing so would of course have the exact opposite effect. Schumpeter's deeply flawed interpretation of J Horsley Palmer's ambiguity, the latter now almost two hundred years old, continues to display quite remarkable properties of immortality.

THE MORE FAMOUS publication between the wars was Keynes's own *General Theory on Employment, Interest and Trade*. He intended his book to be a definitive and permanent statement of how economies work, if indeed that is ever a realistic ambition.. In the event he fell into the familiar trap of ambiguity, sometimes even self-contradiction.

Keynes is best known for his advocacy of deficit spending in order to kick-start an economy out of a recession - the problem which was the historical starting point for his analysis. Thirty years later even that reasonable proposition became the subject of heated debate. It was contested by the monetarists, whose politicised sub-text led them to question every category of government spending.

In retrospect the manufactured controversy over the Public Spending Borrowing Requirement looks like a real-life application of Jonathan Swift's biting satire. His imaginary state was bitterly divided over which end to crack a boiled egg: should it be tackled blunt end or pointed end first? The PSBR debate a surely comes into that category. It has nevertheless dogged successive Chancellors of the Exchequer and their audiences for almost fifty years.

Keynes was wholly mistaken in one vital respect. He jumped to the erroneous conclusion that all money not spent, in his word 'saved' must thereupon be used for investment. The notion is a financial nonsense. Of necessity savings must always equal borrowings, an immutable identity clear to anyone who understands banking. They are opposite sides of the same coin.

By no stretch of imagination will all *borrowing* be used automatically for investment - much of it promptly finances further consumer spending. In any case the definition of 'investment' is scarcely scientific. Especially in the field of public spending it has become a grossly over-used word. If, in our own day, money is borrowed to buy a computer, who is to say whether that purchase will be an investment or just further consumer spending?

That probably depends whether the computer is bought by a business and gradually written off by depreciation, or whether it is bought by a games enthusiast for his or her private entertainment. The shop which sold it, or the bank which made the original loan, cannot know how the computer will be used.

Whether the loan to buy a computer turned out to have financed an 'investment' in Keynes's calculus, or whether it was simply used to increase consumer spending must, inevitably, be indeterminate. Monetarists had meanwhile latched onto a previously discredited formula of economics attributed to the American mathematician Irving Fisher (1867-1947).

An intellectual fossil was dragged out of the museum, dusted off and given an apparently new lease of life. Fisher had suggested that the quantity of money in the economy - difficult to measure at the best of times - multiplied by its "velocity of circulation" - presumably he meant its frequency of circulation - would equal the level of prices multiplied by the volume of transactions. Measuring any one of these quantities is fraught with difficulty. In total the Fisher equation, usually expressed in the form MV = PT, is at best a theoretical plaything, and at worst a serious impediment to an effective understanding of any economy.

WITHOUT DOUBT, IT MOST certainly is not the Philosopher's Stone, which is how it was now regarded for the best part of forty years. Among its numerous infelicities, one should suffice to illustrate its errors. Watch what actually happens in banks. A bank manager noting transactions going through his customers' accounts can see four different kinds of activity:

1. From an account in credit to an account in credit.
2. From an account in debit to an account in debit.
3. From an account in debit to an account in credit.
4. From an account in credit to an account in debit.

In monetarist logic, types one and two should have no effect on the total money supply. Type three would increase the total money supply. Type four would reduce the total money supply, but how far it did so depends on how far it pushed the receiving account out of the red. Even with a fixed "quantity of money" in circulation, for money supply to remain constant would require all transactions in types three and four to cancel one another out. The chances of that ever happening would be infinitesimal.

The bank manager's view also illustrates something else. Negative money in the guise of overdraft accounts proves to be every bit as significant in the workings of the economy as positive money. So when calculating the total money supply in order to feed the Fisher equation, should monetarists have included both the asset and liability side of a bank's balance sheet? That essential input never even occurred to them [8]. In short, the Quantity Theory of Money is a logical nonsense. Money is just one form of credit, and it is the total of credit in all its forms which drives an economy, the fundamental Creditary Principle.

One such component is the huge volume of trade credit, which never figured in the monetarists' calculations either. The important issue is the economic use to which credit of any kind is put.   If anything is to be assessed in order to find some Philosopher's Stone for managing an economy it needs to be, not a quantity theory of money, but a quality theory of credit.

KEYNES HIMSELF WAS ALERT to this necessity. In his wise but little-understood Borrowing (Control and Guarantees) Act of 1946, he was giving the power to the Treasury to call in a significant loan to see how it was being applied. The Act was eventually repealed for lack of use. More generally, the commercial banks of the twenty-first century could be required to categorise the use of their loans, across their entire lending activity, as part of their daily accounting process.

8. *A more comprehensive rebuttal of the Fisher equation is to be found in Geoffrey Gardiner's 1993 book* Towards True Monetarism, *Chapter Fourteen.*

They and their internal auditors know at the outset how a significantly large loan is going to be used - otherwise they should not grant it in the first place. A daily feed from their computers into a central computer could monitor the composition of all bank lending. No longer would Britain's Chancellors of the Exchequer, like Harold Macmillan, be obliged to rely on 'last year's Bradshaw'.

Some loans will finance fresh production, other loans will just inflate the price of existing assets. The balance between the two goes a long way to determining whether a currency will inflate or deflate. This creditary principle never escaped the Japanese, who in the postwar reconstruction of their devastated economy, paid close attention to bank lending. Was it fostering industrial growth or not? In part the so-called 'Japanese Miracle' may be attributed to that diligence, but the targeted investment activity of its industrial Trust Banks had a lot to do with it as well

Britain's Chancellor Geoffrey Howe was way off the mark when he declared, in about 1980, that the Japanese had to be a different kind of human being to explain the success of their economy. The comment was politically and in every other sense absurd. The real difference lay in Japan's more methodical system of banking and finance, and specifically its understanding of credit.

More seriously, Keynes left behind a trail of ambiguity over the correct function of the Bank Rate in the wider economy. To judge by his actions rather than his words, he was wisely opposed to the idea of using it to control anything. As noted above, as long as he remained on the Court of the Bank of England, Bank Rate barely budged from two per cent. It even stayed at that level throughout the public and military spending exigencies of the Second World War. His successors would be hard put to explain how that failed to cause inflation - in fact the reverse happened.

The upshot of Keynes's ambiguity in his book was that the self-styled Keynesians who claimed to adopt his theories did the exact opposite with interest rates. He gave a hint of this contradiction at the Treasury not long before his death when, having listened to what everyone else had to say he then declared *"I think I must be the only non-Keynesian present."*

Five years later the 'Keynesians' of the British Treasury and Bank of England began to raise interest rates, from November 1951 onwards, in a forlorn attempt to conquer inflation. In fact inflation burgeoned as never before. It was another of the twentieth century's major economic disasters. The scene was set for the monetarists to offer a different economic doctrine.

WHERE KEYNES HAD SOUGHT solace in the dubious efficacy of government regulation, the monetarists turned instead to the free market. Some of their influence was most beneficial. Two years after Milton Friedman set the monetarist ball rolling in 1969, the United Kingdom scrapped government regulation of capital movements in and out of the country.

The principal beneficiary was the City of London. Already by 1974 the Eurodollar had been devised; it became a foundation of the City's primacy in financial markets. Within a decade London had over 50 per cent of the world's trading in currencies, Forex. New

York and Tokyo had about 20 per cent each. So all the world's other financial centres put together shared the remaining ten per cent.

In other respects the financial freedom pursued by the monetarists was less beneficial. In 1971 the Bretton Woods agreement regulating currencies at more or less fixed exchange rates and dating from the 1940s was scrapped. It had proved just too inflexible for the rapid relative changes in different countries' economic progress.

However the decision to resort to a free-for all, the making of the currency and financial markets, also abandoned the constraints on bank lending. Without any such constraints banks could go on creating new credit for ever. Roughly speaking that is what they did from the 1970s until the early 1990s, the period of highest inflation. Then under the influence of the Bank of England the Basel Accords were drawn up.

The new rules restricted the total a bank could lend to a multiple of its shareholder's funds, or equity. That principle could yet usefully find a wider application in managing inflation. The result was to cause a sharp contraction in the Japanese financial sector, whose banks had become grossly over-lent. The net effect of that was to halt Japan's boom in its economy and its finance.

However commercial banks still operating within the Basel Accords remained free to fuel the credit boom, and the restraints had no effect on the credit generation of central banks. Much like the South Sea Bubble of three hundred years previously it was a disaster waiting to happen. It did so spectacularly in 2007-08, a financial calamity bringing us back to Chapter One.

D EVELOPMENT OF CREDITARY technique in the second half of the twentieth century also transformed the retail banking sector. In the 1980s Britain abandoned its traditional system for paying workers in notes and cash with weekly wages packets. Instead the commercial banks opened their doors widely and within a decade the vast majority of people now had a bank account instead.

That was very new. It became the natural partner of the credit card, and then of the debit card. A majority of the population could now, within only minimal restraints, design their own overdrafts. That steadily developed as a precarious component of the credit bubble, and at the time of writing the final reckoning for that conundrum is still in the balance. For all the regulatory devices contrived by the new doctrine of monetarism, the tide of inflation continued unabated.

Indeed it speeded up. No matter whether it was the self-styled Keynesians from the early 1950s, or the self-styled monetarists from the early 1970s, the upshot was effectively the same. No one seemed to know how to bring inflation under control. Interest rates continued to be pushed up and up in a mistaken belief they would control it - a technique which Milton Friedman had not advocated.

Only the financial crisis of 2007-2008 brought an abrupt end to the pernicious interest rate habit. In the meantime the value of the pound had fallen, in terms of its purchasing power, by well over ninety per cent. It had been one of the worst experiments in political economy at any time in the twentieth century.

Inflation has to be manufactured. Left to its own devices, the market economy will normally have the opposite effect. Without induced inflation, a punitive price rise in one commodity or service will reduce demand or force less spending on another. A wage rise in one part of the economy will trigger unemployment there or possibly somewhere else. Unless additional and fruitless credit is manufactured artificially, neither will cause true inflation.

Not only governments manufacture credit, of course. Every time a commercial bank makes a loan, its registers a fresh, non-negotiable IOU from a borrower on its books as an asset. At the bank's commercial discretion that has been exchanged for legal tender IOUs registered on the liability side of its books, which then balance. Whether or not the loan is inflationary or deflationary depends entirely on the use to which the loan is put, not on which kind of bank made it or which kind of entity borrowed it.

If the loan is used to finance a new factory or new services, the borrower will only do so if he - or she - can see a way to make the product more cheaply than existing competitors. There is no point making them more expensive. The economic effect of such a business loan will therefore be deflation.

If however the loan is used to buy an existing asset, then there will be no additional production in the economy, merely a profitable exchange of ownership. The result must be asset price inflation, be it shares in a takeover bid or transfers in the domestic housing market. The manufactured spending power will eventually work its way into the general economy, and thus be inflationary. It is the contention of this book that a primary route by which inflation enters the economic mechanism is through asset price inflation, a debilitating economic mechanism process originally remarked upon decades ago.

ITH THAT THE STORY OF economics, with at least some of its prolixities dock'd, about brings us to the point reached at the start of this book. Perhaps it should conclude with some guesses about foreseeable future but, before that, the story should first look at the have-nots of the twentieth century. Why is it that some countries have missed out so conspicuously on the broad prosperity emerging elsewhere? The Third World is a problem for economists too - or is it?

The conventional mantra about 'land, labour, capital' offers little by way of solution. Africa has abundant land, labour running into millions and capital which sadly has been squirreled away by its ruling classes in countries overseas. The banks of Switzerland are brimming with accounts owned by the wealthy of the Third World. A couple of examples will suffice to illustrate a more general pattern.

Kwame Nkrumah was among the first of his kind. He became President of Ghana, the country formerly called the Gold Coast until it gained its independence from Britain in 1957. It was the first British colony to shake off what were regarded as the 'shackles of colonialism'. India, formerly an Empire under the crown, had broken away from British rule just ten years previously.

By the time he was deposed in 1966, Nkrumah had amassed a personal fortune estimated at £75 million. Translated into present values, that is approximately £1.5 billion. In effect he was creaming off personal profit from the Ghanaian economy at the rate of roughly £3 million for every week he was in office. Nice work if you can get it. Moreover that windfall was from a country as generally impoverished as Ghana.

The financial antics of its state Cocoa Marketing Board were notorious on the cocoa market in London; the equivalent activities in the other cocoa producing countries of West Africa such as Nigeria and Ivory Coast were probably little different.[9] The trading profits of those organisations, legitimate in themselves, were being diverting from their organisation's trading account to private bank accounts on a huge scale, and no doubt the man who appointed them demanded his share. The procedure used, though technically permissible in London, would have been illegal in New York.

Robert Mugabe, President of the former British colony of Southern Rhodesia, was another case in point. In its days as part of the British empire, that part of Africa had been a major agricultural producer. Its 'white farmers' were themselves prosperous when their farms were efficient, and generated wages for their workers and a more general prosperity for the country at large.

Under its leader Ian Smith, Rhodesia declared independence from Britain unilaterally in the 1960s, a state of affairs which was to continue until it was resolved only at the Lusaka Commonwealth Conference in 1979. The only other country to have declared unilateral independence from the United Kingdom has been the United States of America. So far that has not been resolved.

~~~~~~~~~~~~~~~~~~~~~~~~~~~~~~~~~~~~

9. *See the author's article:* How to Become a Cocoa Millionaire *published in* Punch, *October 1996.*

Mugabe supposedly acquired one large fortune by seizing Zimbabwe's banking reserves, lost it, and perforce began all over again. He seized the successful farms of white farmers and handing them over to people with few clues about agriculture. Not surprisingly, output shrank. The white farmers were murdered in pursuit of an 'Africanisation' policy. Eventually Zimbabwe was consumed by rampant inflation which wiped out its currency.

As Southern Rhodesia, the country had been one of the most prosperous in Africa south of the Sahara. As Zimbabwe, it became poverty-stricken. Some vital ingredient was clearly missing. Other countries prosper without any significant natural resources. Hong Kong is a case in point. The territory emerged from Japanese occupation in World War Two on its knees. Yet within twenty years its economy, per head, was the strongest in Asia and riding high. What was the magic ingredient?

THE TWO HALVES OF AMERICA, in about 1500, broadly matched in terms of land area, natural resources and economic potential. Half a millennium later, South America was still poor, while North America was the richest place on the planet. What was the magic ingredient which made the difference?

Switzerland is perhaps the extreme example of a small country with virtually no natural resources save hydro-electricity in its mountainous landscape. Yet it has become the richest country per head in the world. The general phenomenon of differing national success attracted the attention of a perceptive Dutchman Fons

Trompenaars, an organisational theorist. In 1983 he received a PhD from the Wharton School of the University of Pennsylvania. The reason was his thesis *"The Organisation of Meaning and the Meaning of Organisation."* Despite its direct relevance to the wealth discrepancy question, his work has so far attracted virtually no attention from professional economists.

In 1981 Trompenaars had started his career in the personnel division of Royal Dutch Shell, working on job classification and management development. Then in 1989 he founded a Centre for International Business Studies, working for such major companies as BP, IBM, Heineken, General Motors, Merrill Lynch, Pfizer and several European banks. Along the way he devised an acid test, and it ran approximately thus : *"You are being driven by a close friend when he has a culpable traffic accident. You are the only substantial witness. Do you report him to the authorities or not?"* Trompenaars was not interested in the rights or wrongs of the matter so much as the attitude of the passenger, and how it was shaped by different national cultures.

For example, the English and Japanese began by asking about the severity of the incident. In tribal countries that was immaterial. In Switzerland, by contrast, the rule book was what really mattered no matter how close the friendship. Fons Trompenaars concluded all societies can be ranged along a continuum from those based on a rules culture to those based on a relationship culture. Only the former can create a viable banking industry, a viable legal system, an architecture of accepted public criticism or uphold the rule of law.

Further implications were outside Trompenaars' remit, but from his analysis we may possibly identify a mainspring of national prosperity. Rules-based societies succeed. Relationship-based societies generally fail to do so. In the latter case corruption - the granting of favours to friends and relations outside the rule book - is endemic. And such corruption is the cancer which always impedes economic development; it has done for centuries. It is symptomatic that the privileged elite of a relationship-driven Third World country are at the front of the queue to lodge their purloined wealth in the banks of a rules-driven countries like Switzerland. Leaders in the West who genuinely seek a solution to the lack of investment and economic expansion in the Third World do not have far to look. It is quite unnecessary to attend glitzy conferences and sumptuous banquets in Paris, or wherever, in order to find an answer.

Elsewhere in the world one leader who has recently recognised much of this is Rodrigo Duterte of the Philippines. As its mayor, he had made his name combatting corruption in the city of Davao on the southern coast of Mindanao. Ordinary Filipinos, the unheard victims of corruption, applauded Duterte's success in Davao. On the back of that he was elected as president in 2016.

He took over from a corrupt regime and became unpopular among those whose own corruption, often at high levels, put them in Duterte's firing line. Such enmity is the inevitable fate of those who take on the task of ridding a country of the problem. More so, if like Duterte the means to do so are potent and crude; he pursued his prey with extra-judicial killings. Yet if the legal system in such a country cannot be relied upon either, there are few other options.

The lesson for those in the West is salutary. If the Third World is to escape from its cycle of corruption and the poverty

which it causes, drastic measures will probably be involved. Those
who find them repugnant should remind themselves of the privilege
of living in societies in which corruption, although it happens, can at
least be exposed. In many countries that is still not the case.

There as a more general problem, one of nomenclature.
Economic 'growth' is a label devised by statisticians. Unhelpfully it
suggests everything sweetly grows larger, like some inflating balloon.
On the ground that is not always the case. Most often, economies
advance because some enterprises die and others replace them. That
means people losing one job and having to find another. In the USA
it has been estimated that fifty percent of jobs in manufacturing
disappear in ten years. Growth is not just a statistical phenomenon.
It can be a social trauma; we should speak of 'economic change'.

WRESTLING WITH THE fickle fate of the twentieth
century, has been challenging enough. It is unrealistic
to characterise it as 'good' or 'bad'; the same could
surely be said all previous eras. The difference has been
that from the early twentieth century a spotlight of media interest has
been shone on its activities. Mass circulation newspapers appeared
at the beginning of it. By the end of it the social media of the
Internet, often generating more heat than light, were taking over.

Some might argue too much public opinionating is now in the
hands of those lacking the ability to reach an informed opinion. The
cult of celebrity has increasingly supplanted calm wisdom.
Anticipating where all that will lead is beyond the compass of the
present writer. Pontificating about the twenty-first century in general

is even more risky. There is little point playing the part of soothsayer, even if many economists fancy their chances. Certain trends are however becoming manifest. The difficulty is working out in advance which will come first, and how they will interact.

The jigsaw puzzle of the future can be assembled into many different pictures. In the internationalisation of economies and society, helped in large measure by modern air transport, greatly amplified by the ease of global communication, one can perhaps see a world heading gradually toward a single community, Marshall McLuhan's prophetic "Global Village".

ULTIMATELY, EVERYONE CAN in principle become a neighbour of everyone else. People working from home, using the Internet, making virtually free telephone calls, can participate in businesses anywhere. They longer need to congregate in costly, city centre jumbo office blocks. The urban management metropolis which flourished in the twentieth century may well begin fade in significance in the twenty-first.

In the twentieth century more and more manufacturing activity became mature. That staple of intercontinental travel, the Boeing 747 jumbo jet, has been in continuous production with successive upgrades since the early 1970s. Such major industries, despite all their substantial capacity for original research, reveal there are finite limits to the potential for further product innovation.

It can be overdone; Concorde has come, and gone, and there seems to be no rush to develop a successor. With cars and aircraft the basic purpose of providing means to move people quickly, in safety and in comfort, and as cheaply as possible, has by and large been fulfilled. Passing the halfway point of the industrial revolution, the trend is increasingly towards cost reduction. With diminishing product differentiation, competition must fall back on price.

In practice that means reducing the number of human wage-earners required to complete a manufacturing task. It has already happened in both the communications and the creditary spheres. The first telephone systems required platoons of operators to connect the calls. Then the dial telephone enabled the customer to do all the necessary routing at no cost to the provider.

For many years after that, international calls did still require a human operator, probably a whole chain of them across the world, to complete the connection. It may seem woefully old-fashioned to a younger generation, but such methods were normal until not so long ago. Today's telephone users can route all the international calls they wish simply from their own key pad.

So the essential keystroking to convert a customer's need into code which can be followed by electronic devices has already been done. With no paid employees involved in the process, that effectively means it is all achieved at no marginal cost to the provider. All that remain are widely-spread capital costs, management overheads and a minute bill for electricity and transmission, but after that the rest is sheer profit.

Should we be surprised that mobile phone companies were some of the most profitable enterprises by the turn of the century? Other communications are comparable ; it costs virtually nothing to make contact over the Internet. A parallel process has transformed banking. Introduction of automated teller machines means banks no longer needed to employ armies of clerks to process pieces of customers' paper. The keystroking to convert a transaction into code which can be understood by a computer has already been done.

Provided the 'chip and pin' technology can be made sufficiently robust to cope with fraud, the essential function of a bank to move money between accounts and among banks can be done at virtually no cost to a commercial bank. Matters have come a long way since the pioneer banks of Renaissance Italy. As with automated telephones, so modern banks just have widely-spread capital costs, management overheads and a minute bill for electricity, but after that the rest could be sheer profit. Shifting money around should, in principle, costs almost nothing.

Beyond that, however, banks still need skilled human staff and clever fraud detection technology to keep the system honest. For the foreseeable future no machine could be programmed to anticipate and eliminate every kind of fiddle. The fraudster or the criminal is constantly on the lookout for new ways to make their own kind of profit from a non-suspecting automated system.

WHAT IS TRUE IN THE communications and creditary sphere is also happening in manufacturing. Peering into the future, we may perhaps envisage an oil production platform which is entirely run by computers. A pipeline then takes away its crude oil output, again with no human intervention. The crude oil is fed into a refinery which is also run by computers and similarly needs no labour force.

The final products are delivered to retailers by tankers driven by computers with no human drivers. At no stage has there been a necessary employee. So there are no wages. In effect the product is free at the point of sale. Only the royalties on design, the salaries of a much slimmed-down management team, and payment of interest on purchases or leasing of capital equipment need to be met.

Were the computers being used in the industry themselves produced in an automated factory with no labour costs, and the oil refinery, or ship, or road tanker were assembled by robots using components with no labour cost either, another large slice of the cost disappears. Henry Ford's concept of standardised design would have reached its ultimate destination. In the final analysis all direct costs are just labour costs, right back to those incurred in the extractive industries mining the original metal ores.

If we were to extrapolate that pattern to the end of the twenty-first century, it could be that most manufactured products would, in effect, be free. Were that to become a general pattern for a maturing industrial economy, it would be following the agricultural economy of a century and more earlier. Over the years the proportion of the labour force employed in agriculture has fallen to a tiny fraction of the original, yet output has increased. Improved technology in everything from plant breeding to combine harvesters continues to add to agricultural efficiency, and that in an industry which, in a sense, is now eleven thousand years old.

If such industrial trends generate price reduction, the upshot would be general, chronic price deflation. Just as it did in the nineteenth century, the purchasing power of money would increase.

Although that might sound attractive after the rampant inflation of the twentieth century, it is nowhere near so desirable as it may seem. In periods of anticipated deflation would-be customers back off. Why buy today when you could buy more cheaply tomorrow?

The consequence of deflation is economic contraction in which everyone becomes poorer. It can be disastrous. That prospect is another reason why practitioners of political economy need to improve their understanding of inflation. Instead of seeking to prevent it as they did less than a century previously, they may even need to start encouraging it. A twenty-first century in which inflation had been over-corrected would not be a pleasant experience.

S O IT IS NOT ALL PLAIN SAILING. While this book was in its final stages of preparation, a profound argument erupted in California, involving Facebook's Mark Zuckerberg, about the ethics of a robot-based society. Some may prefer to argue that artificial intelligence will never be a match for natural stupidity. More seriously, some kind of transnational policing may yet be needed to regulate what is published on the Internet.

The nation state emerged over a period of about four hundred years and reached its zenith in the early twentieth century. The First World War was very much a trial of strength among such countries, some of them like Germany and Italy still quite new. It is to hoped we will never see its like again. If the political sphere is moving in one direction, the creditary sphere is moving the other way. The future now holds out the prospect of local banks of a kind not been seen before (but see p.239). With a minimal clerical staff, a neighbourhood bank manager who knew what was going on in the community could supervise the lending, keeping a watchful eye on people's creditworthiness. There may be a good argument to own and manage such a local bank as a community enterprise.

Need it be a profit distributing limited company? Broadly, it would be risk-avoiding rather than profit-generating. A community chamber of commerce could provide the requisite knowledge of who was a good credit risk, and who was not. That takes us right back to the temple, the commercial structure of ancient Sumer. The French system of a statutory, non-profit distributing Chamber of Commerce which also owns the port, or the airport, is well worth further and careful consideration.

The twenty-first century is also witnessing a shift in energy generation. Without joining the controversy over 'climate change' it seems fossil fuels are on their way out anyway. In Spring 2017 it was announced that for the first time in 130 years, Britain's electricity requirement had been met without burning coal. Countries such as Canada, Norway and Switzerland have long relied on their hydro-electricity. France relies on nuclear power, rather than fossil fuels, for around 70 per cent of its electricity requirements.

Among renewable energy sources, the net benefit of wind farms is coming into question. The current trend is solar power; the price of solar panels is falling steadily. Even better, poor desert countries around the tropics enjoy the most reliable sunshine. They are prime candidates for developing solar energy. If the desert cannot yet be made to bloom, at least it could be made to generate.

With the seeming decline of the nation state, another political era has begun to dawn. No longer can a nation state's frontiers also determine its trading boundaries. But if some pattern of international trading blocs is growing more and more self-evident, the best way to deliver it is still in a state of flux. The politicians are blundering around as ever, and their enterprise has been distorted by national rivalries both obvious and covert.

So the European Union is proving to be little more than a transitory caprice along the way. Despite the rearguard antics of those on its payroll, it has had its day. Its origins lay in the European Economic Community, a political aspiration masquerading as a free trade area. That in turn drew its anti-national inspiration from an outlandish German eccentric, Richard von Coudenhave-Kalergi. Objective critics of the EU might usefully investigate him.

His musings, arguably racist and undeniably crackpot, gained a lot of admirers in the 1930s and they even lingered after World War Two. Although the muddy backwaters of political philosophy are beyond the scope of this book, their influence on the evolving shape of economies cannot be entirely overlooked. His political influence over the ostensibly economic EU has been noteworthy.

Devoid of any such covert political agenda, genuine free trade areas are the most sensible way forward. The resulting trend to a global economy is a means to diminish any prospect of another global war. Just because one of the early, politicised attempts to create a trading bloc fails, that certainly does not condemn the principle. The world's largest free trade area is not the EU anyway, but NAFTA, comprising the United States, Canada and Mexico.

One can foresee the United Kingdom, on leaving the EU, might well join that greater trading bloc instead. A new administration in Washington is already making friendly noises. A NAFTA thus extended might well embrace leading members of the Commonwealth, extending to English-speaking economies such as Australia and New Zealand, probably the resurgent India plus the steadfastly prosperous countries of EFTA.

As noted above a shift in sea transport and other vectors means trade now works globally rather than just continentally. A wider NAFTA's impact on the world's commercial geography could well be profound.

WRITING THIS BOOK HAS taken a long time, for its purpose has been to introduce or at least suggest a new architecture of economics. To achieve that it has been necessary to look at many previous edifices as well. Some are in ruins; some just need repair. There are also those which have been overlooked. By adding all four elements together, maybe a fresh way of teaching the subject could be distilled.

That would be achievement enough. Its students ought then to develop the teaching well beyond anything dreamt of in this philosophy. It would be a conceited author who thought he, or she, had written the final word on any subject - although too many have leapt to that woebegone conclusion.

At best this book is just one further step along a winding road, one strewn with obstacles and misconceptions. Too many economists want to have the final say. They will be disappointed, every one of them. Ask any dozen such how they see the future and you will get at least thirteen different answers.

Least convincing of all has been the computerised "Treasury Model of the Economy". It purports to look two years ahead. Even with the advantage of the most sophisticated computer in the world, and applying around half a dozen immutable laws of physics, the Met Office can just about manage three weeks. Economists perhaps need to ponder that.

Conventional economists often side-step reality by devising a Shangri-La to embrace their theories, a place where everything comes together neatly. In their fantasy world, economic problems are resolved in a magical land they poignantly call the state of Equilibrium. Like the grey havens in Tolkien's ' Lord of the Rings' it is a mythical, even beautiful place which never impinges on our normal existence. In our real world, by conspicuous contrast, things are almost always getting better or getting worse and are usually unpredictable; they never stay the same for very long. This book has been anything but a utopian thesis.

It is in the very nature of political economy always to generate unanticipated change, or if you prefer 'disequilibrium'. Partly because a new technology will invariably create disruption, partly because some businessman or politician will try to upset the applecart to their own advantage, and partly because customers are continually tempted to try something different, then disequilibrium will always be with us.

As volunteered ten pages above, economic soothsaying is a decidedly risky business. Fundamental economic advances will be driven not so much by predictable formulae, rather by serendipity. Far from some ideal construct of eventual harmony, the business school paradigm, an economists' variant of Chaos Theory would be much more fruitful.

The future is, in the main, little more than a random walk. The stock market spends 95% of its time wondering where to go next, and 5% of its time getting there. The financial calamities of 2007-8 and their economic aftermath, felt most strongly in the Anglo-Saxon world, were not only a tough lesson to politicians of all colours but also a wake-up call to economists of all faiths.

As noted at the beginning of Chapter One, amid that financial chaos ordinary people in their tens of millions came to an unhappy realisation that the teaching of economics, as then articulated, was little more than a pantomime. Or as the Queen asked of the LSE in 2009: "Why did no-one see it coming?"

To those economists still caught up in conventional and outdated doctrines of the subject, especially those in the Anglo-Saxon sphere, I would say only this. If it has achieved what it set out to do this book has either given you a preview of a future career or perhaps it has given you a preview of your professional obituary. The eventual choice, as it always is in such matters, is entirely yours.

Folkestone,
August 2017

About the author

Christopher Meakin was born in Sheffield and educated at the city's King Edward VII School. At Keble College, Oxford, he read PPE, edited the weekly undergraduate magazine *Isis*, and created the *John Evelyn* gossip column in the university newspaper *Cherwell*.

After studying economics for six years he began his career as a business journalist on the *Financial Times*, then *The Times*, then Economic Editor of *Industry Week*. He became a trader on London's cocoa market, after which he was policy director of the British Chambers of Commerce, followed by smaller firms director of the Confederation of British Industry. For seven years he worked as an international banker in London and later Hong Kong, thereafter taking charge of financial and media relations for BAT Industries, Britain's third largest company.

From 1974 until 1980 he held a ministerial appointment on the Central Transport Consultative Committee of Great Britain as its expert on railway policy. In 1978 he was elected local councillor for Dulwich village and became Deputy Leader of the Opposition on Southwark Council. In the 1990s he established various small businesses and PR consultancies, and wrote the business feature articles for *Punch* magazine. Since 1996 he has served on the Executive Committee of the Economic Research Council. In 1998 he founded *Gang of Eight*, a long-running transatlantic e-mail forum for economists.

As a freelance journalist he has been published as far afield as Russia and South Africa and appeared *inter alia* in the *Evening Standard*, the *Daily Telegraph*, *Investor's Chronicle*, *Marketing*, *Management Today* and the ERC's quarterly journal. With three adult children from his former marriage, he nowadays lives an uncomplicated bachelor's existence in Folkestone after many years absorbed in the shiremoot of Dulwich.

Bibliography

Andersson, Ingvar
A History of Sweden (trans. Carolyn Hannay)
Weidenfeld and Nicolson 1956.   First published Stockholm, 1943

Basham, A L
The Wonder That Was India
Sidgwick and Jackson, London, 1954
ISBN 0-283-354 57 7

Carradice, Ian
Greek Coins British Museum Press 1995
ISBN 0-7141-2210-6

Cribb, Hoe; Coo, Barrie; Carradice, Ian
The Coin Atlas
Macdonald 1990; Little, Brown and Co 1999
ISBN 0-316-84821-2

Cunliffe, Barry
Origins - the Roots of European Civilisation
BBC Books 1987
ISBN 0 563 20531 1

Cunliffe, Barry (Ed)
Prehistoric Europe - an Illustrated History
Oxford University Press
ISBN 0-19-288 063-2

Gardiner, Geoffrey
Toward True Monetarism
Dulwich Press, London 1993
ISBN 1-897657-01-3

Green, Edwin
Banking - An Illustrated History
Phaidon, Oxford 1989
ISBN 0 14 8 2 570 0

Grice-Hutchinson, Marjorie
The School of Salamanca
OUP 1952. Reprinted Ludwig von Mises Institute, Alabama, 2009

Hewitt, Virginia
The Banker's Art
British Museum Press, 1995
ISBN 0-714 -10879- 0

Hibbert, Christopher
The Rise and Fall of the House of Medici
Allen Lane, London, 1974; Penguin Books 1979

Homer, Trevor
The Book of Origins
Portrait, an imprint of Piatkus
ISBN 0 7499 5100 9

Hoare, C & Co. Bankers : A History   No author shown.
Published privately by the bank.

Ifrah, Georges
The Universal History of Numbers
Harvill Press, London 1998.
Translated from French,   *Histoire Universelle des Chiffres*
Editions Robert Laffont, Paris, 1994
ISBN 1 860 46324 X

Keynes, John Maynard
The General Theory of Employment, Interest and Trade, 1936 et seq.

Larouche, Robert
The Birth of Western Economy
Methuen, London 1961 Trans. from French *Les Origines de l'Economie Occidentale*
Editions Albin Michel, Paris, 1956

Lobley, Douglas
Ships through the Ages
Octopus Books, 1972
ISBN 7064 0018 6

Malin, Stuart and Stott, Carol
The Greenwich Meridian, 1989.
The Ordnance Survey, Southampton.
ISBN   0 319 00191

Marx, Karl
Critique of the Gotha Programme, 1875.
Translated by Foreign Language Press, Peking 1972

Marshall, John
The Guinness Railway Fact Book
Guinness Publishing
ISBN 0-85112-764-9

Montgomery Watt, William
The Majesty that was Islam
Sidgwick and Jackson, 1974
ISBN 0-283-97995-X (Sidgwick & J); 0-312-04714-2 (St Martin's Press)

Mitchell, Stephen; Reeds, Brian (eds)
Coins of England and the United Kingdom
Seaby, London (annual editions)

Nissen, Hans; Damerow, Peter; Englund, Robert
Archaic Bookkeeping - Writing and Techniques of Economic Administration in the Ancient Near East University of Chicago Press.
Trans. from German, Verlag Franzbecker, 1990
ISBN 0 226 58659 6

Nock, O S:
150 Years of Main Line Railways
David & Charles, 1980

Partner, Peter
The Murdered Magicians - the Templars and their Myth
OUP 1981
ISBN 0 850 30534 9

Renfrew, Colin and Bahn, Paul
Archaeology - Theories, Methods and Practice
Thames and Hudson, London, 1991
ISBN 0 500 27867 9

Roberts, J M
The History of the World
Huchinson 1976,   Pelican Books 1980

Saggs, H W F
Civilisation before Greece and Rome
Batsford, London 1989
ISBN 0 713 45277 3

Seldon, Arthur; Pennance, F O;
Everyman's Dictionary of Economics
Dent & Sons, 1976
ISBN 0 460 03028 0

Sigler, L E
translation of *Leonardo Pisano Fibonacci's* **The Book of Squares**
Academic Press Inc 1987
ISBN 0 12 6431130 2

Smith, Adam
The Wealth of Nations 1776 et seq.

Stobart, J C
The Glory That Was Greece
Sidgwick and Jackson
ISBN 0-283-48455-1 and 0-283-35320-1

Swan, Ned
Building the Global Market - a 4000 Year History of Derivatives.
Published privately.